W9-AWC-669

Tim Homan

Hiking Trails

of the

Southern Nantahala
Wilderness

Ellicott Rock
Wilderness

Chattooga
National Wild and Scenic River

PEACHTREE

ATLANTA

ℚ

Published by
PEACHTREE PUBLISHERS, LTD.
1700 Chattahoochee Avenue
Atlanta, Georgia 30318

Text © 2002 by Tim Homan
Cover and interior photographs © 2002 by Mark Morrison
Interior illustrations © 2002 by Vicky Holifield
Maps © 2002 by Mark Morrison

All rights reserved. No part of this publication may be reproduced, stored in a retrieval system, or transmitted in any form or by any means—electronic, mechanical, photocopy, recording, or any other—except for brief quotations in printed reviews, without the prior permission of the publisher.

Book design by Loraine M. Balcsik
Book composition by Robin Sherman

Manufactured in the United States of America

10 9 8 7 6 5 4 3 2 1
First Edition

Library of Congress Cataloging-in-Publication Data

Homan, Tim.
    Hiking trails of the Southern Nantahala Wilderness, the Ellicott Rock Wilderness, and the Chattooga National Wild and Scenic River / Tim Homan.-- 1st ed.
        p. cm.
Includes index.
    ISBN 1-56145-260-2
    1. Hiking--Southern Nantahala Wilderness (Ga. and N.C.)--Guidebooks. 2. Hiking--Ellicott Rock Wilderness--Guidebooks. 3. Hiking--Chattooga River Region (N.C.-Ga. and S.C.)--Guidebooks. 4. Trails--Southern Nantahala Wilderness (Ga. and N.C.)--Guidebooks. 5. Trails--Ellicott Rock Wilderness--Guidebooks. 6. Trails--Chattooga River Region (N.C.-Ga. and S.C.)--Guidebooks. 7. Southern Nantahala Wilderness (Ga. and N.C.)--Guidebooks. 8. Ellicott Rock Wilderness--Guidebooks. 9. Chattooga River Region (N.C.-Ga. and S.C.)--Guidebooks. I. Title.
    GV199.4 .H66 2002
    917.58'2--dc21   2001007767

Acknowledgments

I WISH TO EXTEND SPECIAL THANKS to the following people for their help:

■ David Acton Brown, Steve Craven, Gary Crider, Elizabeth Little, Page Luttrell, Maggie Nettles, Charles Ratliff, and Chuck Wanager for hiking with me;

■ Vicky Holifield for her editing, patience, and artwork;

■ Page Luttrell, my wife, for her typing and computer lessons;

■ Mark Morrison for his maps and photographs;

■ Dr. Charles Wharton for answering questions concerning the Southern Nantahala Wilderness;

■ Loraine Balcsik for her map and design work;

■ Robin Cooper, Mike Crane, and David Heddon (Sumter National Forest); Erin Bronk and Mary Noel (Nantahala National Forest); and John Petrick and Allen Smith (Chattahoochee National Forest) for their time and wilderness or wild river information;

■ Rob Messick for his old-growth forest information.

—*Tim Homan*

Contents

Part I
Southern Nantahala Wilderness

Preface

DURING SPRING, SUMMER, AND FALL of a recent drought year—on weekends, holidays, and vacation days—I walked all of the trails described in this guide at least once, many of them more. For various reasons—pushing an old, malfunctioning measuring wheel, walking shorter trails to reach longer ones, leading groups on dayhikes, looking for a stream the topo map told me I should have seen, searching for the real Ellicott Rock, etc.—I managed to prolong the pleasurable part of the process, the hiking part, into November, long enough to walk six or seven trails three or more times.

On the first go-around, I rolled a measuring wheel—a bright orange, incessantly clicking, spoked mechanism that, to some people, resembles a unicycle. By pushing this pain-in-the-ass apparatus, I was able to record distances to the exact foot (for example, the Fork Mountain Trail measured 33,829 feet), then easily crunch the large numbers to the nearest tenth of a mile. (If a measurement fell exactly between tenths, I rounded the figure upward; mile 1.65, for example, became mile 1.7.)

This time around I didn't feel the burning pain from a single yellow jacket sting, a first, but I did watch two copperheads crawl through camp, another first, early in the morning after a rainy night along the Chattooga. I encountered neither bear nor boar, but saw creatures rarer still: a pair of feathered skyrockets, peregrine falcons patrolling the blue mountain skies surrounding Pickens Nose. In mid-June, I was pinned down for ten anxious minutes atop Standing Indian by a devil of a thunderstorm—gust-driven rain lashed leaves in my face, multi-tined lightning torched the thunderstruck sky, head-drumming hail bounced off my hat near the end. The next time up, two weeks later, the mountain treated me to a clear-weather show, the peak of a heavy-bloom-year flowering of flame azalea and Catawba rhododendron. Later that summer, I lost a third of our backpacking party atop the mountain for almost an entire day (he slept in, broke camp very late, then went the wrong way), but I found calm reassurance and good cheer from an old friend while we waited periodically for the hiker who never caught up with us.

As always, sweat washes away and fatigue is quickly forgotten, replaced by earned memories and easily recalled images of beauty: midnight lightning flashing strobelike across the froth-white face of a waterfall; the startling orange color of a red eft; the bright, star-sequined sky above a Standing Indian camp; large-flowered trilliums whitening the spring woods downslope from outcrop rock; scarlet tanagers and rose-breasted grosbeaks, sunlit and at eye level, perched near the top of Chimney Rock; the veery's spiraling song floating flutelike through a highcountry camp at dusk; swimming in Rock Gorge pools; standing behind the waterfall down in Three Forks; kidding a backpacking buddy because he always fails to remember a spoon, yet never fails to remember a discreet dram of ground softener.

Tim Homan

Scope of the Book

THIS HIKING GUIDE DESCRIBES twenty-five trails or trail sections totaling 114 miles of treadway in or near the Southern Nantahala Wilderness, the Ellicott Rock Wilderness, and the Chattooga National Wild
and Scenic River north of its US 76 bridge. Though close by, the
Southern Nantahala stands high and alone from the other two wildlands. Its easternmost boundary is a relatively short 17 miles from
Ellicott Rock's western perimeter. Ellicott Rock and the Chattooga,
however, are inextricably linked; the river flows through the wilderness, and the wilderness surrounds and protects that 5-mile stretch
of river.

The Southern Nantahala's trail network includes eleven trails or
trail sections totaling 44.9 miles. Chattooga River's trail system em-
braces eight trails or trail sections amounting to 47.7 miles, and Ellicott Rock's system encompasses six trails or trail sections spanning
21.1 miles.

The combined expanse of the two wildernesses and the wild river
is approximately 47,630 acres—74 square miles. This total is less than
that of the added acreages of the three areas. Approximately 870 acres
of the Chattooga corridor through the Ellicott Rock Wilderness are
twice claimed, once by the wilderness and again by the wild river.

About the Area

THE GEOLOGICAL HISTORY of the Southern Blue Ridge is an amalgam of long ago, high above, and far away. Geologists believe the Southern Appalachians are the consequence of three separate Paleozoic orogenies—mountain-building periods. The first orogeny, the Taconic, occurred some 500 million years ago when protocontinents collided following the rifting apart of an ancient landmass. During the Acadian Orogeny, 380–360 million years ago, metamorphism (changes caused by heat and pressure) and igneous intrusion (the injection of molten material from below the earth's surface) substantially altered the structure and composition of proto-Appalachian rock.

The last and most important event in the upheaval took place during the Alleghenian Orogeny (310–260 million years ago), when the earth's crust slowly buckled and folded and lifted for 50 million years as proto-eastern North America smashed against proto-northwestern Africa during the assembly of the supercontinent Pangaea. Geologists broadly agree that this final mountain-raising episode elevated the Appalachians to between 20,000 and 30,000 feet, to Andean or Himalayan magnitude. As soon as the uplift ended, however, geologic eras of erosion began whittling away at the proto-Appalachians. Geologists calculate the Appalachians have lost as much as 4 to 5 miles of height since their Paleozoic zenith.

The seemingly immovable Southern Appalachians—the old, stoop-shouldered mountains we fondly call ours, are travelers. And they have traveled far. Our planet's surface is composed of tectonic plates floating upon the earth's upper mantle. These plates are like self-moving puzzle pieces. They collide with other pieces of the puzzle, rift apart into new configurations, move, then collide with a different combination of pieces like shape-shifting, continent-sized bumper cars. Six hundred million years ago, before the advent of the Appalachians, proto–North America's puzzle piece was floating by itself, most of its landmass below the equator. By the end of the Alleghenian Orogeny, proto–North America had fit its piece, most of it above the equator, into the interlocking puzzle of Pangaea. Since the time of their greatest height, the Appalachians have marched lockstep atop their tectonic plate, the mountains moving and shrinking through time and space as the North American plate drifted northward to its current position.

These ancient peaks and valleys, heaved up and worn down through the eons, did not feel the imprint of human feet until a relatively recent 10,000 years ago when hunters spread throughout the Americas.

Southern Nantahala History

The Cherokee did not inhabit the land of today's preserve. The mountains were too steep, too high, and too cold. The streams lacked the size for high-yield fishing and the wide floodplains needed for farming. Four of the five rivers that have headwaters in the wilderness, however, bear names derived from Cherokee. The Little Tennessee comes from the Cherokee word *Tanasi*, which cannot be translated. Hiwassee is the English rendition of *Ayuhwa si*, which means savanna or meadow. The Tallulah, which originates within the wilderness, acquired its name from *Tululu*, the name of an ancient Cherokee settlement once located along the river south of the Southern Nantahala and north of Tallulah Gorge.

Now the anglicized name of a small mountain range, a river, a national forest, and this wildland, Nantahala comes from *Nun daye li*, a former Cherokee settlement nestled beside what we now call the Nantahala River. The words mean "middle sun" or "midday sun." The Cherokee referred to the Nantahala Gorge as the land of the noonday sun because the high cliffs walling in the river blocked the direct light of the sun until nearly noon.

The name of the Southern Nantahala's tallest peak, Standing Indian, is a loose translation of the Cherokee phrase—*Yun wi-tsulenun-yi*, "where the man stood." According to ancient legend, a vicious winged monster swept down upon a village and snatched up a Cherokee child. The huge creature carried the screaming youngster to its cave lair high in the cliffs of a nearby mountain. Frightened Cherokees from across their nation gathered to beseech the Great Spirit for help in slaying the monster. After days of prayer, a blinding bolt of lightning and a deafening thunderclap rent the clear heavens, shattering much of the mountaintop and killing the beast and its offspring. The lightning was so powerful it destroyed the forest, creating a grassy, bald mountaintop that remained tree-less for many centuries.

A Cherokee warrior, posted as a lookout near the monster's cave, not only was killed by the lightning but also was turned to stone, some said as punishment for being a poor sentry. Most of his figure has been worn away by the onslaught of time; all that remains of the standing Indian is a pillar of stone with an ill-defined head at its top.

The first written references to the Cherokee and their moun-tains, the Appalachians, occurred in the journals chronicling De-Soto's murderous rampage through the South in the mid–sixteenth century. DeSoto named the mountains out of grudging respect for the Apalachee Indians. More than a century after DeSoto marched through Cherokee territory, colonists from the Carolinas and Vir-ginia began trading with the tribe. By 1716, merchants from Charleston, South Carolina, had established a lucrative deer-hide trade with the Cherokee. After the hide market peaked in the 1750s, traders developed a profitable ginseng enterprise with the tribe.

From 1810 to 1825, small numbers of whites settled the flatter, more inviting land of the four counties currently surrounding the Southern Nantahala. In 1828, the year prospectors discovered gold in the North Georgia mountains, the pace of settlement quickened dra-matically. Greed for gold and land brought an influx of settlers, and the tide they rushed in on washed the native inhabitants away. The United States Army forced all the remaining Cherokee—except for the few who escaped capture—from the Southern Appalachians in 1838. (See the Chattooga River History, page 13, for more information con-cerning the Cherokee and the events that precipitated their removal.)

By 1840, much of the southeastern Blue Ridge in Georgia and North Carolina was owned by whites who had flocked to the region as a result of the gold rush and the land lotteries, which had awarded to homesteaders 40- and 160-acre tracts of mountain land. The fertile bottomlands along the major watercourses were homesteaded and farmed first; three-quarters of the mountainous land was left as a forested commons.

Southern Appalachian farmers used their forested land, and that of their neighbors, as a free-range forage area for their livestock. They herded their cattle, hogs, and sheep up to highcountry crests for lush summer grazing, and they fattened their hogs on the forest chestnuts in the fall. They built corrals and herder cabins up on the ridges. Whiteoak Stamp, the name of a Blue Ridge gap along the western perimeter of North Carolina's portion of the zoned wildland, received its name from the corralled livestock that stomped and stamped the ground to bare dirt.

Falling crop yields and primogeniture inheritance forced succeeding generations higher and higher into the hills. A few even built cabins in the mountains above 3,000 feet. While many of the coves and ridges of today's Southern Nantahala were grazed by free-range livestock, most of the actual farming and settlement took place within Georgia's share of the wilderness, particularly Georgia's narrow southwestern section. Here, at the lowest elevations in the two-state wilderness, coves spill north, south, and west away from a long, east-to-west-running lead. Several named coves—Stillhouse, Milksick, and Burnt Cabin—attest to settler use and occupation. Because the walk from the cove-bound cabins was short here, farmers from either side of the crest cultivated small plots in the gaps and on the level sections of the lead.

Even before the Civil War, many of the original farms had been abandoned for new land further west. Many of the landowners in the four counties that now contain the preserve left their land to fight in the Civil War. Those who managed to make it back alive faced fields grown over with saplings. Starting in the early 1870s, and continuing into the early 1900s, much of Southern Appalachia was up for grabs. Politicians, businessmen, and prominent journalists promoted the region's potential for investment, encouraging carpetbaggers to exploit the mountains' remaining mineral and timber wealth. Northern industrialists bought steep, forested land, often sight unseen, and often with no purpose beyond personal empire and hunting preserve. By 1900, however, the timber boom was in full whipsaw swing in the Southern Blue Ridge.

Starting around 1910, timber companies and private landholders logged nearly all of today's wilderness at one time or another. The large-scale commercial cutting ceased by the late 1930s; small timber companies and individual owners continued to skid out old growth and salvage dead chestnut until the early 1960s. Especially on the North Carolina side, rugged terrain and high elevations kept the sawyers at bay for a time. But the old-growth forests rich with huge hemlock, oak, maple, poplar, chestnut, and cherry were far too valuable to bypass for long. The forests blanketing the upper Nantahala River basin were widely known for their bragging-size trees, large even by Southern Appalachian standards.

Ritter Lumber Company logged North Carolina's upper Nantahala River valley in and outside of the wilderness. The company sold large tracts of mountain land to the U.S. Forest Service from 1912 to 1920. A compromise deal offered a carrot for the company and a stick for the government. Ritter's carrot was the timber rights on these parcels for twenty years after government purchase, but the government stick forced Ritter to leave all trees under 14 inches in diameter. In 1920, Ritter sold 15,000 acres of highcountry in the uppermost Nantahala watershed—land now within and bordering the designated wilderness—to the Forest Service.

Using government capital and narrow-gauge steam locomotives, Ritter pushed their operation further up the Nantahala River and began felling trees on the 15,000 acres in 1927. The main rail line followed the river and its major tributaries higher and higher into the old-growth forests; spur lines chugged up the smaller streams into coves. One of the largest logging camps sprawled across Whiteoak Bottoms, the current site of Standing Indian Campground.

During the first decades of the 1900s, Morse Brothers Lumber Company constructed a rail line toward the high mountains of the Blue Ridge from another direction, northward from Georgia up the Tallulah River. The company extended their line, logging as they went, into North Carolina toward the Tallulah's northernmost headwaters.

Morse Brothers sold their leavings in North Carolina and Georgia's present-day portion of the reserve east of the Tallulah River to the Forest Service in 1932.

In Georgia's narrow section of the wilderness from the Tallulah River west to Hightower Bald, the Forest Service acquired their acreage from numerous small owners between 1932 and 1937. The most recent acquisition in that part of the wildland came in 1977, when the Forest Service bought from the Nature Conservancy some property the Conservancy had been holding for preservation. The two largest landholders in Georgia's wider section of the wilderness west of Hightower Bald, Pfister and Vogel Land Company and Irvington Investment Company, sold their tracts to the government, Pfister first, in 1936 and 1942.

In 1963, the Dorothy Thomas Foundation bought a 1,196-acre property in the upper Tallulah River basin in Dorothy's memory. Nearly all of this sizeable tract was located east of the Tallulah River, south of Case Knife Gap, southwest of the Blue Ridge, and north of Bull Cove. The foundation established a Girl Scout camp on the banks of the Tallulah River. The girls had plenty of room to roam. They had their own waterfalls, their own trail network, including a sidepath leading to the Appalachian Trail, and their own 5,000-foot mountain—Big Scaly.

The foundation sponsored the remote North Carolina camp until the Forest Service purchased the property early in 1984. A ski-resort company made offers to buy the high-elevation mountain acreage, but the foundation, determined to preserve the land, refused and sold it to the Forest Service on the condition that the government would incorporate the parcel into the Southern Nantahala Wilderness. The government agreed, and the deal became fortuitous reality. If this private inholding had been developed, the integrity of the wilderness would have been greatly diminished; the wilderness would have been divided into two sections with practically no core left in the middle.

Congress created the two-state, 23,714-acre Southern Nantahala Wilderness in 1984. The North Carolina Wilderness Act of 1984, Public Law 98-324, designated the initial 11,944 acres on

June 19, 1984. The Georgia Wilderness Act of 1984, Public Law 98-514, designated 11,770 additional acres on October 19, 1984. Stretching east to west along the Georgia (Chattahoochee National Forest)–North Carolina (Nantahala National Forest) line, this oddly shaped preserve also spills into four counties—Towns and Rabun in Georgia; Clay and Macon in North Carolina—and four national forest ranger districts—Brasstown and Tallulah in Georgia; Tusquitee and Wayah in North Carolina.

The Southern Nantahala encompasses 37 square miles, most of those miles empty of designated trails. Its widest north-to-south dimension, just east of center, is 6¾ miles. The wildland's greatest east-to-west length, from Jumpoff Ridge along the westernmost edge to Brushy Ridge on the easternmost perimeter, is slightly over 14 miles measured as if the two ridges were in direct east-to-west line. The narrowest point in the wilderness, near Hightower Bald and Montgomery Corner, is less than a mile measured north to south.

Located completely within the Blue Ridge Physiographic Province, the Southern Nantahala Wilderness features steep, rugged terrain notched by cascading streams. The wilderness encompasses numerous mountains over 4,000 feet in elevation and four peaks above 5,000 feet. These four summits—Big Scaly (5,060 feet), Little Bald Knob (5,050 feet), Ridgepole Mountain (5,060 feet), and Standing Indian (5,499 feet)—are the southernmost 5,000-footers in the Appalachian chain. Its high point only one-third mile north of the Georgia line, Little Bald Knob is the southernmost 5,000-foot mountain in the eastern half of the United States. Standing Indian, by far the highest crown in the wilderness, was known as the Grandstand of the Southern Appalachians until the 1960s, when its firetower was dismantled.

Georgia's share of the Southern Nantahala—long east to west and often somewhat skimpy north to south—is divided into two sections by FS 70 and the private property along the Tallulah River. The much smaller eastern section does not have a single mile of designated trail. Dicks Knob, one of Georgia's tallest peaks at 4,630 feet, surpasses all others in this part of the wilderness.

Georgia's much larger western section includes only one designated treadway, a short stretch of the Appalachian Trail atop the Blue

Ridge. Gated Forest Service roads led into this section when the Southern Nantahala became wilderness in 1984. Although none of these former roads have been maintained as trails by the Forest Service, no doubt a few have been kept at least partially passable by hunters and adventurous hikers.

The focal point of Georgia's western section is the nearly 6-mile-long ridgeline roller-coastering to the west away from the Blue Ridge. This high, east-to-west-running crest connects a string of named gaps and high points, most of the balds and knobs above 4,000 feet. Hightower Bald, the first hump west of the Blue Ridge, is the section's highest peak (4,588 feet). Flowing away from Georgia's westernmost wilderness border, Upper Bell Creek leaves the Southern Nantahala at 2,240 feet, the lowest elevation in the entire preserve.

North Carolina's contiguous half of the wilderness is a wonderland of waterfalls, wildflowers, cliffs, cascading streams, rock outcrop vistas, and rich coves. North Carolina claims all four of the Southern Nantahala's 5,000-foot-high mountains, most of the Blue Ridge, and all but 3 miles of the entire trail system.

The Tennessee Valley Divide, a major hydrological boundary, follows the keel of the Blue Ridge as it curves into a high-walled half-circle within the wilderness. Here, to either side of the Georgia–North Carolina line, the defining crest of the Blue Ridge bends northeastward then back southeastward into an inch-worm-shaped arch open to the south. Because of the divide and the Southern Nantahala's long east-to-west sprawl, the wilderness sheds rainfall, over 90 inches per year at the highest elevations, into the headwaters of five rivers and two major drainages.

East of Little Ridgepole Mountain, Betty Creek courses toward the Little Tennessee River. All of the streams arising under the Blue Ridge arch, including the Coleman River, funnel toward the Tallulah. West of the divide from Blue Ridge Gap to Bly Gap, the branches spilling north and south from the wilderness head to the Hiwassee River. Further north, from Bly Gap to Chunky Gal Mountain, all of the gathering waters gliding west away from the wildland also flow to the Hiwassee. From Chunky Gal around the northernmost tip of the wilderness, then southeast to Mooney Gap, every brook above the Blue Ridge arch sloshes toward the Nantahala River.

The Nantahala, Little Tennessee, and Hiwassee send their mountain water to the Tennesseee River. Its highest headwaters a scant one-quarter mile south of Deep Gap, the Tallulah River cascades south out of its hemmed-in basin toward Tugaloo Lake, where it joins the Chattooga. Here in the Southern Nantahala, rivulets sliding seaward from springs less than one-half mile apart follow vastly different routes to the salty oceans. The Tennessee-bound rivers add to our country's largest drainage; they join waters from Montana and Pennsylvania on their way down the Mississippi to the Gulf of Mexico. The Tallulah, however, is a headwater stream of the Savannah River, which mingles with the Atlantic after a comparatively brief journey of a few hundred miles.

Most of the Southern Nantahala Wilderness is cloaked in a moist, breathing forest of broadleafs. Only two conifers, the hemlock and white pine, regularly reach the canopy in this wilderness. Much more common and widespread of the two, the hemlock is most plentiful in stream ravines, moist coves, and on north slopes. Where found atop highcountry ridges, the hemlock usually remains a short-trunked, low-limbed understory tree. The white pine is most common on the lower elevation, south-facing slopes of Georgia's southwestern segment of the wilderness. The white becomes increasingly scarce above 3,800 feet.

The oak-hickory forest community covers most of the Southern Nantahala. While this general forest classification occurs at all elevations, it is most uniform from the lowest elevations to the transition zone at 4,000–4,200 feet. A component of the oak-hickory community, the cove hardwood forest, renowned for its giant trees and spring wildflowers, flourishes on moist north-facing slopes and in sheltered coves and ravines from approximately 2,700 feet to 4,000 feet. Especially on north-facing slopes above the transition zone, the northern hardwood forest, identified by indicator species such as sugar maple and yellow birch, increasingly replaces the oak-hickory community.

While well over 90 percent of the Southern Nantahala Wilderness was logged at one time or another, timber companies left small pockets of old growth largely undisturbed because of their inaccessibility—various combinations of too high, too steep, and too cliff bound. Some of these pockets were probably high-graded for valuable species; others, especially those at the highest elevations, may have been left alone because of poor-form boles. Dr. Charles Wharton, Georgia's preeminent field biologist and long-time Beech Creek resident, believes small old-growth tracts remain on at least six sites: in the uppermost Kilby Creek watershed east of Beech Gap, in the high cliffs at the head of Beech Creek, on Big Scaly's crown, on the steep slopes immediately south of Big Scaly's peak, on Standing Indian's highest southwestern slope dropping into Rough Cove, and on the pitches to either side of Whiteoak Stamp.

If you bushwhack off Standing Indian's ridgeline southeast of its high point, you will discover, especially on the northeast side, many poor-form old-growth yellow birch and northern red oak. The Western North Carolina Alliance and Southern Appalachian Forest Coalition have researched potential old-growth sites in upper Betty Creek valley—the steep slopes west of Pickens Nose and east of Little Ridgepole Mountain's crest.

The bog turtle is the only threatened or endangered wildlife species known to exist within the wilderness. The upper Tallulah basin, especially the Beech Creek valley, is a unique island of small mammal diversity. This low-elevation refugium harbors a relict population of vole, shrew, and mole species normally confined to much higher elevations in the Southern Appalachians or boreal environments far to the north.

The Southern Nantahala also provides refuge for rare plants such as the Blue Ridge St. John's-wort and the federally listed and very rare Biltmore sedge. In addition to several other rare sedges and lichens, the North Carolina Heritage Program lists three wildflowers found in the wilderness—large purple-fringed orchid, creeping sunrose, and granitic-dome bluet—as significantly rare in their state.

The Southern Nantahala Wilderness trail system encompasses ten paths totaling 44.9 miles. The routes range in length from the

0.2-mile Betty Gap Trail to the 23.3-mile segment of the Appalachian Trail (described in two sections), stretching from Blue Ridge Gap to Mooney Gap. With the lone exception of Pickens Nose Trail, all of the other treadways are connected, directly or otherwise. An imaginative walker can start at any trailhead, except the Pickens Nose Trailhead, and hike to any other trailhead by linking one or more trails or sections of trails. Approximately 8.0 miles of the network lie outside of the wilderness.

Chattooga River History

The Cherokee called their longer rivers, such as the Chattooga, *Yun wi Gunahi ta*, the "Long Man." They personified the living waters as a giant, powerful and always flowing, with his head resting in the mountains and his feet stretching down into the lowlands. The voice of the Long Man, the river god, constantly spoke in the sounds of mountain water to those few who could understand the message.

The Long Man was associated with the moon; on every new moon, including winter ones, the Cherokee went to water. Everyone who was able gathered at the river, and upon the priest's command plunged naked into the cold open vein of the earth. This purification ritual helped ensure long life. The monthly dip into deity usually took place at a riverbend, where the supplicants could face upstream toward the rising sun.

The Cherokee hunted and fished and farmed along the *Tsatu gi*, the river we know as the Chattooga. James Mooney, author of *Myths of the Cherokee and Sacred Formulas of the Cherokee*, believed the Cherokee word is of Creek origin. Just as Europeans borrowed and butchered Cherokee words, the Cherokee incorporated words from other tribes and bent them to their tongue. According to Mooney, possible Cherokee derivations come from their words *gatu gia*, meaning "I sip" or "he drank by sips," or *gatu gi*—"he has crossed the stream and come out upon the other side."

In 1730, the Carolina General Assembly proclaimed that "the safety of the colonists does under God depend upon the friendship of the Cherokees." The powerful Cherokee—the *Ani Yunwiya*, the principal people—were all that stood between the English settlers and the

French-led tribal Americans to the west. The Cherokee, who called the Southern Appalachians the "great blue hills of God," were the mountaineers of the region. At their zenith, they held an area of approximately 40,000 square miles, land destined to become portions of Virginia, Tennessee, Georgia, Alabama, Kentucky, and the Carolinas.

A mid–eighteenth century map depicting "Cherokee Indian Towns and Principal Paths" showed three Cherokee trails, in addition to the important Cherokee Path, crossing the Chattooga. *Kusa Nunnahi*, the Creek Trading Trail, passed over the river north of Burrells Ford. Further south, another trading track forded the stream near Earls Ford. Today's US 76 follows the third and southernmost Cherokee path across the river.

Russell Field, the Carolina floodplain south of the Highway 28 bridge over the Chattooga, was once the site of a Cherokee settlement called Chattooga Town. Archeological investigation has revealed that the town, which had no more than fifteen scattered dwellings and a large council house, stood on the site of a former Creek village. Chattooga Town, with an estimated population of only ninety, was the smallest of the Cherokee's Lower Towns. Despite its small size, Chattooga Town was an important outpost because of its location along the Cherokee Path—a major trade route once running from the Lower Towns across the mountains to the Cherokee's Middle and Overhill Towns.

The once-mighty Cherokee knew little but suffering, heartache, and strife during the fifty-year period from 1735 to 1785. Disease, dependence upon English trade goods, frequent forced land cessions, and warfare—against the English, the colonists, and other tribes— left them a much smaller and weaker nation. Because of their proximity to the Carolina frontier, the Lower Towns were the first to experience the severe terms of the traders, the mass death of imported epidemic, and the full fury of European-style warfare. Quick decline first came to the Lower Towns in 1738 and 1739, when smallpox carried to the Carolinas aboard slave ships decimated the Cherokee, killing nearly half of their nation within a year.

The next calamity struck with the French and Indian War, which began in 1754. Tied to the British through trade, the reluctant Cherokee were bullied into loyalty against the French, who treated tribal Americans much better than the British. The British demanded territorial cessions, permission to build forts in Cherokee country, and angered the Cherokee with their arrogance and neglect during military campaigns. Injustices went unredressed, and resentments festered. Some of the Lower Town Cherokee took the warpath against the Carolina British. South Carolina's governor declared war against the Cherokee in November of 1759, an unthinkable act before the smallpox epidemic. Further negotiations and more Lower Town concessions led to increased British demands and renewed Cherokee hostility.

In June of 1760, Colonel Montgomery and his force of 1,600 troops attacked and destroyed one Lower Town village after another, burning them to the ground, cutting down the orchards and cornfields, killing defenders, taking prisoners, and generally driving much of the population into the mountains before them. While Chattooga Town may have ceased to function as a community before Montgomery's raids, it most certainly had been abandoned by the end of 1760. The Cherokee formally ceded their last strip of land in northwesternmost South Carolina in 1816.

During the Revolutionary War, the Cherokee sealed their fate by allying themselves with the British. As soon as the revolutionary forces won the war, state militias marched against the Cherokee, seeking vengeance and land. By the early 1800s, the states of Georgia, Tennessee, and North Carolina were demanding the removal of the Cherokee to the west.

After years of debate and court battles, tribal representatives signed the Treaty of New Echota in 1835, relinquishing all their land in the east in return for much drier land located in the Indian Territory of Oklahoma. After more bitter debate, and despite a Cherokee petition containing 15,665 signatures declaring the agreement a fraud, Congress ratified the New Echota treaty in 1836. When it became obvious that thousands of Cherokee were unwilling to leave their homeland, the U.S. Congress passed the Indian Removal Act of 1838.

General Winfield Scott was ordered to conduct the removal: a harsh journey known as the "Trail of Tears." The cost of their removal was deducted from the 4.5 million dollars the Cherokee received for their remaining eastern holdings. Those few who escaped the soldier's net took hungry refuge in the high mountains of western North Carolina, and became, after amnesty, the nucleus of the eastern band of the Cherokee.

After DeSoto's murderous foray through the mountains in the mid–sixteenth century, the first Europeans to interact with the Cherokee on a regular basis were traders from Charlestown. Starting in 1716, Charlestown became the hub of a lucrative hide trade, primarily deerskin, in the Carolinas. Trade routes radiated from the coast onto established Indian paths leading to the backcountry.

During the late 1820s, the yellow magnet gold lured larger numbers of whites into the Chattooga region. One early gold mine was located along Ammons Branch, two miles from the river. After the gold ran out, the remaining settlers turned to agriculture, most locating their farms in the valleys between the main ridges well away from the river.

Local tradition holds that the lands adjacent to the Chattooga were not occupied by settlers during the early days after the Revolutionary War. According to the Chattooga Wild and Scenic River Study Report, the earliest known settlement in the Chattooga Gorge occurred in 1830, near Monroe House, where about 50 acres of bottomland were cleared and farmed. Other early settlers, mainly Scotch-Irish, came to farm on the floodplains at Burrells Ford and near present-day Russell Bridge (Highway 28). Most of the farms along the Chattooga were small. Over time, the descendants of the original owners extended their fields onto the steep slopes of hillsides and hollows. Poor farming practices and erosion eventually reduced most of the mountain farms to subsistence level.

By the late 1800s and the early 1900s, timber barons began buying up mountain land in the Chattooga River drainage. The timber companies hired the cash-starved farmers for cheap labor, and began the highly destructive logging typical of the Southern Appalachians. In the early years of the last century, lumberjacks used the Chattooga to transport logs to sawmills downriver. The river was not deep enough to float a winter's cutting, so "splash dams" were constructed to pool the timber until the higher waters of spring. Then the dams were blown and the boles rode the flood down to the mills. Splash dam remnants can still be found on the West Fork Chattooga River.

Most of the river's watershed was cut over with no provision for reforestation. In response to the widespread watershed destruction, the U.S. Congress passed the Weeks Act in 1911. This act provided the Forest Service with the money and authority to purchase cutover lands and to protect and restore watersheds in many critical areas throughout the eastern United States. The Forest Service—through erosion control, fire suppression, and reforestation—fought to heal the logged-over and farmed-out slopes. During the mid-1930s, Depression-era CCC workers helped in the conservation effort. Those hard-working folks planted trees, checked erosion, and constructed roads, trails, and campgrounds. The CCC boys built the Walhalla Fish Hatchery, located near the banks of the East Fork Chattooga River.

By the early 1960s, the Forest Service and Georgia Power owned most of the land bordering the Chattooga south of Whiteside Cove Road in North Carolina. Georgia Power had purchased their tracts for potential hydroelectric sites: dams. But no dams were built right away. Except for the Chattooga's last few miles, which are buried beneath Tugaloo Lake, the river managed to flow rambunctious and free into the midsixties, a time as turbulent as Bull Sluice. The more progressive political climate of that decade combined with the growing influence of the environmental movement—which had aroused public sentiment against dams—prompted an act protecting some of our last undomesticated rivers.

The Wild and Scenic Rivers Act became Public Law 90-542 on October 2, 1968. In addition to the "instant eight" rivers designated with the act, the U.S. Congress listed twenty-seven other potentially more controversial rivers, including the Chattooga, to be studied for possible inclusion in the National Wild and Scenic Rivers System. While the Forest Service was busy conducting its study, cameramen were filming whitewater sequences for the movie *Deliverance* along the river. The movie opened in 1972; the Chattooga became a star, an overnight celebrity. Floater use on that river rose from roughly 800 in 1971 to 21,000 in 1973.

The Forest Service study recommended the Chattooga for inclusion. On May 10, 1974, Public Law 93-279 designated 56.9 miles of the Chattooga and the West Fork of the Chattooga as a National Wild and Scenic River. The river's designation was the first of its kind in the South, and the first addition to the system after the original act. This legislation established a protective corridor, now encompassing approximately 15,800 acres, extending a quarter-mile on average to either side of the river. The national wild and scenic corridor begins at Whiteside Cove Road in North Carolina and continues downstream along the main river for 49.6 miles to Tugaloo Lake. A second corridor safeguards 7.3 miles of the West Fork Chattooga from its confluence with the main river upstream to nearly a mile above Three Forks.

The Wild and Scenic Rivers Act of 1968 specified three classifications—rankings reflecting past river modification—which determined future management. The Chattooga incorporates all three categories: it has 39.8 miles of wild river, 2.5 miles of scenic river, and 14.6 miles of recreational river.

In 1974, when the Chattooga first gained system status, the river corridor passed through several sections of private property, including one tract with several small, bankside homes (now removed) near the Highway 28 bridge. Since that time the Forest Service, which manages the Chattooga, has acquired through purchase or exchange nearly all of the privately held land within the river corridor. To its credit, Georgia Power did not impede the Forest Service study and final recommendation. The Forest Service acquired Georgia Power's holdings largely through land swap deals.

Pushed by heavy rainfall, sometimes over 80 inches per year, and pulled by steep escarpment slopes, the Chattooga's first whitewater runs start south of the Blue Ridge, where the famed crest doubles as the Tennessee Valley Divide. The highcountry headwaters—a dendritic pattern of rollicking rivulets, branches, and creeks—are bounded by Chattooga Ridge to the northeast, the Blue Ridge–Tennessee Valley Divide to the north, and the northern slopes of Whiteside Mountain to the west. The Chattooga's loftiest blue-line rivulet, well west of the gathering river, comes to life and light at 4,080 feet on Whiteside's northwest slope. The northern springs start their journeys in that narrow strip of mountainous terrain south of the Blue Ridge and north of US 64 near Cashiers, North Carolina. The river's northernmost spring begins its tumble toward the Atlantic northwest of Cashiers, at approximately 3,800 feet.

The upper Chattooga courses through Jackson County, North Carolina. Downstream from Chattooga Cliffs near Bull Pen Mountain, the river becomes the boundary between two North Carolina counties, Jackson to the east and Macon to the west. Further downriver, where it leaves North Carolina and the Nantahala National Forest at Ellicott Rock, the Chattooga serves as the state line between Georgia's Rabun County (Chattahoochee National Forest) and South Carolina's Oconee County (Sumter National Forest) to its flatwater end at Tugaloo Lake.

The Chattooga is an escarpment river. More specifically, the Chattooga cascades down the Southeastern Blue Ridge Escarpment—an abrupt, clifflike landform, delineating the unmistakable boundary between the high mountains of the Blue Ridge and the gentle rolling hills of the Piedmont. On their 2,000-foot descents toward the upper Piedmont, the Chattooga and other rivers have cut deep, beautiful gorges into the massive face of this escarpment. These deeply cleft, V-shaped gorges are the result of millions of years of erosive force.

Except for the wide valley where Highway 28 crosses the Chattooga, the river remains entrenched between rocky, heavily forested slopes plunging into deep, narrow gorges. The stream cascades through the steepest portion of the gorge, the escarpment, in its first 20 miles. The final 33 miles wind through a wider, less defined gorge hemmed in by lower, less precipitous mountains.

The Chattooga's full length is approximately 53 miles. The northernmost 3 miles, which flow primarily through private property, were excluded from the wild and scenic river corridor. The protective buffer begins downstream from Whiteside Cove Road at approximately 2,800 feet. The 50-mile rush of wild and scenic water drops about 1,910 feet—38 feet per mile—to its end at Tugaloo Lake (890 feet).

From the beginning of the wild and scenic river corridor south of Timber Ridge, the Chattooga surges generally southward to the North Carolina border at Ellicott Rock. Along the way, the quickly growing stream slips below Chattooga Cliffs—a long band of nearly sheer bluffs, smooth and often colored with lichen, 400 to 600 feet above the east side of the river. The Chattooga shoals into the Ellicott Rock Wilderness below Bull Pen Bridge. In the heart of the wilderness immediately south of the North Carolina line, the now wider river bends southwestward and continues rolling in that direction for over 40 miles to its end. After the channel turns to the southwest, Chattooga Ridge more closely parallels the river on the South Carolina side. This long crest of low mountains, rising 900 feet above the flow in places, divides the Chattooga watershed from the upper Piedmont.

Below Burrells Ford Bridge, where the watercourse leaves the wilderness, a series of ridges forces the river to snake to one side, then the other. The stretch pouring from Big Bend Falls through Rock Gorge is particularly rugged and beautiful. In Rock Gorge, jagged bedrock ledges and huge boulders fallen from old bluff lines squeeze the stream into powerful sluices, many only 5 to 10 feet wide. Near Reed Mountain, the Chattooga slows down, passes beneath Russell Bridge (Highway 28), then glides past the wide floodplain of Long Bottom.

About a mile downstream from the bridge, Floating Section II begins at its launch ramp off Highway 28. (Floating Section I is the lower 4 miles of the West Fork Chattooga to the main river.) Normally shallow, Section II often slides swiftly over a cobble bottom between easy drops over low ledges. Several Class 2 rapids and one Class 3, Big Shoals, present the only challenges for inexperienced boaters. Floating Section III, a 14-mile-long wildwater run from Earls Ford to US 76, forces you to paddle, portage, or line a total of seven Class 3 or Class 4 rapids. Most dangerous is Section III's last rapid—Bull Sluice, a booming, boat-holding Class 5. Only expert or intermediate boaters willing to scout should attempt this section.

Bull Sluice serves as a reminder and warning of potentially dangerous whitewater to come. Below the US 76 bridge, the 7 miles of Floating Section IV test the skill and nerve of intermediate-to-expert kayakers and expert canoeists. Woodall Shoals, the river's only legally paddled Class 6, makes you scout ways to avoid its hydraulic in high water. The homestretch is a whooping climax of four Class 5 rapids in quick succession—Corkscrew, Crack-in-the-Rock, Jaw Bone, and Sockem Dog.

Tugaloo Lake drowned the Chattooga's last few miles of rapids. A short distance uplake from today's Tugaloo Dam, the Chattooga and Tallulah Rivers once flowed together to form the Tugaloo, which quickly swerved to the southeast. Geologists believe the Savannah's headwaters were forced into at least one major change in direction. Until relatively recent geological times, the Tugaloo sloshed to the southwest as a major tributary of the Chattahoochee, joining a drainage emptying into the Gulf of Mexico. Through a process known as "stream capture" the Savannah River gradually eroded back up into its northern headland until it cut into the Tugaloo's channel, thereby diverting Chattooga River water to the Atlantic.

The Chattooga is the only mountain river in the three-state area of the Carolinas and Georgia without substantial commercial, agricultural, or residential development. With the exception of five road crossings, visitor access facilities, and one historical site (Russell Farmstead), the river rushes past thick forest unbroken by field or farm. Few virgin stands remain along the river. Most of the Chattooga watershed supports a medium-aged to mature second-growth forest. In this region, the Southeastern Escarpment of the Blue Ridge, the oak-hickory forest of the mountains changes abruptly to the oak-pine forest of the upper Piedmont.

The oak-hickory forest predominates from headwaters to Bull Pen Bridge. From Bull Pen southward to Burrells Ford, the two forest types compete almost to a draw. Below Burrells Ford, however, the corridor forest becomes increasingly oak-pine, especially on dry slopes and ridges. The Chattooga corridor provides refuge for two rare plant species—the shrub called mountain camellia and the wildflower Oconee bells.

The rock in the Chattooga drainage is composed primarily of meta-sediments—sandstones and shales—deposited 750 to 600 million years ago during the late Precambrian Period. During the next period, the Paleozoic, these sedimentary layers were metamorphosed by extreme heat and pressure, intruded by igneous rock, and folded during mountain formation. Most of the rock formations found in the Chattooga Gorge are highly metamorphosed sediments or igneous intrusions. The dominant surface rocks along the Chattooga and its tributaries are composed of gneiss, granite, schist, and quartzite.

North of US 76, the Chattooga River trail system features ten footpaths totaling 68.8 miles. These figures include the Ellicott Rock Wilderness trail network and two sections of the Foothills National Recreation Trail (counted as one trail) described in this guide as Chattooga River Trail approach routes. The shortest hike is the 0.5-mile Spoonauger Falls Trail, and the longest, divided into four sections, is the 37.5-mile Chattooga River Trail.

Ellicott Rock History

Ellicott Rock's geological, ecological, and cultural histories are essentially the same as those for the larger and much longer Chattooga National Wild and Scenic River, which divides the wilderness into nearly equal east and west sections. Cherokee history specific to today's wilderness consists of a trading path and a small village of unknown duration. *Kusa Nunnahi*, the Creek Trading Trail, skirted the southern slopes of Ellicott Mountain and followed Indian Camp Branch downstream to the East Fork Chattooga. It then switched streams and paralleled the East Fork downriver, crossed it, and forded the Chattooga about a half-mile below the mouth of the East Fork.

In 1761 Commissioner of Indian Affairs John Stuart drew a map depicting extant Cherokee villages. He located a town named Kanuga along Indian Camp Branch, which flows near the eastern edge of our present-day wilderness. After the Cherokee sided with the British in the Revolutionary War, Colonel Williamson and his colonial militia attacked and destroyed Kanuga during the early months of the conflict.

The unique feature of the Ellicott Rock area is the story of the survey of the thirty-fifth parallel. When King George II issued Georgia's Crown Charter in 1732, he established the colony's border with North Carolina at the thirty-fifth parallel. While this royal demarcation appeared simple enough on paper, it soon proved to be problematic in the wild, Cherokee-warrior sprawl of the Southern Appalachians. During the years before the Revolutionary War, the two colonies argued over the location of the boundary; each one claimed that the elusive parallel ran to its advantage, giving it more territory. In the late 1700s, when the new national government still seemed weak and remote, the mountainous region near the disputed boundary became a no-man's land known as the Orphan Strip—a refuge where scofflaws and other shady characters hid from proven jurisdiction.

In December of 1810, Georgia's Governor Mitchell and the state legislature decided to solve this problem once and for all, or so they hoped. Governor Mitchell appointed Andrew Ellicott, a highly competent surveyor from Pennsylvania, to survey and mark the dividing line between the two contentious states. Ellicott accepted the appointment, began work in September of 1811, and completed the task on December 26 of that same year. He submitted his final report, bad news for Georgia, to the legislature in March of 1812. No doubt Governor Mitchell wished he had waited for North Carolina to initiate the survey. Georgia not only bore the entire expense of the survey and experienced bitter financial dealings with the shrewd and perhaps somewhat shady Ellicott, but the state also lost an entire county to North Carolina. No part of what was then Walton County, claimed by Georgia, survived south of the newly surveyed boundary. Intermittent squabbling continued, and longer and more accurate lines were verified in later years.

In 1813 the two Carolinas decided their states needed a clear demarcation of their shared border, again the thirty-fifth parallel at the Chattooga River. The states appointed commissioners who, in turn, hired surveyors to establish markers along the dividing line. Written accounts vary in particulars—the precise letterings and distances between markers—but concur in the main facts. When the Carolina crew reached the Chattooga, they could not locate Ellicott's marker, reportedly NC-GA 1811 chiseled in rock on the eastern bank of the river. They continued with their reckoning of the parallel, a remarkably accurate one, and put steel to another rock, again reportedly 500 feet downriver from Ellicott's boundary mark. On the east bank of the Chattooga, on slanting rock near the water line, the Carolina surveyors carved three lines: LAT 35/AD 1813/NC + SC.

Occasionally discovered by curious hikers, those three lines have long been erroneously known as Ellicott Rock. This uninspiring inscription is now known as Commissioner's Rock. Thus far, the only other chiseled survey marker I have found is the riverbank rock inscribed with the letters NC 15 feet upstream from Commissioner's Rock.

Commissioner's Rock

The first Europeans to enter our remnant wilderness came on the Creek trading trail called *Kusa Nunnahi*, probably in the early 1700s, to seek the Cherokee deerskin trade. Much later, during the 1820s, the reckless frenzy of gold fever swept through the Chattooga region. Fortune seekers ransacked the banks of Ammons Branch, which runs beside Ellicott Rock's northwestern boundary near Bull Pen Road. The earliest recorded settlement in the Chattooga Gorge, south of the wilderness, did not occur until 1830. Within the wilderness, the only early and relatively long-term settlement, perhaps beginning in the 1830s or 1840s, took place in the Chattooga floodplain north of Burrells Ford. Forest Service documents state that several fields on the South Carolina side of the river remained in cultivation until 1910, when the last family to live in the bottom sold out and moved away.

The early 1900s were a good time to leave the area. The small family farms along the Chattooga were failing, and timber barons were buying up forested land. They hired cash-starved mountaineers for cheap labor and put them to work on the large-scale, cut-and-run logging operations.

As was the case throughout the Southern Appalachians, the Forest Service acquired Chattooga River land after most of it had been commercially logged, usually by large timber companies eager to sell stumplands to the federal government. In North Carolina's share of the preserve, the Forest Service purchased most of the acreage from the Macon County Land Company in 1914 and the White Water River Lumber Company in 1945. Macon County Land Company logged their property before the sale; White Water River cut their holdings from 1915 to 1925.

The Forest Service obtained Georgia's quarter portion of the designated wildland from three primary sources—Three State Lumber Company in 1921, White Water River Lumber Company in 1944, and a land-swap deal with Georgia Power in 1973. Three State Lumber timbered their mountainous terrain before the sale, and White Water River took their trees out from 1915 to approximately 1925. In South Carolina, Sumter National Forest procured tracts in 1940 and 1948 from White Water River, which felled its forests at the same time as in the other two states.

The U.S. Forest Service rode to the rescue of steep-sided, thin-hided lands all too often suffering from the triple insults of logging, slash fire, and erosion. They stopped the worst of the erosion, restored watersheds, and helped the earth to heal with its own natural glory of trees. Blighted chestnuts were salvaged at scattered locations in the 1950s and the early 1960s. A very small percentage of today's feral land was logged a second time. The last timber sale occurred along North Carolina's Ellicott Rock Trail in the early 1980s, before the wilderness addition of 1984.

In February of 1966, the regional forester established the 3,332-acre Ellicott Rock Scenic Area to protect the tract's trout steams, old-growth forests, and historical markers. Most of the scenic area, 2,809 acres, preserved land in South Carolina. The remainder of the tract was split between North Carolina and Georgia. On May 10, 1974, Congress added the Chattooga River to the National Wild and Scenic River System, creating a protected corridor averaging one-quarter mile wide to either side of the river. This corridor included land within and adjacent to the scenic area.

Early the next year, January 3, 1975, Public Law 93-622 converted the scenic area into the Ellicott Rock Wilderness. Spurred by demand for Chattooga River watershed protection and more wilderness, Congress nearly tripled Ellicott Rock's size in 1984. In that year legislators enacted two separate bills, both adding much needed elbow room to the wilderness. On June 19, 1984, the North Carolina Wilderness Act (Public Law 98-324) expanded the Nantahala National Forest's allotment of wilderness by approximately 3,200 acres. On October 19, 1984, the Georgia Wilderness Act (Public Law 98-514) increased the Chattahoochee National Forest's piece of the Rock by approximately 1,950 acres. These two enlargements boosted the zoned wildland to its current size—9,012 acres. South Carolina failed to act upon the Forest Service's recommendation for an addition in the Sumter National Forest. For now, until the next round of potential additions, North Carolina preserves 4,022 acres, South Carolina 2,809 acres, and Georgia 2,181 acres.

Today's version of the wilderness is busier than ever with boundaries—boundaries intersecting boundaries, boundaries within boundaries. The perimeter of this modest preserve spills into or across three states, four counties, three national forests and their ranger districts, and one national wild and scenic river. The North Carolina line runs generally east to west across the wilderness, slightly north of center. The Chattooga River rushes generally north to south through Ellicott Rock, somewhat west of center. In the heart of the wilderness, where the land and liquid borders intersect, is the exact and only place where Georgia (Rabun County), North Carolina (Jackson and Macon Counties), and South Carolina (Oconee County) meet. In North Carolina's section of the wilderness, the Chattooga divides the two counties, Macon to the west, Jackson to the east. Downstream from the North Carolina line, the Chattooga separates South Carolina and Georgia.

The Nantahala National Forest's Highlands Ranger District administers North Carolina's share of the wilderness; the Chattahoochee National Forest's Tallulah Ranger District manages Georgia's parcel, and the Sumter National Forest's Andrew Pickens Ranger District oversees South Carolina's acreage. Even the Chattooga National Wild and Scenic River has boundaries within Ellicott Rock, a doubly protected corridor of approximately 870 acres to either side of the river.

Roughly rectangular—it has four lumpy sides and is somewhat longer east to west than north to south—the wilderness encompasses slightly more than 14 square miles, enough room for exploration away from the beaten path if you've a body and mind to venture. Ellicott Rock's greatest east-to-west reach is approximately 5 miles, and its furthest north-to-south span is slightly less than 3 miles. The wildland lies completely within the Blue Ridge Physiographic Province. Although the mountains rise to less-than-impressive heights, many of their slopes, especially those slanting toward the deeply incised streams, are surprisingly steep. Ellicott Mountain (3,740 feet), Glade Mountain (3,672 feet), and Red Side Mountain (3,490 feet)—all without trails—hump up the highest. The Rock's lowest point, where Harden Creek enters the Chattooga near Burrells Ford Bridge, is 2,030 feet.

Like the arms of a candelabra, the grain of the land funnels toward the Chattooga River gorge, the most prominent and unifying feature in the wilderness. To the east of the river, most of the larger crests, including Chattooga Ridge and Fork and Medlin Mountains, orient north to south or northeast to southwest. To the west of the Chattooga, the long ridge connecting Glade and Red Side Mountains trends northwest to southeast. Flowing between the funneling ridges, the river's main wilderness tributaries—Glade and Harden Creeks from the west, East Fork Chattooga and Bad and Fowler Creeks from the east—drop sharply to join the Chattooga's more deeply entrenched channel.

Ellicott Rock straddles yet another boundary: an abrupt transition zone from the oak-hickory forest of the Blue Ridge to the oak-pine forest of the upper Piedmont. North of Bull Pen Road, the land rapidly gains loft and the cooler, moister oak-hickory forest clearly holds sway. South of Burrells Ford Road, the mountains quickly become lower, drier, and warmer, more suited to the oak-pine forest. The wilderness itself is a mix of the two major forest communities. In general, the high moist exposures are likely to be oak-hickory, the low dry exposures tend to be oak-pine.

Several Forest Service documents state that significant portions of the original Ellicott Rock Scenic Area were never commercially logged. While I did notice occasional old-growth trees—blackgum, white pine, and hemlock mostly—I did not, to my knowledge, see any large stands of old growth along the trails winding through the former scenic area. It is certainly possible that tracts of old growth exist in the upper coves, stream valleys, and high ridges away from the widely spaced trails.

The Ellicott Rock Wilderness trail network connects six paths totaling 21.1 miles. The routes range in length from the 0.5-mile Spoonauger Falls Trail to the 6.4-mile Fork Mountain Trail. All six trails either parallel or lead to the South's wildest mountain river, the Chattooga. Three trails—Ellicott Rock, Bad Creek, and the Chattooga River—converge near the two historical survey markers, Ellicott Rock and Commissioner's Rock. Approximately 1.7 miles of the trail system lie outside of the wilderness.

Note: For background material on the Blue Ridge area, I am especially indebted to two articles that appeared in the 1997 Georgia Wildlife Federation publication called *The Blue Ridge:* "Living on the the Land: Blue Ridge Life and Culture," by Donald Davis, and "The Natural History of the Blue Ridge," by Charles Wharton.

Things To Know Before You Go

WILDERNESS AND WILD-RIVER HIKING brings many rewards—wide views of undisturbed mountains; bouldery slopes covered with spring wildflowers; clear, cold, cascading streams—but this kind of hiking also presents challenges. The following information will help dayhikers and backpackers plan for trips and will help them become aware of what to expect on Southern Nantahala, Ellicott Rock, and Chattooga River trails.

Forest Service Rules

In addition to the standard rules that apply to all wildernesses and national wild and scenic rivers, the Forest Service has further codified a few formal rules to protect the specific wildlands described in this guide. Thus far they have enacted only three extra regulations, one for the Southern Nantahala Wilderness and two for the Ellicott Rock Wilderness and the Chattooga National Wild and Scenic River. Within the boundaries of the Southern Nantahala, the maximum size limit for all private or organized groups is ten. Within the Ellicott Rock Wilderness and the protected Chattooga Corridor, you must camp at least one-quarter of a mile away from any open road and at least 50 feet away from any stream or designated trail.

Road Closures

The only weather-related road closures occur along North Carolina's northern border of the Southern Nantahala Wilderness. Forest Service 67 (reached from Access Point 1) and FS 83 (reached from Access Point 2) link to provide the most important route near the northeastern perimeter of the wilderness. Both of these dirt-gravel roads are gated every winter. They are usually blocked between December 15 and January 1 and do not reopen until sometime between March 15 and early April. The Wayah Ranger District administers both of these roads, which may close earlier or open later as the weather warrants.

The Deep Gap Road (FS 71, Access Point 5) also closes every winter. The dates are roughly the same as those given for FS 67 and FS 83. Wayah Ranger District manages one length of Deep Gap Road, and the Tusquitee Ranger District oversees the other; both districts have their own gates and may not coordinate openings and closings to the exact hour. As always, if in doubt, call the ranger districts. (Phone numbers are provided on page 260.)

Trail Usage

With the lone exception of a 1.2-mile segment of the Beech Gap Trail, which shares its treadway with the Big Indian Loop Horse Trail, all of the remaining mileage included in this guide is designated foot travel only.

Deadfalls and Trail Maintenance

Wilderness trails are by regulation maintained to a more primitive standard than nonwilderness trails. This standard includes an acceptable number of deadfalls per mile. Under normal circumstances, wilderness trails can easily be kept passable. After blizzards, hurricanes, and tornadoes, however, when the number of deadfalls becomes problematic, when trails most need maintenance, the prohibition against chain saws in wilderness makes clearing the way slow and strenuous. While power tools can be employed within the Chattooga National Wild and Scenic River corridor in an emergency, fire fighting for instance, they are rarely if ever used for trail maintenance.

With the exception of Beech Creek, Deep Gap, and Wateroak Falls, all of the trails included in this guide are usually well maintained, often to an impressive level. Beech Creek and Deep Gap are maintained to a more primitive standard by design. Wateroak Falls is not a designated trail, and therefore is not maintained by the Forest Service at all.

Car-camping Sites

As long as you do not block a gate or ignore posted signs and regulations, you have the right to camp more or less where you want in most of our publicly owned national forests. The exception to that permission is the Sumter National Forest, where you must camp at designated sites, primitive or otherwise. If you would like a few amenities in the other two national forests, the Nantahala and the Chattahoochee, the U.S. Forest Service provides designated camping areas—primitive, semiprimitive, and developed. With the exception of group campgrounds, all of the other camps are first come, first served. Primitive campsites may offer vault toilets and fire rings only. Semiprimitive camps provide a few more appurtenances such as tent pads, picnic tables, and lantern posts. They may or may not have potable water.

Developed campgrounds are deluxe. They supply plenty of drinking water, and some, such as Standing Indian, are appointed with indoor plumbing and showers. In general, the primitive and semi-primitive camps are no fee or fee-pay, while the developed sites are definitely fee-pay. At present, the typical cost for a primitive or semi-primitive fee-pay camp is three or four dollars. The most expensive tent pads near the trails detailed in this guide, those at Standing Indian, require a twelve-dollar payment. After a substantial upgrade, no-fee campgrounds usually convert to fee-pay. Rates, as you may assume, are subject to upward change.

Nantahala National Forest's Wayah Ranger District administers three campgrounds north of the Southern Nantahala Wilderness— Standing Indian (developed, fee-pay), Kimsey Creek Group (developed, fee-pay, reservation required), and Hurricane Creek (primitive, fee-pay). Kimsey Creek is located on the outskirts of Standing Indian Campground. Hurricane Creek, which tends to be a horse-rider camp, straddles FS 67 a little over 2 miles beyond the prominently signed entrance to Standing Indian (from US 64).

Chattahoochee National Forest's Tallulah Ranger District maintains three campgrounds south of the Southern Nantahala Wilderness. Nestled along the scenic Tallulah River off Tallulah River Road

(FS 70), all three camps—Tallulah River, Sandy Bottom, and Tate Branch—are developed and fee-pay. Closer to the Chattooga River, the Tallulah Ranger District also maintains a small campground known as West Fork or Overflow (primitive, fee-pay, walk-in) beside the bank of the West Fork Chattooga River. This little-known campground is located on the left side of Overflow Creek Road (FS 86) well before you reach Three Forks Trail from Warwoman Road.

In the Nantahala National Forest near the northwest boundary of the Ellicott Rock Wilderness, the Highlands Ranger District operates Ammons Branch Campground (semiprimitive, no fee, no water). Ammons Branch is situated on the southwest side of Bull Pen Road less than a mile northwest from the Ellicott Rock Trailhead.

Across the Chattooga in South Carolina, Sumter National Forest's Andrew Pickens Ranger District regulates two campgrounds—Burrells Ford (semiprimitive, no fee, one-quarter-mile walk in) and Cherry Hill (developed, fee-pay)—both south of the Ellicott Rock Wilderness. You will find the large, prominently signed parking area for Burrells Ford Campground off Burrells Ford Road a few tenths mile from the Burrells Ford Bridge over the Chattooga River. Cherry Hill is sited on the east side of SC 107, the side opposite Big Bend Road and Moody Spring Picnic Area, approximately 1.5 miles south of the Burrells Ford Road–SC 107 intersection. The Andrew Pickens Ranger District also oversees two primitive, no-fee camps, Long Bottom Ford and Earls Ford, both located along the Chattooga south of Highway 28's Russell Bridge over the river.

Many of the national forest campgrounds close during the cold weather off-season. As of now, West Fork, Tate Branch (no water in winter), Ammons Branch, and the fords—Earls, Long Bottom, and Burrells—remain open year round. Sandy Bottom and Tallulah River both close on the first weekend in November and reopen the Wednesday before trout season opens on the last Saturday in March. Standing Indian usually closes after the end of November and reopens during the first weekend of April. Hurricane Creek remains open as long as FS 67 remains open (see Road Closures on page 27). Cherry Hill's variable timetable depends upon the weather and personnel. It normally closes between October 15 and November 15 and normally reopens between March 15 and April 15. As always, these dates are subject to change; if you are cutting it close, call the Forest Service.

In addition to the federal campgrounds, two excellent state parks—Georgia's Black Rock Mountain and South Carolina's Oconee—feature numerous campsites relatively near many of the trails in this guide. East of the Southern Nantahala Wilderness and just west of Mountain City, Black Rock Mountain State Park is only slightly more than 10 miles from the US 441–Coweeta Lab Road intersection (Access Point 2). Call 1-800-864-7275 for reservations. Located a few miles northeast of the SC 28–SC 107 intersection north of Walhalla, Oconee State Park is especially handy to the Ellicott Rock Wilderness and the Chattooga River approach trails originating off SC 107. Call 1-864-638-5353 for reservations.

Hunting Seasons

Hunting is a legal and somewhat popular pastime within both wildernesses and the Chattooga National Wild and Scenic River corridor. Various overlapping hunting seasons occur throughout much of autumn and early winter. In spring, hunters attempt to call turkey within shotgun range. To further complicate matters for hikers and hunters, the three states—Georgia, South Carolina, and North Carolina—have different seasons and different laws.

Keep in mind that relatively few nonmounted big-game hunters venture more than a quarter of a mile from a road. Even though the trails are designated foot travel only, hunters on horseback occasionally make camps deep within the Southern Nantahala Wilderness, usually in the Tallulah River basin near Beech Creek Trail. If you want to hike these wilderness trails during hunting season, wearing an orange vest is definitely a good idea.

National forests have been designated as wildlife management areas in South Carolina; Sunday hunting is illegal on these lands. In North Carolina, national forests are part of the State Game Lands, and no hunting is allowed on Sundays. Georgia's Chattahoochee National Forest includes both Wildlife Management Areas, which have short, highly regulated seasons, and non–WMA lands, which follow the much longer general statewide seasons. Georgia's share of the Ellicott Rock Wilderness, the Chattooga River corridor, and its portion of the Southern Nantahala Wilderness where there is a trail (the AT) are located outside of the WMAs. Georgia hunters may shoot on Sundays.

For more information, contact the following offices:

Georgia

Game Management
2150 Dawsonville Highway
Gainesville, GA 30501
(770) 535-5700
www.gohuntgeorgia.com

North Carolina

North Carolina Wildlife
  Transaction Management
NCWRC
1709 Mail Service Center
Raleigh, NC 27699-1709
(919) 662-4370
www.ncwildlife.org

South Carolina

South Carolina Department
  of Natural Resources
153 Hopewell Road
Pendleton, SC 29670
(864) 654-1671
www.scdnr.state.us

How To Use This Guide

WITH THE LONE EXCEPTION of the Southern Nantahala's Big Indian Loop Horse Trail, this guidebook details all of the twenty-five trails or sections of trails (see trail usage on page 28) within or leading to the Southern Nantahala Wilderness, the Ellicott Rock Wilderness, and the Chattooga National Wild and Scenic River north of US 76. The routes are grouped geographically; a list of trails and a basic map are provided at the beginning of each section.

Trail Descriptions

A concise, at-a-glance summary of essential trail information appears at the beginning of each route description. You can quickly refer to a trail's length, difficulty rating (often for both dayhiking and backpacking), and its starting and ending points with elevations given. Also provided here are the trail junctions, topographic quadrangles, blaze descriptions, ranger districts and national forests, plus a brief listing of some of the trail's outstanding features.

Following this information listing you will find a complete description of the course, usually in the direction most frequently walked, with special attention given to the type of terrain, stream crossings, trail junctions, and interior mileages to prominent physical features. At the conclusion of most trail narratives, a section called Nature Notes features some of the flora and fauna you may encounter while walking a particular path.

Finally, the directions or references will lead you to the exact trailhead or—if there is more than one tread leading from a trailhead—to the specific walkway.

When using this guide, keep in mind that trails often change, are often rerouted by man or nature. To be sure of current conditions, contact the appropriate ranger district office before planning a hike.

Trail Ratings

Difficulty ratings are inherently subjective and relative; there are no standardized norms that fit all the possibilities. Useful systems, however, are those that achieve consistency by limiting this subjectivity and relativity to a single region and a single source. To this end, I have walked and rated all of the trails described in this guide. Even if you do not agree with my ratings, I hope that you will find them consistent and, after a trip or two, useful.

The trail ratings utilized in this book were based upon the usual criteria: the rate of elevation change, the way that elevation change is accomplished, the difficulty of a route compared to others described in this guide, the length of the trail, and the effect the hike had on my legs and lungs. In general, to reflect the cumulative effect of the grade, the longer trails were usually rated as slightly more difficult than shorter trails with roughly the same elevation change per mile. Rough footing, stream crossings, and fords were usually given only minimal consideration: they are simply part of wildland walking.

This rating system is also based on two assumptions. The first is that this scheme, or any other, does not apply to either end of the fitness-spectrum bell curve—those in excellent condition and those in poor condition. Hikers who are able to run long distances with little effort already know that ratings are meaningless for them. Conversely, people who become winded while searching for their remotes would find difficulty classifications equally inaccurate, although much harder to ignore.

The other assumption is that a very high percentage of the people who walk or want to walk in the mountains exercise, at least occasionally. After all, if you rarely exercise, it probably would be unwise to attempt a wilderness route ranked more difficult than easy to moderate. Thus, this approach is designed to accommodate those people who work out, at least sporadically, and who fall somewhere in that broad, general category between slightly below fair condition and slightly better than good condition.

This guide utilizes three categories of difficulty: Easy, Moderate, and Strenuous. As you will notice, many trails have been assigned two designations. These split designations are used to help bridge fitness levels when trail difficulty falls between obvious gradations. For instance, a trail may be rated "Dayhiking In: Easy to Moderate." A person in good cardiovascular condition would consider this trail to be easy. A hiker in fair shape would probably rate the route as easy to moderate, and a walker with a poor fitness level would probably find it moderate, perhaps even harder.

The decision to walk a certain trail is a commonsense personal judgment. When planning a trip, you should be aware of the trail's difficulty, not intimidated by it; you should think of the rating as a recommendation, not a warning. If you keep the intended mileage reasonable, walk at a comfortable pace, take frequent rest stops and are energized by mountain beauty, you will often be surprised at what you can accomplish. If you want to walk a tougher trail and think you're ready, go for it.

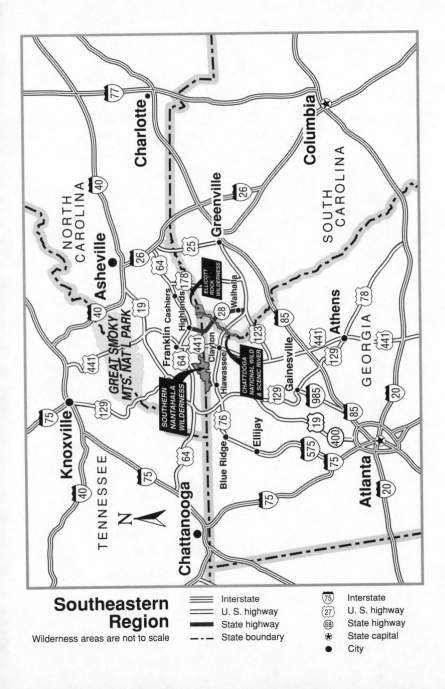

Southeastern Region

Wilderness areas are not to scale

═══	Interstate
══	U. S. highway
▬▬	State highway
─·─·─	State boundary

🛡75	Interstate
〔27〕	U. S. highway
〔68〕	State highway
✪	State capital
●	City

The hiker has a unique opportunity to experience the perspective-altering impact inherent in the combination of solitude, time, immersion in the natural order and the beauty of the planet...

—Jan D. Curran

Southern Nantahala Wilderness

Regional Directions and Access Points

THE SOUTHERN NANTAHALA WILDERNESS straddles the Georgia-North Carolina border between Dillard, Georgia, to the east and Hiawassee, Georgia, to the west. An 84-mile-long combination of state and federal highways makes a complete circuit—four sided and four cornered—around a larger area with the wilderness located somewhat in the middle. This circuit is defined by four sides and four intersections; three of the intersections are located in towns. The eastern side of the loop, US 441, stretches approximately 21.0 miles from the US 441–US 76 West intersection in Clayton, Georgia, to the US 441–US 64 West intersection in Franklin, North Carolina. The northern link spans approximately 28.5 miles from the US 64 West–US 441 intersection in Franklin to the US 64–NC 175 intersection east of Hayesville, North Carolina. The western leg runs slightly more than 7.5 miles from the US 64–NC 175 intersection to the US 76–GA 75 intersection in Hiawassee, Georgia (NC 175 switches to GA 75 at the state line). Completing the crooked loop, the southern segment extends a little more than 27.0 miles from the US 76–GA 75 intersection in Hiawassee to the US 76–US 441 intersection in Clayton.

The Southern Nantahala section of this guide utilizes a two-tiered system of directions. This arrangement is designed to avoid repetition, yet enable hikers to reach the five access points—two from the south, one from the east, and two from the north. The following introductory directions are those to the five access points: the highway circuit–wilderness approach road junctions. The numbers of the access points correspond to the numbers on the regional map (page 45). These directions lead hikers from the two nearest corners of the circuit, the two nearest intersections—one from the east and the other from the west, for example—to the access-point approach roads that lead toward the trailheads.

The second tier of directions, those following each trail description, begins at one or two of the closest access points. Final directions steer you from the access points to the exact trailheads.

Access Point 1

This access point is the three-way US 64–West Old Murphy Road intersection located along that stretch of US 64 between Franklin, North Carolina, to the east, and Hayesville, North Carolina, to the west.

Approach from the east: From the US 64–US 441 (Business 441) intersection in Franklin, travel US 64 West for approximately 12.0 miles to the left turn onto paved West Old Murphy Road. This turn is marked with signs for Wallace Gap and Standing Indian Campground in addition to the road sign.

Approach from the west: From the US 64–NC 175 intersection east of Hayesville, travel US 64 East approximately 16.5 miles to the right turn onto paved West Old Murphy Road. This turn is marked with signs for Wallace Gap and Standing Indian Campground in addition to the road sign.

Access Point 2

This access point is the three-way US 441–Coweeta Lab Road intersection just south of the small community of Otto, North Carolina. Otto is located along that segment of US 441 between Clayton, Georgia, to the south, and Franklin, North Carolina, to the north.

Approach from the south: From the US 441–US 76 West intersection in Clayton, travel US 441 North for approximately 12.2 miles to the left turn onto paved Coweeta Lab Road (SR 1110). This turn is marked with a road sign and a prominent brown-and-white Coweeta Hydrologic Lab sign.

Approach from the north: From the US 441 (Business 441)–US 64 intersection in Franklin, travel US 441 South slightly more than 8.5 miles to the right turn onto paved Coweeta Lab Road (SR 1110). This turn is marked with a road sign and a large brown-and-white Coweeta Hydrologic Lab sign.

Access Point 3

This access point is the three-way US 76–Persimmon Road intersection located along that segment of US 76 between Clayton, Georgia, to the east, and Hiawassee, Georgia, to the west.

Approach from the east: From the US 76 West–US 441 intersection in Clayton, turn onto US 76 West (a left turn if you approach this junction from the south on US 441 North) and travel slightly more than 8.0 miles to the right turn onto paved Persimmon Road, designated with two signs, one for the road and the other for the National Forest Campgrounds along the Tallulah River. If the road sign is missing, look for the volunteer fire department at the beginning of Persimmon Road.

Approach from the west: From the US 76–GA 75 intersection in Hiawassee, where GA 75 heads north toward North Carolina, proceed slightly more than 19.0 miles on US 76 East before turning left onto paved Persimmon Road. This turn is designated with two official signs, one for the road and the other for the National Forest Campgrounds along the Tallulah River. If the road sign is missing, look for the volunteer fire department at the beginning of Persimmon Road.

Access Point 4

This access point is the three-way US 76–Upper Hightower Road intersection located along that stretch of US 76 between Clayton, Georgia, to the east, and Hiawassee, Georgia, to the west.

Approach from the east: From the US 76 West–US 441 intersection in Clayton, turn onto US 76 West (a left turn if you approach this junction from the south on US 441 North) and travel US 76 West for approximately 18.7 miles to the right turn onto paved Upper Hightower Road. This turn is marked with signs for the road and Mount Pleasant Church of God at its entrance.

Approach from the west: From the US 76–GA 75 intersection in Hiawassee, where GA 75 heads north toward North Carolina, travel US 76 East for approximately 8.5 miles to the left turn onto paved Upper Hightower Road. Upper Hightower Baptist Church is located on the left side of the highway just before the turn, which is marked by signs for the road and Mount Pleasant Church of God at its entrance.

Access Point 5

This access point is the three-way US 64–Deep Gap Road intersection located along that segment of US 64 between Franklin, North Carolina, to the east, and Hayesville, North Carolina, to the west.

Approach from the east: From the US 64–US 441 (Business 441) intersection in Franklin, travel US 64 West for approximately 14.6 miles to the left turn onto paved Deep Gap Road (FS 71), usually marked with a small brown sign for Deep Gap.

Approach from the west: From the US 64–NC 175 intersection east of Hayesville, travel US 64 East for approximately 13.8 miles to the right turn onto paved Deep Gap Road (FS 71), usually designated with a small brown sign for Deep Gap.

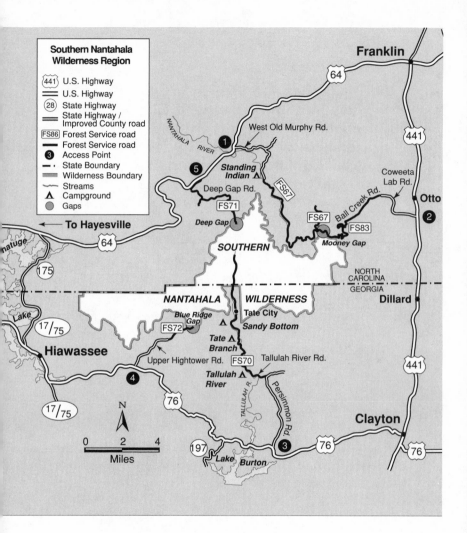

Southern Nantahala Wilderness Region

441	U.S. Highway
═══	U.S. Highway
28	State Highway
▬▬▬	State Highway / Improved County road
FS86	Forest Service road
▬▬	Forest Service road
3	Access Point
·–·	State Boundary
▓▓▓	Wilderness Boundary
∿∿	Streams
▲	Campground
●	Gaps

Franklin

64

441

NANTAHALA RIVER

West Old Murphy Rd.

1

5

Standing Indian ▲

Coweeta Lab Rd.

Otto

2

Deep Gap Rd.

FS67

FS71

Ball Creek Rd.

Deep Gap ●

FS67

FS83

SOUTHERN

Mooney Gap ●

← To Hayesville

64

175

natuge

Lake

17/75

NORTH CAROLINA

GEORGIA

Dillard

NANTAHALA   **WILDERNESS**

Blue Ridge Gap ●

Tate City ▲

FS72

Sandy Bottom

Hiawassee

Tate ▲ Branch

Upper Hightower Rd.

FS70

Tallulah River Rd.

4

Tallulah ▲ River

441

17/75

76

N

TALLULAH R.

Persimmon Rd.

Clayton

0   2   4

Miles

197

Lake Burton

3

76

76

I thought as I sat there this was the quiet we knew in our distant past, when it was part of our minds and spirits. We have not forgotten and never will though the scream and roar of jet engines, the grinding vibrations of cities, and the constant bombardment of electronic noise may seem to have blunted our senses forever. We can live with such clamor, it is true, but we pay a price and do so at our peril. The loss of quiet in our lives is one of the great tragedies of civilization, and to have known even for a moment the silence of the wilderness is one of our most precious memories.

—Sigurd Olson

Southern Nantahala Wilderness
Western Section

Left: High Falls
Right: Large-flowered trillium
near Beech Creek Trail

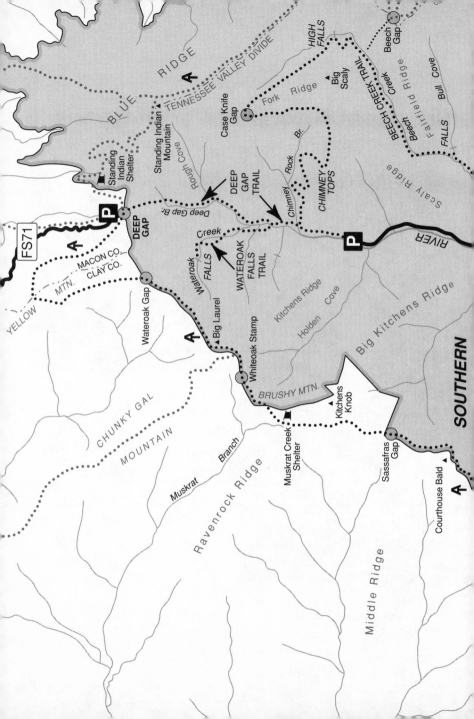

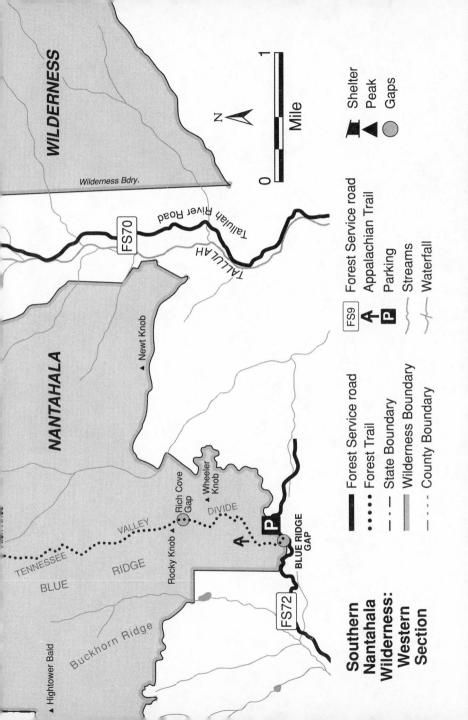

WILDERNESS

NANTAHALA

Wilderness Bdry.

FS70

Talulah River Road

TALULAH

▲ Newt Knob

Rich Cove
Gap

Wheeler
Knob

DIVIDE

Rocky Knob ▲

VALLEY

BLUE RIDGE
GAP

P

FS72

TENNESSEE

BLUE

RIDGE

Buckhorn Ridge

▲ Hightower Bald

N

Mile

0   1

**Southern
Nantahala
Wilderness:
Western
Section**

━━━ Forest Service road
••••• Forest Trail
– ·· – State Boundary
▬▬▬ Wilderness Boundary
– ··· – County Boundary

FS9 Forest Service road
↗ Appalachian Trail
P Parking
∿ Streams
⋎ Waterfall

🛏 Shelter
▲ Peak
● Gaps

Beech Creek Trail

Length 7.0 miles

- **Dayhiking** Moderate in either direction
- **Backpacking** Moderate to Strenuous in either direction
- **Vehicular Access at Either End** Southern (lower elevation) terminus of the near loop at the Beech Creek Trailhead off Tallulah River Road, 2,600 feet; northern (higher elevation) terminus is the Tallulah River Trailhead (end of Tallulah River Road), 2,830 feet
- **Trail Junctions** Deep Gap, Wateroak Falls, unmaintained sidepaths (see description)
- **Topographic Quadrangles** Rainbow Springs NC, Hightower Bald GA-NC
- **Blaze** No official Forest Service blazing
- **RD/NF** Tusquitee/Nantahala
- **Features** Tallulah River; Chimney Rock; winter views; spring wildflower display; Beech Creek and its numerous cascades; rock outcrops; High Falls

THIS TRAIL DEFIES A SHORT, SIMPLE, LINEAR DESCRIPTION. It features far too many attractions and sidepaths demanding digression. First, Beech Creek's configuration, a near loop, is unusual within wilderness trail systems. Unmaintained routes lead left and right to a rock-climb overlook, two waterfalls, and a gap on the Appalachian Trail. If you poke around a bit near the beginning of the loop, you can find remains of the former Girl Scout camp. Just beyond the sidepath to High Falls, you'll have no trouble spotting the mining operation ruins.

More clifflike rock outcrops line this course than any other Southern Appalachian trail I have hiked. The wildflower display, especially the extensive colonies of two trillium species, is impressive in early May. Near the middle of the loop, winter views of the surrounding ridges last until the second week of May. Last, but certainly not least, the final half of this loop often closely parallels its namesake stream—a clear, cold brook that tumbles and falls 2,180 feet in a little more than 3.5 miles from its beginning spring near Case Knife Gap to Tallulah River Road.

Like Deep Gap, Beech Creek traverses the upper Tallulah River basin, a drainage emphatically delineated by a high, sweeping, bell-shaped arc in the Blue Ridge. Here the famous ridge doubles as the Tennessee Valley Divide. All of the water south of the divide flows into the Tallulah, a Savannah River headwater stream that quickly enters Georgia.

Combined with a 1.2-mile segment of Tallulah River Road, Beech Creek Trail forms a complete loop, ending exactly where it begins. This route is described as it is most often and most easily walked, in a clockwise direction from the end of Tallulah River Road up to Case Knife Gap, then down with Beech Creek back to the road.

Starting at the road-blocking boulders, Beech Creek follows the gradual upgrade of an old road (it was still traveled by high-clearance vehicles until wilderness designation), which is the trail for all but the final 0.5 mile of the near loop. From trailhead to Girl Scout camp, the track often closely follows the scenic, creek-sized Tallulah River, here only 2 miles downstream from its highest headwater spring. The sheltering Tallulah valley supports a remarkably cool and moist hemlock-hardwood forest, especially notable for its species composition in a habitat below 3,000 feet and so close to the north Georgia border. Here among the expected beech, sweet birch, silverbell, yellow buckeye, yellow poplar, and northern red oak, two northern hardwoods—sugar maple and yellow birch (curly bark)—are growing very close to their southern limit in this part of the Southern Appalachians. If global warming proves to be as severe as many predict, the warmer temperatures will probably push these two species higher up the mountain.

At 0.3 mile the roadbed trail enters the former Girl Scout camp. To the right of the route saplings mark the site of a field that was, with the exception of a few fruit trees, totally open when Congress designated the land as legal and biological wilderness in 1984. The walkway reaches its only officially maintained and signed junction at 0.4 mile. Deep Gap Trail leads to the left; Beech Creek Trail, just getting warmed up, continues straight ahead before curving to the right and climbing slightly harder into a stand of tall yellow poplar. Two-tenths mile beyond the fork, a rounded switchback curls beside Chimney Rock Branch, last call permanent water before the Beech Creek springs. On the rich wildflower slope before the next turn, rattlesnake ferns are easily identified by their unusual fertile stalks, held erect above their lacy foliage from midspring through early fall.

Continuing to change exposures as it winds to the northeast toward Case Knife Gap, the path traverses lush north- and northwest-facing slopes full of spring wildflowers. The long north-facing slope furnishes good looks at Standing Indian's 5,200-foot-high wall to the left (40 degrees to 60 degrees). The steady, easy ascent passes through rhododendron tunnels to a drier forest ruled by oaks—chestnut, scarlet, and northern red. At mile 1.2 the course gains elevation harder (short, easy to moderate) for the first time. Three-tenths mile further, it slants uphill even sharper, moderate at worst, to the crest (mile 1.7) of a westward-dropping spur from nearby Big Scaly—a ho-hum 5,060-foot peak in Standing Indian's shadow.

The treadway turns left onto the ridgeline before quickly slabbing to the left onto slope where chestnut logs from blight-felled trees that died 65 to 70 years ago are still slowly decaying. After gaining the spur top a second time, Beech Creek slips onto the northwest-facing slope again and ascends steadily (easy or easy to moderate) through an open hardwood forest with a largely herbaceous understory. At mile 2.1, well below the ridgeline, the route passes a worn loafing spot beside three or four boulders on the left side of the woods road. Opposite the boulders, a small cairn marks the sidepath that angles up and to the right, leading 0.1 to 0.2 mile through scenic terrain to Chimney Rock.

Located on Big Scaly's upper-west slope, Chimney Rock is a large and unusual outcrop, significantly higher than wide and open to air all the way around. Starting from the rock's lower left side, a scramble up through rhododendron takes you to the upslope side. At the far upslope corner a foot- and hand-hold rock-climb route leads to the 360-degree panorama from the cap. The conical peak at 325 degrees is 5,020-foot Yellow Mountain. To the north, the high hump of Standing Indian breaks the mile-high barrier at 5,499 feet. From late April through early summer, this high perch is an excellent place to spot two of Southern Appalachia's most beautiful songbirds—the scarlet tanager and the rose-breasted grosbeak—in the eye-level and below-eye-level canopy of the surrounding trees.

Because we live in the land of the free and the frequently sued, Chimney Rock requires a disclaimer. Actually, a stern warning is the only responsible choice here. Although the rock's exposure is not sheer, a fall from the upper or middle sections will probably kill you. Young, fit, self-assured hikers will probably slither up in a hurry and think it's no big deal. Confident middle-aged hikers in reasonably good shape will think it's a challenge and go up haltingly. But if you are neither strong nor confident and are afraid of heights, Chimney Rock is no place for you. Don't let any prodding cheerleader convince you otherwise. As always, you undertake wilderness activities at your own risk. Just remember: natural selection never sleeps, and the dumb shall suffer.

Beyond the sidepath to Chimney Rock, the main trail climbs harder as it heads north on the western slope of Fork Ridge, a named Big Scaly spur. The often-rocky upgrades alternate between easy and easy to moderate, with a few short moderate pulls to make you work a little harder for your beauty. Two intermittent Chimney Rock Branch feeders, the first a waterslide and the second a regular rivulet, cross the track at mile 2.3 and 2.5. Up here above 4,000 feet, not a hemlock is in sight; all of the trees larger than rhododendron are hardwoods, increasingly oak. Along this stretch the wilderness walkway offers steady winter views of the Blue Ridge to the west and northwest. Above 4,500 feet, beech and yellow birch mix with the oaks. The treadway levels as it passes through the trail's high point— Case Knife Gap (4,740 feet) at mile 3.1. The planted fir trees in the gap have not fared well; most have died since the mid-1980s.

Once through the gap, the route swings to the southeast and heads down, gradually at first, the upper Beech Creek valley between 5,000-foot peaks. Standing Indian's wall-like ridge bulks high above the track to the left (northeast); nearby Big Scaly hems in the valley to the right (southwest). The next 0.8 mile, all level or gentle down, provides the trail's easiest walking. Dense rhododendron clumps darken the woods; occasional old-growth trees—mostly gnarled, poor-form northern red oaks and yellow birch—escaped last millennium's logging. Just to the left of the trail at mile 3.3, Beech Creek's highest headwater spring flows cold and clear out of the black dirt. If you poke around in the rhododendron on the other side of the spring, you will find rusting strips of tin, remains of the former shelter that stood on the site until the late 1980s.

Narrowed to path by the lush vegetation, the course closely follows the shining stream, which quickly grows from the numerous seeps and springs. The rich northeast-facing slope above the creek nourishes an unusually lavish and diverse spring wildflower display. At mile 3.9 the often-rocky treadway begins a series of sharper downgrades (most easy to moderate, some moderate) as it switchbacks to the south away from, then back to, Beech Creek. The stream descends sharply here too, falling in short cascades, sluices, and slides between boulders or over bedrock ledges. Tall, gray outcrops line the near upslope as the walkway bends further away from the entrenched creek. A particularly high (70 to 90 feet) and scenic set of cliffs continues straight ahead where the route switchbacks down and to the left at mile 4.3. The descent proceeds through open, rocky, hardwood slopes where extensive large-flowered trillium colonies bloom below the outcrops in early May.

Where the roadbed trail doglegs to the right at mile 4.5, a usually signed sidepath to the left leads 0.1 mile down a very rich wildflower slope to High Falls. Approximately 75 to 80 feet tall, this small-volume falls is not much to look at during drought. But on a sunny day after the right amount of rain, the froth fans out into a dazzling lacework, joining and splitting in a repeated pattern as the white skeins spill down the wide rockface.

Beyond the sidepath to the beautiful falls, the main trail descends steadily (moderate at first, then easy), downslope from another impressive set of rock outcrops. The track switchbacks to the right and down alongside Beech Creek at mile 4.8. To the left on the outside of the curve, a homemade, non–Forest Service sign points (or did when I hiked the trail) to an unofficial sidetrail leading, so the sign said, 0.5 mile to Beech Gap on the Appalachian Trail. I wheeled this unmaintained track to see if it was really 0.5 mile long, and if it really led to Beech Gap. It was, and it did. This blue-blazed AT connector is the steepest trail, official or otherwise, that I have ever walked or wheeled. It is so steep that when I stopped to catch my breath I had to lean backwards against a tree.

Almost immediately after veering above its namesake stream, the course passes a stacked-rock ruin, where corundum was crushed during the mining days. For the next 1.1 miles, from the switchback at mile 4.8 to the creek crossing at mile 5.9, the route works its way down the watershed to the southwest, closely following Beech Creek's wilderness-clear water. Steady downslope views offer excellent looks at the stream's numerous low falls and short white surges. The overall easy-to-moderate downstream run leads through a predominantly deciduous forest of tall second-growth trees. Hemlock is the only conifer in sight. To the right of the path at mile 5.4, a wet-weather rivulet spills down a 15-foot-high double-ledge drop.

The downgrade crosses Beech Creek just below a bank-to-bank ledge at mile 5.9. One-tenth mile beyond the first crossing, the trail rock-steps a Beech Creek feeder flowing out of Bull Cove. (Just before you cross the branch, a faint path to the left heads approximately 120 yards upstream to the 40-foot-high Bull Cove Falls, a small-volume waterfall.) The no-sweat hiking continues, at one point through a memorable, trail-crowding gauntlet of poison ivy. At mile 6.5 the treadway swerves to the right and down off the old road, which continues straight ahead into saplings. The final segment of the trail was rerouted off the road grade to avoid private property.

Less than 0.1 mile after the turn onto path, the track crosses Beech Creek for the second time. Now the walking slants up the slope—easy, then moderate-to-strenuous, then easy again—through a drier, south-facing forest. The ascent ends at mile 6.8, where the course passes through a gap in Scaly Ridge before dropping to the trail's southern end at Tallulah River Road. Two of the descents along this poorly routed downgrade are very steep.

Nature Notes

Beech Creek's hardwood forest harbors an impressive spring wildflower display. Not only does this route offer diversity and abundance, but it also allows hikers to walk up and back into spring, to find freshly minted wildflowers high in the shadow of Standing Indian weeks after the blooms have withered down below. In early May, as the canopy closes overhead, extensive colonies of Vasey's and large-flowered trillium blossom at the lower elevations while windflower and trout lily still bless the highcountry near Case Knife Gap. The Vasey's rich, carmine-colored corollas are the largest among Southern Appalachian trilliums. This striking flower is far more numerous here than along any other trail I have ever walked.

You may find many other wildflowers near this trail. The speckled wood lily blooms beside the path to Chimney Rock; waterleaf and sweet cicely grow along the sidetrail to High Falls. Two other trilliums—wake robin and Catesby's—bloom alongside mayapple, yellow mandarin, and lousewort. You may also see hepatica, rue anemone, umbrella-leaf, foamflower, bloodroot, blue cohosh, showy orchis, and toothwort blooming during April or May.

Along Beech Creek's first half, which affords numerous views down hardwood slopes, you can pick out the distinctive bark of the black cherry trees from a relatively long distance. Its dark bark sticks out in a stand, especially in the diverse cove hardwood forest, where most of the species exhibit light gray or grayish brown boles. Cherry bark, broken into small platy scales with upturned edges, is dark brownish gray to nearly black. The centers of the scales often appear slick and shiny.

This species is one of the earliest hardwoods to leaf out in the southern mountains. As far as I know, only the yellow buckeye breaks bud substantially earlier within this wilderness. The foliage, twigs, and bark of the black cherry emit the distinctive aroma of bitter almond or hydrocyanic acid. The alternate, finely saw-toothed leaves—oblong and sharp pointed at the tip—are 2 to 6 inches long and ¾ to 2 inches wide. When eaten fresh and raw, the leaves release prussic acid, a poison. Black cherry leaves have probably killed more Southern Appalachian livestock than any other plant.

black cherry

The black cherry trees along this trail flower in late April or May when the leaves are not yet fully grown. Unfolding from the ends of the outermost branches, numerous small white corollas with orange stamens cluster tightly on racemes 4 to 6 inches long. You probably won't see the blossoms on the taller trees without binoculars, but if you happen upon a low-hanging bloom, a strong whiff at close range will make you squint your eyes and wrinkle your nose.

The black is the largest native cherry in North America. This species reaches its largest proportions in the deep, rich, well-watered soils of the southern mountains, where it thrives from the lowest elevations to approximately 5,500 feet. People accustomed to the small, scraggly specimens (easily identified by their heavy infestations of tent caterpillars) along the roadsides of Piedmont Georgia and the Carolinas can hardly believe the stature and beauty of mountain-grown cherries. Achieving their best growth in coves and on north-facing slopes, the largest second-growth blacks already have grown 70 to 90 feet tall and 6 to 9 feet in circumference. In the Great Smoky Mountains National Park, a virgin-forest lunker along Ramsay Cascades Trail measures 124 feet in height and slightly over 13 feet in circumference.

Throughout its huge range, this hardwood is dispersed by birds and other animals that void the seeds well away from their meals. When the seeds hit the soil, wrapped in their pre-fertilized packets, they take root and grow on most sites except the very wet and very dry. The northeastern portion of the black cherry's widely disjunct range stretches from central Florida up to Nova Scotia, west to northernmost Wisconsin, then southward to east Texas. Following mountains from north-central Arizona to southern Mexico, the southwestern portion of its range is linear and much smaller. The southernmost limit of this tree's range is a pocket of mountainous habitat in Guatemala.

Birds and other wildlife, including bears, eat cherries when they ripen in late summer. Bears crave and concentrate on the fruits when they are the tastiest, usually in August and September. The bruins climb right up, crawl out onto limbs, and begin feasting. Biologists estimate bears can gain as much as 3 pounds per day eating cherries alone. Back when there were more large cherries and more bears, woodsmen considered "cherry bears" to be particularly irritable and best left alone.

Early mountaineers also harvested wild cherries and no doubt became belligerent themselves from time to time. In *A Natural History of Trees*, Donald Culross Peattie describes a cherry-flavored libation: "In the days when our woods were rich with such fine old cherry trees, the Appalachian pioneers invented a drink called cherry bounce; juice pressed from the fruits was infused in brandy or rum to make a cordial which, though bitter, was in high favor among the old-time mountaineers."

From just beyond the Beech Creek–Deep Gap junction to nearly mile 1.0, you will have no trouble finding the unusual rattlesnake fern on the rich, wildflower slopes above and below the old roadbed. This native fern is easily detected by its forked stem; one branch of the fork holds the fertile stalk (the spore-bearing part), and the other the sterile blade (the leafy part). The fertile stalk continues straight up from the fork; the blade leans away from the fertile stalk at an approximate 45-degree angle.

Usually 8 to 24 inches in height, the deciduous fronds (the entire leaf from the ground up) appear in April and last until frost. Branching from the base of the blade, the conspicuous, 6- to 14-inch-long fertile stalk withers earlier in the fall than the rest of the plant. The sporangia cluster densely on short alternate stems. The appearance of these sporangia probably led to the reptilian name; someone must have thought the clusters resembled the buzzing end of a rattlesnake.

Highly variable in size and wider than tall, the broadly triangular sterile blades (the leafy part) are usually 5 to 12 inches in length. The opposite-stemmed foliage has evolved to delicately filigreed lace. This primitive, nonflowering plant is common throughout much of the Southern Appalachians in moist deciduous forests, particularly those with rich, well-drained soils. Its range is transcontinental: it is found throughout large portions of North America, Europe, and Asia. In North America the rattlesnake fern grows throughout most of the eastern U.S., across much of southern Canada, and, surprisingly, up the moist, moderate West Coast all the way to Alaska.

rattlesnake fern

Directions

Beech Creek Trail nearly forms a complete loop. The route has either-end vehicular access—two trailheads 1.2 miles apart on Tallulah River Road. These two trailheads can be most easily reached from Access Point 3. (See the detailed description of the Access Points on page 40.) Closely paralleling and crossing its namesake stream, Tallulah River Road affords numerous excellent views of the Tallulah's trout pools, shallow riffles, and boulder-clogged cascades.

Access Point 3: From the US 76–Persimmon Road intersection, travel paved Persimmon Road straight ahead for approximately 4.2 miles, then turn left onto paved Tallulah River Road (FS 70), designated with a road sign and a brown-and-white national forest sign for campgrounds and the Southern Nantahala Wilderness.

Follow scenic Tallulah River Road to the north. (The pavement ends after 1.5 miles.) The road enters Tate City after 5.0 miles, crosses the bridge over Beech Creek after 7.1 miles, and enters North Carolina after 7.3 miles. From the Tallulah River Road–Persimmon Road junction, it is approximately 7.8 miles to the southern trailhead and approximately 9.0 miles to the dead-end northern trailhead. A Beech Creek sign points to the large parking area (turnaround loop and plenty of pull-in parking) for the southern trailhead on the left side of the road. Marked by a numbered (378) carsonite Forest Service sign and sometimes a wooden sign further in, the southern end of Beech Creek Trail begins 55 yards before and across the road from the parking area's entrance.

The northern trailhead, known as the Tallulah River Trailhead, is impossible to miss; it is the parking area/turnaround at the boulder-blocked end of Tallulah River Road. The trail is the old road that continues straight ahead beyond the boulders and bulletin board.

Notes

Deep Gap Trail

Length 2.5 miles

- **Dayhiking** (low to high) Moderate
- **Dayhiking** (high to low) Easy to Moderate
- **Backpacking** (low to high) Moderate to Strenuous
- **Backpacking** (high to low) Moderate
- **Vehicular Access At Either End** Southern (lower elevation) terminus at Tallulah River Trailhead (end of Tallulah River Road), 2,830 feet; northern (higher elevation) terminus at Deep Gap Trailhead, 4,340 feet
- **Trail Junctions** Beech Creek, Wateroak Falls, Appalachian (end of Section 1 and beginning of Section 2 at Deep Gap), Kimsey Creek (at Deep Gap, nonwilderness and not included in this guide)
- **Topographic Quadrangle** Rainbow Springs NC
- **Blaze** No official Forest Service blazing
- **RD/NF** Tusquitee/Nantahala
- **Features** Tallulah River; Deep Gap Branch; AT approach

DEEP **G**AP **T**RAIL **PROVIDES A GOOD ROUTE** into the Southern Nantahala from the Georgia side of the wilderness. Combined with an equal length (2.5 miles) of the Appalachian Trail, Deep Gap offers dayhikers and backpackers a relatively easy, 10-mile round trip to the top of 5,499-foot-high Standing Indian Mountain.

Like Beech Creek, this north-south trail traverses the upper Tallulah basin, a drainage unequivocally delineated by a high, sweeping, horseshoe-shaped curve in the Blue Ridge. All water flowing within the basin is forced southward into Georgia and finally into the Atlantic at Savannah. Bisecting the upper end of the basin, Deep Gap closely parallels or loosely follows Atlantic-bound water—the Tallulah River then Deep Gap Branch—for most of its length as it rises toward the prominent notch in the middle of the horseshoe. Walked low to high, this route's beginning and end are street-shoe strolls compared to its short, steep middle, one of the sharpest grades described in this guide. Much of this trail once passed through privately owned land lightly used as a Girl Scout camp. Deep Gap was just one link in the camp's wide network of footpaths.

This trail is described as it is most often walked, from low to high, from south to north, from river to ridge. The initial treadway rises easily up the former roadbed, still wide and well graveled. Here at the beginning, three trails—Deep Gap, Beech Creek, and Wateroak Falls—share the same course. Down and to the left, the Tallulah River, less than 2 miles downstream from its northernmost headwater spring, flows cold and clear and shallow through mossy rocks. The cool, moist, riverine habitat supports rhododendron, hemlock, and a diverse, second-growth mix of northern and cove hardwoods— yellow poplar, northern red oak, white ash, striped and sugar maple, beech, basswood, yellow buckeye, and the birches, yellow and sweet.

The walkway narrows to single-file path through encroaching vegetation before arriving at the lower edge of a former field now filled with sapling hardwoods. When I first saw this human-made meadow in the fall of 1985, a year after its legal and biological designation as wilderness, the grassy field was totally open except for a few fruit trees. The track skirts the lower edge of the young forest on the gentle but rocky upgrade of a washed-out woods road to Deep Gap's first junction at 0.4 mile. Beech Creek Trail continues straight ahead at the often signed, obvious fork; Deep Gap and Wateroak Falls turn left. The now two-trail treadway passes a Deep Gap sign (#377 routed on post) and crosses very shallow Chimney Rock Branch in quick succession.

Once across the thin-water tributary, the wilderness walkway curls up and to the right with the rocky old road. The open forest in the flat between the trail and the Tallulah was once the camp's tenting site. The easy uphill hiking continues through hemlock and hardwoods (including three species of oak) to the second fork, this one beside the riverbank at 0.7 mile. Wateroak Falls Trail crosses the creek-sized stream. Guided by a second sign, Deep Gap skirts the bank, makes a short, warm-up elevation gain, then dips back down toward the Tallulah, where it picks up another roadbed. The mild grades continue as the track parallels the river through rhododendron. The canopy is composed primarily of moist-site broadleafs; the large, heart-shaped leaves of basswood saplings are particularly common.

This trail gains 1,500 feet of elevation over its 2.5-mile length. By the time you reach mile 1.2 and rock-step across Deep Gap Branch, a fast-dropping Tallulah feeder four strides across, you will be wondering when the ascent will begin. Your answer is not long in coming. After crossing the branch, the path passes through a rich, lower-slope forest lush with ferns and herbaceous wildflowers; in the spring look for yellow mandarin, blue cohosh, showy orchis, foamflower, and wake robin and Catesby's trilliums. The trail climbs for the first time, a short 90-yard-long pitch, before rock-stepping over Deep Gap Branch again. Steeper banks make this crossing more challenging than the last one. The course continues its ascent in the fork between two headwater streams; to the right an unnamed Deep Gap Branch tributary spills noisily down from Rough Cove.

At mile 1.4 the treadway begins a strenuous (moderate to strenuous overall) upslope run, frequently zigzagging in tight switchbacks. Now on steep, south-facing slope well above water, the footpath rises through drier-slope hardwoods—red maple, hickory, chestnut oak, sassafras, blackgum, sourwood, and a few chestnut saplings. Evergreens dominate the understory; galax and trailing arbutus cover the ground beneath the mountain laurel and the glossy rhododendron. The hard hiking eases up after 0.2 mile, and the trail returns to moist habitat above uppermost Deep Gap Branch. Back on former road again, the walkway works its way up the watershed on undemanding grades roughly parallel to the small stream. Not a single pine is rooted along the entire trail and the hemlock has been left behind down below; now the moist-site canopy is totally deciduous.

After crossing one of the branch's uppermost rivulets, the single-file footpath swings to the right onto another woods road at mile 2.1. The final segment, heading north across a slope higher to the left, is as sidewalk flat as a trail can be in the Southern Appalachians.

Extensive colonies of lousewort, an easily recognized perennial wild-flower, often flank the treadway. The northern end of the trail enters sunlight and the gravel parking area in Deep Gap. You can continue walking to the left or the right on the long green tunnel—the Appalachian Trail. A right turn onto the white-blazed AT and 2.5 miles of fairly easy hiking will set your feet atop Standing Indian Mountain, the Southern Nantahala's highest peak.

All of the wilderness trails heading south from Forest Service roads north of the wilderness are well maintained. Beech Creek and Deep Gap, the two designated trails located in the bowl of the Blue Ridge are maintained to a more primitive standard. You may want to carry a folding backpacker's saw to help clear the way.

Nature Notes

Basswood, a large and distinctive yet often unrecognized tree, thrives along most of this trail. Its large-leaved saplings are especially numerous and no-ticeable beside the segment from mile *American basswood* 0.7 to 1.2. This broadleaf competes for the canopy and is often a significant component within its preferred habitat—hardwood cove, north-facing slope, and stream valley—throughout the Southern Nantahala Wilderness below 4,200 feet. The botanical controversy concerning the basswood's genus, *Tilia*, has waned for now. Current literature lumps all basswoods into one species—the American basswood (*Tilia americana*)—with three varieties (Carolina, white, and American).

Basswood is sometimes known as linden, a name German settlers transferred from a *Tilia* species in Europe, and as bee-tree, because honeybees swarm to its fragrant blossoms. The common name basswood, which is recognized by botanists and foresters, comes from the fibers in the tree's inner bark, called bast, which Native Americans stripped to make rope.

This hardwood is identified by its large, alternate, heart-shaped leaves, which are sharply pointed, coarsely toothed, and usually 4 to 6 inches long and almost as wide. The larger leaves of the saplings often measure as much as 8 inches long and 6 inches wide. Bark on a maturing second-growth trunk is light to medium gray. Slight furrows rising in broken lines split the bark into vertical patterns. Especially in once- and twice-cut forests, basswood often occurs in multiboled clumps. A mature specimen usually can be distinguished from a distance by its sapling ring—a circle of sprouts growing from the tree's base.

Commonly 60 to 90 feet in height and 2 to 3 feet in diameter (these are southern mountain dimensions), the forest-grown basswood features a straight bole clear of branches to half its total height. The largest basswood in North Carolina stands 116 feet high and measures an impressive 18 feet 7 inches around at 4½ feet from the ground. Some old-timers have held bark and bole together for over 400 years.

At least three or four easily overlooked clumps of lousewort flank the trail along the first 2.1 miles before its final switchback onto level roadbed. But after that last turn, extensive colonies of this semiparasitic perennial are hard to miss when they are blooming by the hundreds to either side of the walkway. A member of the Snapdragon family, this unusual wildflower with the unflattering name is quickly identified with or without blossoms. The larger dark green basal leaves are 3 to 6 inches long, and deeply and regularly cut into toothed, fernlike lobes. A few smaller leaves alternate along the flowering stems, which are usually between 6 and 15 inches high.

lousewort

Lousewort flowers form a dense terminal cluster or spike, 1 inch or more in diameter, consisting of a twisted whorl of tubular, two-lipped blossoms. The odd-looking corollas are slender and from ¾ to

1 inch long. Double toothed at its apex, the larger upper lip arches beaklike over the smaller, three-toothed lower lip. Most Southern Appalachian colonies produce bicolored blooms. The upper lip is usually maroonish brown or burgundy, while the lower lip is creamy white, yellow, or brownish yellow. This species usually blooms along the Deep Gap Trail from May 5 to May 25.

Distributed widely across the eastern U.S., this common native herb occurs from northwestern Florida to east Texas, northward to south-central Manitoba, then eastward across southern Quebec to Maine. Within its extensive range, the lousewort is most plentiful in rich, moist woods, primarily open and deciduous, up to approximately 5,200 feet.

Lousewort has a colorful history. Medieval Europeans firmly believed their livestock became infested with lice after grazing on or near their version of this perennial. ("Wort" is the old English word for plant.) When Europeans colonized North America, they transferred their old-world superstitions to the new-world species. At the same time peasants were worrying about livestock lice, Native Americans were happily grinding up the herb's roots for an aphrodisiac potion. One culture's pest magnet was another's love elixir. Computer-age physicians use this wildflower in the treatment of Bell's palsy, an affliction affecting facial nerves.

Directions

Deep Gap has either-end vehicular access. Because of this trail's short length (2.5 miles) and very long shuttle distance (approximately 60 miles one way), however, most hikers begin and end at the same trailhead. The directions to Deep Gap's southern (lower elevation) terminus are exactly the same as those to Beech Creek's northern, Tallulah River trailhead. This trailhead is impossible to miss; it is the parking area/turnaround at the boulder-blocked end of Tallulah River Road. The trail begins on the old roadbed continuing straight ahead beyond the boulders and bulletin board. (See Beech Creek, page 60, for directions to its northern end at the Tallulah River trailhead.)

The directions to this route's northern (higher elevation) terminus at Deep Gap are exactly the same as those for Section 2's western terminus at Deep Gap. (See Section 2 of the Appalachian Trail, page 95, for directions to its western trailhead at Deep Gap.)

The unblazed Deep Gap Trail, an old woods road, enters the forest to the back of the pull-in spaces straight ahead from Deep Gap Road's entrance into the parking area. The white-blazed Appalachian Trail crosses the far end of the parking area, perpendicular to Deep Gap's entrance.

Notes

Wateroak Falls Trail

Length 1.3 miles

- ■ **Dayhiking** Moderate
- ■ **Backpacking** Not suitable
- ■ **Start** Tallulah River Trailhead (end of Tallulah River Road), 2,830 feet
- ■ **End** Wateroak Falls, 3,320 feet
- ■ **Trail Junctions** Beech Creek, Deep Gap
- ■ **Topographic Quadrangle** Rainbow Springs NC
- ■ **Blaze** No official Forest Service blazing
- ■ **RD/NF** Tusquitee/Nantahala
- ■ **Features** Tallulah River; Wateroak Creek; Wateroak Falls

WATEROAK FALLS IS NEITHER DESIGNATED nor maintained as an official Forest Service trail. This track was once part of a network of footpaths walked by locals and Girl Scouts, whose camp beside the Tallulah River stood less than a winding mile away from the falls. I first hiked to Wateroak Falls in 1987, by mistake, while trying to find the Deep Gap Trail. At that time, a few years after the Dorothy Thomas Foundation sold 1,196 acres to the Forest Service for inclusion within the Southern Nantahala Wilderness, the route to the falls was open, occasionally flagged, and fairly easy to follow. Since that time, however, fewer feet have roughed the forest floor all the way to the falls, and the infrequently trod walkway has grown faint.

Wateroak Falls Trail shares the same former roadbed with Beech Creek and Deep Gap Trails for its first 0.4 mile. Where Beech Creek and Deep Gap split apart near Chimney Rock Branch, Wateroak Falls follows Deep Gap for the next 0.3 mile to the Tallulah River. Since this first stretch already has been described in the previous two trails, and the next segment has been detailed in the preceding trail, Deep Gap, this narrative of Wateroak Falls Trail begins at 0.7 mile, where Wateroak Falls forks away from Deep Gap at the Tallulah River.

Just before its first ascent (a very short one), Deep Gap closely skirts the bank of the Tallulah. At the point where Deep Gap comes closest to the water, Wateroak Falls Trail crosses the creek-sized river, normally an easy rock-step after leaf-out at the highest elevations. On its own now, the route follows the bed of a former woods road and continues its easy upgrade parallel to the Tallulah. The forest overhead consists of rhododendron, hemlock, and hardwoods—mainly oaks, yellow poplar, basswood, sugar maple, sweet and yellow birch, hickory, and white ash. Here the hiking, on the edge of the washed-out road, angles further up and away from the river. One tenth mile after rock-hopping the Tallulah, the track crosses a permanent water rivulet and continues its mild uphill run still parallel to the river on well-defined and intact roadbed. Rattlesnake plantain, a small orchid, flourishes in unusually large colonies along this stretch.

At 1.0 mile the trail comes to and crosses Wateroak Creek, a Tallulah tributary. Once across the creek, the course switches streams, turns to the left up and away from the river, then follows the feeder to the falls. So far, so good, but until a recognizable treadway becomes reestablished, hiking the short remainder can be tricky. The footpath, sometimes worn and sometimes not, heads uphill on or near a logging spur close beside the brook, which should be on your left. The few cutbark blazes were probably hacked when someone chopped away homemade paint blazes. You'll have to weave your way around deadfalls and through rhododendron archways.

After heading up the branch-sized creek for almost exactly 0.1 mile, you should pass beside a low clump of four small, close-set boulders. Continue upstream for another 50 yards, then turn left and cross the tributary where you can see a well-defined treadway leading uphill on the far bank. Now the trail climbs sharply on well-defined path (if deadfalls don't move it) for 75 yards before crossing a seep and climbing hard again for 30 yards. With 0.1 mile remaining, you should see a clifflike rockface across the water. Angle down toward the standing rock, then make a switchback to the right and down to where you can lower yourself to stream level. Cross Wateroak Creek for the third and final time, scramble up the bank just downstream from the crag, then work your way to the base of the falls.

When the water flows full, twin white ribbons splash their way down the wide rockface ledge. As the flow falters after leaf-out on the high ridges, most of the slide rollicks down the far left side of the 45- to 50-foot falls. Instead of plunging into a catch pool, the water wends through a jumble of mossy boulders and mouldering logs. Wateroak Falls is the drop of a small-volume stream. By early June of a recent drought year, the waterfall had been diminished to two listless streaks.

Directions

The directions to Wateroak Falls Trail are exactly the same as those to Beech Creek Trail's northern, Tallulah River Trailhead. (See Beech Creek, page 60, for directions to its northern [dead-end], Tallulah River Trailhead from Access Point 3.)

Notes

Appalachian National Scenic Trail
(Section 1: Blue Ridge Gap to Deep Gap)

Length 10.1 miles

- **Dayhiking** Moderate in either direction
- **Backpacking** Moderate to Strenuous in either direction
- **Vehicular Access At Either End** Southwestern (lower elevation) terminus at Blue Ridge Gap Trailhead, 3,020 feet; northeastern (higher elevation) terminus at Deep Gap Trailhead, 4,340 feet
- **Trail Junctions** Chunky Gal (nonwilderness trail not included in this guide), Deep Gap (at Deep Gap), Appalachian (Section 2 at Deep Gap, trail continues southwest from Blue Ridge Gap to southern terminus at Springer Mountain), Kimsey Creek (at Deep Gap, nonwilderness trail not included in this guide)
- **Topographic Quadrangles** Hightower Bald GA-NC, Rainbow Springs NC
- **Blazes** White paint rectangle for AT, blue paint rectangle for most sidetrails and paths leading to shelters or water
- **RD/NF** Tallulah/Chattahoochee, Tusquitee/Nantahala
- **Features** Winter views; rock outcrops; year-round views; flame azalea display

TWENTY-THREE MILES OF ONE OF THE WORLD'S most famous hiking trails wind through the Southern Nantahala Wilderness. That trail, of course, is the Appalachian National Scenic Trail—the long green tunnel. Completed in 1937, the AT is now a linear component of the National Park system, the only unit entirely managed by volunteers. From its southern terminus atop Georgia's Springer

Mountain, the Appalachian Trail beckons walkers onward and upward for approximately 2,167 miles to its northern terminus atop Maine's Mount Katahdin in Baxter State Park.

Most would-be thru-hikers, those who attempt to walk the entire trail in one year, start at Springer Mountain and walk north with the spring. When AT hikers enter the wilderness at Blue Ridge Gap, they are just getting warmed up; they are still in their first of fourteen states, their first national forest—the Chattahoochee. Here in the Southern Nantahala, where the AT passes over 5,499-foot Standing Indian, northbound trekkers encounter their first short stretch of mile-high hiking.

For ease of description, I have divided the Southern Nantahala's 23.3-mile segment of the AT into two accessible sections, each suitable for a long dayhike or a leisurely two- or three-day backpacking trip. The two sections are described as they are most often walked, from southwest to northeast, from Georgia to North Carolina.

Starting at Blue Ridge Gap (3,020 feet), Section 1 enters the wilderness and rises easily on wide path through white pine and diverse hardwoods. The track gains the crest of the ridge descending southward from Wheeler Knob after 0.1 mile. Not only does this ridge lead to a named peak, but it is also part of the Tennessee Valley Divide and the famed Blue Ridge. Here the AT gains elevation (easy or easy to moderate) on or near the ridgetop. On the way up, the route slips onto sunrise slope, switchbacks up to and over the crest onto the sunset pitch, then follows the ridgeline through a maturing forest dominated by oaks.

At mile 0.6 the treadway slants off the backbone of the ridge into a predominantly deciduous, west-slope woods where sassafras saplings thrive in rootsucker colonies. For the next 0.6 mile the gentle grades—crossing the creases over spurs and around hollows—skirt the upper-west flank of Wheeler Knob. Look for sweet birch, yellow poplar, striped maple, and black cherry where the forest is north-facing and moist. At mile 1.0 a blue-blazed sidepath leads left to an intermittent water source, dry as a burned bone during drought. A short distance beyond the blue blazes, a look to the left (west-northwest) offers a partial view of Buckhorn Ridge—a major spur dropping to the southeast from Hightower Bald. A gradual upslope run brings the AT back to ridgecrest at a shallow, narrow saddle—Rich Cove Gap (3,450 feet)—at mile 1.2.

Beyond the gap, the ridge rises sharply toward Rocky Knob. Section 1, however, half-circles around the knob's upper-east slope. Along the way, which includes an initial short, easy-to-moderate ascent, the track affords another hole-in-the-canopy prospect of high rolling humps to the east-northeast. The course dips to a gap at mile 1.4 before riding the crest back up through an all hardwood forest that includes oaks (white, chestnut, and northern red), pignut hickory, red maple, blackgum, and sourwood. Ranging almost due north, the ridgetop walkway follows the nearly effortless grades of the keel to mile 1.7, where it starts down, easy to moderate at first, to the short flat of the next gap at mile 1.9.

Here the ridgeline mounts northward toward Rich Knob's 4,152-foot crown. As the route swings around minor knobs and bumps along the way, it gains elevation from gap to higher gap. Now the AT climbs (easy, moderate, then easy to moderate) as it bypasses a slight knob on western slope. After regaining the spine, the treadway descends to and levels through a slight gap at mile 2.2, then ascends again. A sidepath at mile 2.3 leads to an outcrop offering a partial, over-the-trees look-off to the south-southwest. Beyond the sidepath, the walking heads down through mountain laurel and rhododendron before slabbing to the right off the crest at mile 2.5.

Rather than plodding up and over the top of Rich Knob, the next 0.6 mile makes a much easier end run around its upper-east flank, slowly angling upslope starting at approximately 3,700 feet. Much of this stretch traverses steep, scenic terrain—boulders and slabs of outcrop rock thrust their lichened grays above the lush layers of herbaceous greens. As the well-constructed sidehill path works its way above 3,800 feet, the higher elevation, the eastern exposure, and the state-line latitude combine to make the forest cool and moist enough for two northern hardwoods—sugar maple and yellow birch. The easy walking enters North Carolina at the signed boundary, turns left at a campsite beside an intermittent spring, advances back up to crestline, then bends right and quickly enters Bly Gap (3,840 feet) at mile 3.2. The AT's first named feature in North Carolina, Bly is an open loafing spot, marked, for now at least, by a crooked and sway-boled northern red oak, a convenient leaning post for back and pack. The slope downhill and to the left of the gap was open in the late 1970s (the first time I dropped pack at the oak); the trees have steadily stolen the view since that time.

Beyond the saddle, the Appalachian Trail curves to the northeast and traverses mountainous terrain by its most famous method—roller-coastering through gaps and over peaks—for most of the next 1.9 miles. On the way up to the first peak, Sharp Top, Section 1 climbs for the first time above 4,000 feet, where it remains for the rest of Section 1 and all of Section 2. The track makes an overall moderate upridge run through hardwoods and around jutting outcrop on nar-row crest. The boot-worn treadway switchbacks then tunnels through rhododendron as it passes to the left (northwest) and just below Sharp Top's high point (4,340 feet) at mile 3.6.

Losing elevation toward the next trough in the sine curve course, the dark path angles onto moist northwest slope through a diverse forest, where all the trees above rhododendron level are deciduous. Sweet and yellow birch, sugar and striped maple, yellow poplar, white and northern red oak, cucumbertree, black cherry, basswood, and white ash are among the many species found here. At mile 3.7 a par-tial view of Middle Ridge opens to the north-northwest. Further down, you might catch a quick glimpse of the route's next high point—the sharp, conical crown of Courthouse Bald. The course continues uphill to the next gap (4,180 feet), shallow and unnamed, at mile 4.0. Above the saddle, the trailside understory is a solid aster garden in late summer and early fall.

The snaky, switchbacking climb to Courthouse Bald begins with a short moderate pull and reaches its toughest grade—an 85-yard-long upridge grunt (moderate to strenuous)—at mile 4.2. Here AT volunteers have skillfully constructed a series of switchbacks—a hiker's version of landlubber locks—to reduce leg strain while keep-ing the trail on or near the often sharply rising and rocky ridgetop. Beyond two partial summer views, the first to the left of the trail and the other to the right, a sidepath opposite a switchback at mile 4.4

leads left to an outcrop overlook open to the west. Lake Chatuge lies shining due west. The towered top of Brasstown Bald, Georgia's highest peak, is obvious well away to the southwest. The distant rolling swell of old mountains rises rounded and worn against the hazy sky.

A final easy-to-moderate upgrade finishes the ascent to Courthouse Bald (4,700 feet). The track levels, skirts below the summit around the eastern edge of the crown through a broadleaf forest above rhododendron, mountain laurel, and flame azalea, then begins the 0.6-mile descent, enlivened by short, sharp pitches, at mile 4.5. The wilderness walkway works its way down on or near the ridgecrest, usually on the uppermost east slope, where gaps in the foliage offer peeks at the Southern Nantahala's chief mountain— Standing Indian—to the northeast. After leveling through Sassafras Gap (4,260 feet) at mile 5.1, the white-blazed footpath gains elevation on a steady, 0.2-mile-long, easy-to-moderate grade below and to the west of the keel.

Following a spur back toward the high ridge, the route settles into a steady mild gradient, traveling along the upper west flank of Brushy Mountain, which has two named high points: Kitchens Knob to the south and Whiteoak Stamp to the north. (Stamps and stomps—former sites of corralled livestock—are occasional place names throughout the Southern Appalachians, especially in the former highcountry pastures of summer.) The sugar maple is now noticeably more common in this high, west-facing forest, still all hardwood, than just a few miles downtrail to the south. The gradual upslope run continues—through a rhododendron breezeway and over a bridged rivulet still running in early October of a recent hard-drought year—to Brushy Mountain's spine (mile 5.8) south of Whiteoak Stamp. After a short, more or less level segment, the wide path ventures down through a shiny gnarl of rhododendron with northern red oak boles poking up through the evergreen tangle. At mile 5.9 a topknot of ridgecrest rock just to the left affords another vista open to the west, like the one at mile 4.4. You can spot the nippled top of Brasstown Bald at 235 degrees; look for Blood Mountain, to the left of Brasstown and further away, at 230 degrees.

Persevering toward Maine and Mount Katahdin, still months of hard hiking and over 2,000 miles away, the track slowly descends through dark rhododendron. A blue-blazed sidepath to the left leads approximately 0.5 mile to an open outcrop view from Ravenrock Ridge. Thirty yards further at mile 6.0, Section 1 crosses a two-plank bridge over a headwater rivulet of Muskrat Branch. Muskrat Shelter—with benches, table, and valet pack parking—stands to the right just across the year-round water.

Bearing to the northeast from the shelter, the AT advances on undemanding grades, upslope to the right, through a moist forest where flame azalea and two small trees, witch-hazel and mountain winterberry (a deciduous holly), are common. Fern colonies often cloak the forest floor here. Reaching ridgeline at mile 6.3, the course makes a short, easy-to-moderate downhill run before starting back up through a great interwoven archway of rhododendron. The next 0.4 mile is Section 1's tamest walking. The trail, level or nearly so, proceeds on a wide, unusually flat spur top east of Whiteoak Stamp's high point. At mile 6.8 the bare dirt walkway passes through a shallow saddle (4,540 feet), an open area with old roads, before ascending a steady mild grade to the left (north) of the rising crest. The forest, which includes white ash, is still all deciduous—not a hemlock nor a pine in sight.

After rounding a spur falling westward from Big Laurel, the treadway arrives at its signed junction with blue-blazed Chunky Gal Trail (Big Butt Mountain is not far away) at mile 7.1. This connection is the southeastern end of Chunky Gal—a 5.5-mile nonwilderness trail that follows its namesake mountain to the northwest away from the AT. Heading northeast from the junction, Section 1 curls around the upper sunset pitch of Big Laurel (the worst walking is a short moderate downgrade) and returns to the backbone of the Blue Ridge at mile 7.3. The north- and northwest-facing forest, full of yellow birch, is increasingly moist. Here Section 1 passes its first clump of hobblebush, a viburnum shrub identified by its large, heart-shaped leaves, paired opposite one another at even intervals along branch stems. Buckeyes become more common and hemlocks appear as the gentle-grade track maintains its course on or near the crest. After passing through a slight gap (4,500 feet) at mile 7.6, the treadway immediately slabs onto northwest slope, where the trees, primarily northern red oak and yellow birch, have grown to larger girths. The treadway dips with the crestline to Wateroak Gap (4,460 feet) at mile 7.9. (Just as there are no muskrats at Muskrat Shelter, there are no water oaks at Wateroak Gap.)

Measured by a ruler on a flat map, the distance between Wateroak Gap and Deep Gap is only 0.6 mile. Yellow Mountain's 4,970-foot southeastern knob, however, stands squarely and steeply between the two gaps. Rather than routing the trail up and over the peak, or half-circling it around to the south, the trail builders constructed a long, finger-shaped meander out and around Yellow Mountain's high point (5,020 feet). Entirely outside of the wilderness, this flattened, three-quarter loop leads north from Wateroak Gap, crosses over Yellow Mountain's keel north of and several hundred feet below its peak, then continues south and southeast to complete the roundabout to Deep Gap.

Once through Wateroak Gap, the route almost immediately veers to the left of the ridgetop before bending parallel to Yellow Mountain's crest. The often rocky grades of the next mile angle steadily and easily upslope. Boulder fields, scattered tumbles of rock, enliven the mountainside. Summer views through the foliage feature good old Chunky Gal Mountain, the next long ridgeline to the west. The trail proceeds upward to mile 8.9, where it crosses over Yellow Mountain's spine (4,780 feet) and starts the turn toward the south.

With the exception of a few very short, steeper descents, the remainder of Section 1 sticks with mild grades on moist, east-facing slope—most of them easy downhill and many of them boulder-field rocky. The course passes another patch of hobblebush, then at mile 9.3 the trail makes a zigzag, double-switchback drop past a rockwall outcrop to the left.

The cove and northern hardwood forest shading the final stretch is luxuriantly rich—a partial tally includes yellow poplar, yellow buckeye, silverbell, black cherry, basswood, beech, two types of birch, and three kinds of oak and maple. Spring wildflowers thrive among the boulders, especially in the hollows. The giant and jagged leaves of the umbrella-leaf are difficult to miss at the rocky seepage runs. One last downhill leads your feet—those essential hiking appendages oddly omitted from the hiker symbol—to the trailhead parking area at Deep Gap, 4,341 feet at the bench mark.

Nature Notes

The Solomon's seal, common in rich, moist habitat at all but the highest elevations, is often among the first wildflowers Southern Appalachian hikers learn. With its tall, gracefully arching stem and its two rows of large, prominently veined leaves, this native perennial is distinctive and easy to spot where it arcs over the edge of a trail. Usually 2 to 3 feet high, and sometimes nearly 4, the Solomon's seal quickly grows into one of the tallest nonwoody plants in the late-spring forest. If you find a clump of extraordinarily robust, jungle-sized specimens of this

Solomon's seal

plant, you might have located a subspecies called great Solomon's seal.

Unlike many wildflowers, this herb can be identified easily without its blooms; its size, leaf shape, and leaf arrangement distinguish it from other plants. The smooth, light green leaves—sessile (stalkless), untoothed, and broadly lanceolate to ovate in outline—occur alternately in two rows along the stem. Normally 2½ to 5½ inches long, the leaves are clearly patterned with lengthwise parallel veins.

The small (½ to ¾ inch long), cylindrical, whitish green blossoms of the Solomon's seal are inconspicuous. Flowering stems hang hidden below the leaf axils along much of the upper stalk. Each stem supports a cluster of one to five corollas ending with a flare of six short, downward-pointing lobes. The flowers open from mid-April through May, depending upon elevation. Dark blue berries replace the blossoms in late summer and early fall.

A member of the Lily family, the Solomon's seal received its name from the shape of the scars left on the underground rhizome after the leaf stalk breaks off in the fall. The circular scars were thought to resemble King Solomon's official seal. These rhizome scars also indicate an individual plant's age; each autumn produces a new seal. By counting the scars, botanists have determined that some of these graceful wildflowers live more than fifty years.

false Solomon's seal

Found in the same rich, moist habitat as its close relative, the false Solomon's seal—a similar member of the Lily family—is even more common than the Solomon's seal. This herbaceous perennial, also known as Solomon's plume and false spikenard, shares the stooped, arching growth habit and the double row of alternate leaves with the Solomon's seal. Roughly similar in size and shape, the leaves of both plants have prominent and parallel lengthwise veins—a Lily family characteristic.

While the foliage and growth habit of these two native wildflowers are nearly alike, the shape, size, number, and location of their blossoms distinguishes the two species. A plumelike cluster of corollas, often 4 or more inches long, graces the arching tip of the false Solomon's seal. This pyramidal tuft contains numerous tiny, cream white flowers with enlarged, feathery stamens. The individual star-shaped blooms span only ⅛ inch or less. By late summer the panicle of flowers has transformed into an aggregation of small red berries.

Blooming at about the same time as the true Solomon's seal, the somewhat shorter (1 to 3 feet tall) and less arched stem of the false Solomon's seal noticeably zigzags from one leaf to the next.

Directions

Section 1 of the Appalachian Trail has either-end vehicular access. Its southwestern trailhead at Blue Ridge Gap can be most easily reached from Access Point 4, and its northeastern trailhead at Deep Gap can be most easily reached from Access Point 5. (See the detailed description of the Access Points on page 40.)

Southwestern trailhead at Blue Ridge Gap

Access Point 4: From the US 76–Upper Hightower Road junction, travel paved Upper Hightower Road straight ahead or right (where the road narrows, continue straight at the Charlies Creek Road sign, if it is still up) for approximately 3.7 miles to where the road forks. Paved Upper Hightower Creek Road drops down and to the left; dirt-gravel FS 72, usually designated by a small Forest Service sign, heads up and to the right. Follow FS 72 for approximately 1.0 mile to the pull-off parking where the white-blazed AT crosses the road at Blue Ridge Gap. To walk toward the Southern Nantahala Wilderness and Deep Gap, follow the AT to the northwest (to the left from the way you came) at the blazed post and wooden steps.

Forest Service 72 becomes increasingly steep and rough as it climbs toward the gap. The last few tenths of a mile are impassible for regular-clearance vehicles. Six-cylinder pickups and four-wheel drive vehicles may be able to negotiate the road all the way to the gap. If you are driving a conventional vehicle, you will have to drive as far as practical, pull off, then walk.

Northeastern trailhead at Deep Gap

Access Point 5: From the US 64–Deep Gap Road junction, travel Deep Gap Road (FS 71) for approximately 6.0 miles (pavement ends after 0.8 mile) to the large gravel, pull-in parking area in Deep Gap. The white-blazed Appalachian Trail crosses the back end of the parking area. When you face the back of the parking area and look straight ahead from the way you came in, the northeastern end of Section 1 (the end of Section 1 as described in this guide) will be to your right, and the western end of Section 2 will be to your left.

The love of wilderness is more than a hunger for what is always beyond reach, it is also an expression of loyalty to the earth, (the earth which bore us and sustains us), the only home we shall ever know, the only paradise we will ever need—if only we had the eyes to see.

—Edward Abbey

Southern Nantahala Wilderness
Eastern Section

Pickens Nose

Trails

Appalachian Trail,
  Section 2

Lower Ridge

Beech Gap

Big Laurel Falls

Timber Ridge

Betty Creek Gap

Pickens Nose

Southern Nantahala Wilderness: Eastern Section

▬▬ Forest Service road	Shelter
•••• Forest Trail	▲ Peak
– – State Boundary	● Gaps
▬▬ Wilderness Boundary	
–•– County Boundary	

[FS9] Forest Service road	
← Appalachian Trail	
P Parking	
∼ Streams	
≁ Waterfall	

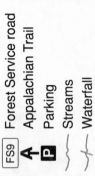

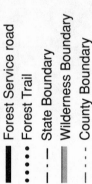

N

0 ___ Mile ___ 1

STANDING
INDIAN
CAMPGROUND

Whiteoak
Bottoms Creek

TRAIL

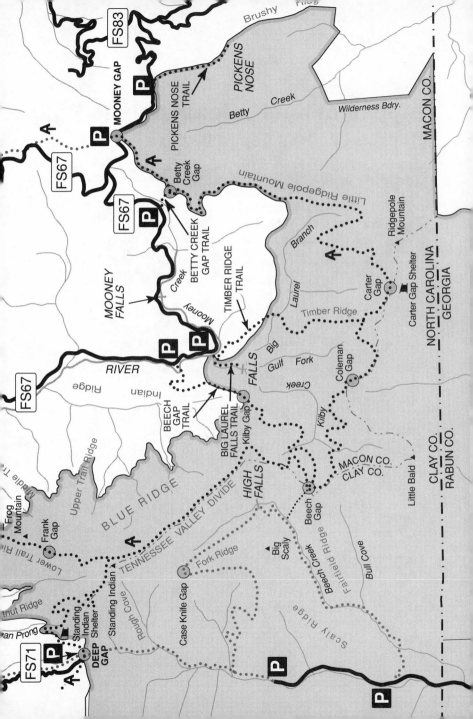

Appalachian National Scenic Trail
(Section 2: Deep Gap to Mooney Gap)

Length 13.2 miles

- **Dayhiking** Easy to Moderate in either direction
- **Backpacking** Moderate in either direction
- **Vehicular Access At Either End** Western (lower elevation) terminus at Deep Gap Trailhead, 4,340 feet; eastern (higher elevation) terminus at Mooney Gap Trailhead, 4,490 feet
- **Trail Junctions** Appalachian (Section 1 at Deep Gap, trail continues northeast from Mooney Gap to northern terminus in Maine), Deep Gap (at Deep Gap), Kimsey Creek (at Deep Gap, nonwilderness trail not included in this guide), Lower Ridge, Beech Gap, Timber Ridge, Betty Creek Gap
- **Topographic Quadrangles** Rainbow Springs NC, Prentiss NC, Dillard GA-NC
- **Blazes** White paint rectangle for AT, blue paint rectangle for most sidetrails and paths leading to shelters or water
- **RD/NF** Wayah/Nantahala
- **Features** Winter views; year-round vistas; Standing Indian; old-growth trees; flowering shrub display

S ECTION 2, AT 13.2 MILES, IS THE LONGEST section of trail described in this guide, and it is the highest by far. Before heading east and northeast, this segment of the AT finishes the half-loop around the upper Tallulah River basin. Offering over 2 miles of highcountry hiking above 5,000 feet, Section 2 follows the Blue Ridge and Tennessee Valley Divide up and over Standing Indian: the highest peak (5,499 feet) in the Southern Nantahala Wilderness. Although a modest mountain by Southern Appalachian standards, Standing Indian is taller than Maine's highest, the revered Mount Katahdin, and it surpasses New York's loftiest summit, Mount Marcy in the famed Adirondacks. Back when a fire tower topped its crown, Standing Indian was known as the "Grandstand of the Southern Appalachians." Today, the mountain is known primarily for three features: its southwestward view, its flowering shrub display, and its elevation—the first place northbound thru-hikers break the 5,000-foot barrier.

Compared to Section 1 and to much of Georgia's AT mileage, Section 2 is fairly easy walking. The stretch from Deep Gap to Mooney Gap has no sustained grades more difficult than easy to moderate.

Beginning to the left of the parking area in Deep Gap (4,341 feet at the bench mark), Section 2 slowly gains elevation outside of the wilderness on a rich, moist, spring-wildflower slope. The second-growth forest is entirely deciduous above rhododendron height. Trees requiring cool and moist conditions—northern hardwoods such as sugar maple and yellow birch—thrive on this north-and northwest-facing slope. Other broadleafs in the mosaic include beech, basswood, black cherry, sweet birch, yellow buckeye, silverbell, red and striped maple, serviceberry, northern red oak, witch-hazel, and soon-to-die chestnut saplings. To the left (west) partial summer views reveal Yellow Mountain's long, nearby ridgeline, which tops out at 5,000 feet. The route ties into the old fire tower road at 0.4 mile and continues the mild upgrade past chestnut logs still slowly rotting on the forest floor. At 0.6 mile the white-blazed track enters the wilderness at the prominent gray sign.

Seventy-five yards beyond the Southern Nantahala sign, the AT turns right onto a spur and follows its crest to the south through a drier forest where chestnut oak is common. At 0.9 mile a signed, blue-blazed sidepath leads uphill and to the right to the deluxe Standing Indian Shelter. Another path heads to the left and downhill to the site of the former shelter and Little Lyman Prong, a Nantahala River headwater stream. Little Lyman is the last easily accessible, dry-weather water between here and Beech Gap.

The wide walkway continues its gradual ascent on or near ridgetop until mile 1.2, where it slabs onto northwest-facing slope. Yellow birch—identified by its vertically curling, papery bark (a great fire starter in a pinch)—and beech saplings become increasingly abundant. Dense colonies of New York and hay-scented ferns pattern the forest floor. The rocky roadbed treadway switchbacks to the right at mile 1.4, the first in a winding series of switchbacks leading to Standing Indian's scalp. After an often steady and undemanding upgrade on moist slope, the white-blazed trail switchbacks sharply up and to the left at mile 1.7. Opposite the switch, a hole in the canopy affords a framed view to the southwest; Georgia's highest peak, 4,784-foot Brasstown Bald, is distinguished by its thimble-shaped observation tower at 240 degrees.

At mile 1.9 the wilderness walkway switchbacks up and to the right into overarching rhododendron. For the next 0.3 mile, until the route reaches Standing Indian's western crest, the course switchbacks left, then right, at frequent intervals. After curling onto the southern edge of the ridgeline at mile 2.2, the track follows the narrow spine for a short distance through Catawba rhododendron and squat, wind-twisted trees before slipping to the left onto north slope. Here Section 2 rises slightly as it swings to the north around the mountain's high point. At mile 2.5 you will arrive at a signed, four-way junction (5,440 feet).

The usually signed and always blue-blazed path leading down to the left (north) is Lower Ridge Trail. The wide, usually signed and always blue-blazed path to the right heads 0.1 mile to Standing Indian's bench-marked summit (5,499 feet) and look-off open from southwest to almost north. The steep-walled bowl of the upper Tallulah River basin falls away at your feet. Lake Chatuge glimmers due west. The western wall of the Tallulah watershed, a string of Blue Ridge peaks—Courthouse Bald, Kitchens Knob, Whiteoak Stamp, Big Laurel—rises as the first row of ridges to the southwest and west.

Approximately 40 yards before the four-way junction, a sidepath to the left drops down to a wet-weather spring. This spring is intermittent and highly unreliable. The hotter and drier the year, the farther down the seepage run you have to walk to find water. During mid-September of a recent drought year, a friend and I searched way, way down the steep seepage slope, and came back up much hotter and thirstier for our efforts. Good thing my friend packed a wee dram of ground softener.

Large patches of the mountaintop forest are composed primarily of two species: short, low-limbed northern red oaks poking up through knotty and twisted clumps of Catawba rhododendron. Quartzite rocks lie scattered across the crown or piled into dirty white fire-ring circles. Mica was mined out of the pits that follow the quartzite veins downslope.

Proceeding from the junction, the highcountry trail loses elevation slowly along the uppermost north slope before bending southward onto the bouldery eastern flank. At mile 2.9 the footpath angles onto the keel of the long, wall-like ridge—still part of the Blue Ridge—that descends gradually to the southeast away from Standing Indian. The next 1.1 miles closely follow the crest. With the exception of a few short uphills, the treadway alternates easy downridge runs with nearly level stretches, frequently tunneling through rhododendron or mountain laurel. After 0.2 mile atop the ridgeline, you will pass a sunny rock-slab opening to the right, a good rest and refueling spot. The southeast-facing ridgetop supports a drier forest of red maple, chestnut oak, mountain laurel, chestnut saplings, some small hemlock, and an occasional white pine. Spared because of their poor form and high elevation, old-growth northern red oak and yellow birch still survive on the uppermost slope to the left.

At mile 4.0, where the main ridge splits into diverging spurs, Section 2 drops down to the left, to the north slope, and descends through rich forest before turning south. Here the trees are larger, the forest more open than above. Several northern red oaks along this scenic segment measured from 9 to 10½ feet in circumference. After winding southward, the downgrade passes through drier, denser woods affording occasional partial summer views of peaks to the left. The route switchbacks onto spur top at mile 4.5 before curving back onto slope and switching again at mile 4.6. Flame azalea and mountain winterberry (a deciduous holly) are now common components of the understory.

After crossing the spur from west to east, the boot-worn track settles into easy walking on the east slope. Here the hardwood forest includes witch-hazel, white oak, cucumbertree, and Fraser magnolia. At mile 5.1 and 5.3 the path rounds the heads of shallow hollows. A double orange blaze and sign mark the boundary of the Standing Indian Bear Sanctuary. The course levels and gains the ridgeline again at Beech Gap (4,420 feet)—a worn watering and loafing place and trail junction at mile 5.4. Usually signed, the blue-blazed Beech Gap Trail leads downhill to the left. As the signs indicate, water can be found and filtered to either side of the gap. The Kilby Creek feeder to the left, down the Beech Gap Trail, has a reliable flow even in drought.

The next stretch, the 1.8-mile segment from Beech Gap to Coleman Gap, sweeps eastward over spurs and around hollows on the northern slopes of Little Bald Knob. Once through Beech Gap, the AT quickly veers off the keel onto eastern slope, heads back to crest at mile 5.5, then bears off onto the other side of the ridgeline. After bypassing the high point of a very slight knob, the course crosses the backbone of the ridge again, this time onto the north slope of Little Bald Knob, where it remains from mile 5.7 all the way to Coleman Gap. At mile 5.9 the trail begins a long grade, essentially level or slightly down, that also lasts to Coleman Gap, Section 2's lowest saddle. Several old-growth hemlocks, saplings long before the logging, stand (let's hope they survive until you pass by) in the north-slope hollow at mile 6.1. One-tenth mile beyond the large hemlocks, the footpath crosses a Kilby Creek feeder—a permanent water branch. The steady descent continues, rounding hollow after hollow.

After passing through usually signed Coleman Gap (4,220 feet), a wide pack-drop loafing spot at mile 7.2, the wilderness walkway quickly slants upslope to the left of the spine, then switchbacks up to and over the fold to the right side, the sunset side where mountain laurel is much more common. A steady easy climb brings the treadway back to keel at mile 7.5. Here, with the exception of one dip, the upridge run advances through a forest dominated by red maple and three oaks—chestnut, white, northern red. Dense monocultural colonies of New York fern occasionally flank the path. At mile 7.8, where the ridgeline rises more sharply toward an unnamed knob at the southern end of Timber Ridge, the AT doglegs to the left (northeast), off of the crest, as it half-loops around the knob.

The gradual elevation gain continues through moist-site hardwoods, including striped maple and two types of birch, yellow and sweet. Witch-hazel arches over the trail; beds of hay-scented ferns mingle with the shorter New York ferns. Section 2 levels before arriving at its blue-blazed, usually signed Timber Ridge Trail junction (4,660 feet) to the left at mile 8.2. Now the route heads down to the southeast as it finishes the half circle over Timber Ridge and around the knob. The predominantly deciduous north-slope forest—sugar maple, white ash, silverbell, yellow buckeye, and basswood—is cool, lush, open. The mild grade ranges down onto the main ridge, passes through a rhododendron breezeway, then levels in Carter Gap (4,520 feet) at mile 8.6. A blue-blazed sidepath to the left leads to water, past the old shelter, which may be removed soon. Sixty yards past the first sidepath, a "shelter" sign points to the right, toward the blue-blazed sidepath leading 55 paces to the most recent model of the Carter Gap Shelter—an elongated A-frame design with built-in benches and a table under the roof.

Beyond Carter Gap, Section 2 makes a long, somewhat flattened, three-quarter loop to the north, around and well below Ridgepole Mountain's northern high point (5,060 feet). The no-sweat upgrade quickly slips to the left of the ridge's spine onto northwest-facing slope, where chestnut oak and flame azalea are much more common than before Carter Gap. At mile 9.1 and again at mile 9.2, the track rounds hollows notched with wet-weather rivulets—Gulf Branch headwaters. The effortless elevation gain proceeds on Ridgepole's western slope, through a drier, oak-canopied forest where flame azalea is seldom out of sight. At mile 9.7 the wide sidehill path crosses over Ridgepole's northern spur and begins a downslope descent to the southeast, back toward the main crest connecting Ridgepole and Little Ridgepole Mountains. After curling to the north, the walkway reaches Little Ridgepole's spine (mile 10.3) and its wind-stunted oaks poking up through a near heath bald. One-tenth of a mile further, a short sidepath to the right leads to a view open from northeast to southeast. Whiteside Mountain's cliff-face and mesalike crown rise to nearly 5,000 feet at 75 degrees. Further to the right, at 105 degrees, stands the high, tower-topped peak of Georgia's Rabun Bald. To the left through the short trees, you can look across the upper Betty Creek valley and spot the nearby cliffs on the western flank of Brushy Ridge (the Pickens Nose ridge).

Maintaining its northward course, the AT plods along level or slowly up on Little Ridgepole's crest to mile 10.6, where it leaves the ridgetop to swing around the western side of a low knob. After venturing over a slight spur at mile 10.8, the treadway loses elevation through woods where chestnut saplings remain common, then returns to the ridgeline at mile 11.1. Here the long green tunnel continues level or easy down on or near the crest to mile 11.4 before slabbing to the right onto sunrise slope.

For the next 0.4 mile the track—a steady undemanding grade—works its way down east slope, then north, until it reaches the crest again at mile 11.8. After remaining on the ridge for only a few yards, Section 2 bends to the right and down onto north-facing slope again. The gentle downhill run wends through a moist forest of tall, maturing, second-growth trees. Still descending, the wide path angles to the right and down off a spur top at mile 12.1. Following a switchback, the walkway dips to Betty Creek Gap's flat camping area (4,300 feet) and junction at mile 12.4. Betty Creek Gap Trail, blue-blazed and usually signed, leads left (northwest) to water, Mooney Branch. A large gray Southern Nantahala Wilderness sign is posted prominently in the gap.

Rising gradually from the saddle, Section 2 avoids the high point of the next ridgeline bump by wandering onto southeast slope to the right of the crest. The track regains the ridgetop northeast of the knob at mile 12.8 before climbing harder—easy to moderate for 0.1 mile—as it slabs onto slope to the right of the keel again. At mile 13.0 the Appalachian Trail makes a short, easy-to-moderate dip before gently ascending, past the wilderness sign, to FS 83 at Mooney Gap (4,490 feet).

Nature Notes

Although backpackers may see mini-bears (gorp-stealing mice) at the shelters, the red squirrel is often the only four-legged mammal dayhikers encounter along this high-elevation section of the AT. This curious, rust-red rodent is the smallest diurnal tree squirrel throughout its vast range. The red squirrel's head and body measure a mere 7 to 8 inches in length; its expressive, reddish brown tail adds another 4 to 6 inches. Easily recognized, this feisty little creature is colored dull red to grayish red on its back and sides, white on its belly. During summer a black strip separates the white from the red; a white ring encircles the dark eyes year-round.

A decidedly northern species, the red squirrel is one of the most widespread mammals in North America. It enters the Deep South of the eastern United States only down the narrow corridor of the Southern Appalachians. The southern limit of the eastern portion of its huge range is northeasternmost Georgia. Further north in the U.S.—from West Virginia and western Maryland northeastward throughout New England and westward through the heavily forested regions of the Great Lake states to the prairie—its range is continuous and solid. Several million square miles of habitat stretch across all of Canada's heavily forested terrain to where the taiga turns to tundra in northern Alaska. Another wider peninsula of habitat extends from western Canada down the Rocky Mountain cordillera all the way to Mexico.

This animal's range is so immense its common name has regional variations. In the Southern Appalachians, it is often called boomer or mountain boomer. Many eastern Canadians know it as the pine squirrel; in the Rockies, the rodent's name changes to chickaree. Folks in the north country of Minnesota and Ontario sometimes refer to the same animal as the fairydiddle.

Although often common in any habitat within its range, this species seems to be most abundant in mixed broadleaf-conifer forests. Unlike gray squirrels, boomers are intensely territorial, chattering at and chasing away all grays and other reds. This fierce defense of home ensures a solitary life, at least until mating season. Territorial adaptations have also given the boomer a wider range of vocalizations and a spirited boldness lacking in many larger squirrels.

Occasionally, when you sit down for a break, one of these compulsive little critters will fairydiddle in for a closer look from a low perch, then scold you with an insistent, ratchetlike *chirr* while waving its tail forward in quick twitches. Except for the *chirr*, most of the red squirrel's extensive repertoire of sounds—squeaks and trills, chucks and chirps—could pass for bird noise.

In general, the smaller the mammal, the faster its metabolism races. The boomer's metabolic rate, its ability to withstand cold, and the ease with which it finds food during winter, keeps it active during the day throughout the year. An omnivore like the bear, the red squirrel eats bird eggs, nestlings, buds, flowers, seeds, fruit, nuts, and fungi (even amanita mushrooms). This busy harvester is well known for its bushel-sized caches of nuts and conifer seeds and its hoards of mushrooms. Because they move such a high volume of mushrooms through the forest, they are important dispersal agents of fungal spores. During spring, red squirrels gnaw through sugar maple bark for a taste of the sweet sap. They even lap sap oozing from sapsucker holes.

Standing Indian's crown is dark with scattered clumps of Catawba rhododendron. Many people rank this species as the most beautiful flowering shrub in the Southern Appalachians. It's easy to see why. The deep pink to rose-lavender blossoms—bell shaped, five lobed, and about 2 inches across—are striking. In years when flowering is heavy, these evergreen heaths produce large ornate clusters of corsagelike blossoms. The dark magenta buds are even more richly colored than the corollas. This 4- to 10-foot-high shrub usually reaches peak bloom atop Standing Indian sometime between June 10 and June 25.

When neither shrub is in flower or full bud, it is often difficult to distinguish Catawba from rosebay rhododendron. Without delving into taxonomic detail, botanists list three fairly reliable ways to differentiate these similar heaths. The first two are physical differences; the third is habitat. The Catawba usually bears leaves that are noticeably smaller (3 to 6 inches long) than those of the white to pale-pink flowering rosebay (5 to 10 inches long). Often 10 to 20 feet in height at maturity, rosebay rhododendron is also taller than the Catawba. And whereas the rosebay is most abundant on moist slopes and streamsides at lower and middle elevations, the Catawba is most often found at higher elevations (above 3,800 feet) on upper slopes and narrow, rocky, thin-soiled ridges. The Catawba often occurs in extensive understory stands beneath open ridgetop forests or in heath balds, also known as "hells"—almost pure thickets that exclude trees.

The Catawba is the dominant shrub of the Southern Appalachian heath balds. People time their visits to Roan Mountain, Shining Rock Wilderness, and Great Smoky Mountains National Park to admire this rhododendron at peak bloom. A Southern Appalachian endemic, the Catawba's northern limit is somewhere in or near Shenandoah National Park.

Catawba rhododendron

Directions

Section 2 of the Appalachian Trail has either-end vehicular access. Its western trailhead at Deep Gap can be most easily reached from Access Point 5, and its eastern trailhead at Mooney Gap can be most easily reached from Access Points 1 and 2. (See the detailed description of the Access Points on page 40.)

Western trailhead at Deep Gap

Access Point 5: From the US 64–Deep Gap Road junction, travel Deep Gap Road (FS 71) for approximately 6.0 miles (pavement ends after 0.8 mile) to the large gravel, pull-in parking area in Deep Gap. The white-blazed Appalachian Trail crosses the back end of the parking area. When you face the back of the parking area and look straight ahead from the way you came in, the western end of Section 2 (the beginning of Section 2 as described in this guide) will be to your left, and the northeastern end of Section 1 will be to your right.

Eastern trailhead at Mooney Gap

Access Point 1: From the US 64–West Old Murphy Road intersection, travel West Old Murphy Road for approximately 1.9 miles before turning right onto paved FS 67 at the prominent Standing Indian Campground sign. Continue straight ahead on FS 67 (the road turns dirt-gravel after 2.2 miles) for approximately 10.0 miles to its three-way junction with FS 83. Here where FS 67 turns up and to the left (north) toward Albert Mountain, proceed straight ahead on FS 83 for approximately 0.5 mile to a small, pull-in parking area to the left side of the road. The white-blazed Appalachian Trail crosses FS 83 just before the parking area. Walking the signed AT to the south, across the road from the parking area, quickly leads you into the Southern Nantahala Wilderness toward Deep Gap.

Access Point 2: From the US 441–Coweeta Lab Road intersection, travel Coweeta Lab Road and FS 83 (Ball Creek Road) approximately 9.4 miles to the small pull-in parking area to the right side of the road. This parking spot is approximately 0.7 mile beyond the signed Pickens Nose Trailhead. The white-blazed Appalachian Trail crosses FS 83 just beyond the parking area. Walking the signed AT to the south, across the road from the parking area, quickly leads you into the Southern Nantahala Wilderness toward Deep Gap.

There is no turn from Coweeta Lab Road onto FS 83; the road changes to FS 83 where the route becomes dirt-gravel after approximately 3.2 miles. After traveling approximately 7.2 miles from the highway, follow the main dirt-gravel road (FS 83) up and to the right at the junction.

Lower Ridge Trail

Length 4.1 miles

- ■ **Dayhiking In** Moderate
- ■ **Dayhiking Out** Easy to Moderate
- ■ **Backpacking In** Moderate to Strenuous
- ■ **Backpacking Out** Moderate
- ■ **Start** Lower Ridge Trailhead at the Nantahala River in Standing Indian Campground, 3,380 feet
- ■ **End** Appalachian Trail (Section 2) near high point of Standing Indian, 5,440 feet
- ■ **Trail Junctions** Appalachian (Section 2), Kimsey Creek (at trailhead, nonwilderness trail not included in this guide), Park Creek (at trailhead, nonwilderness trail not included in this guide), Park Ridge (at trailhead, nonwilderness trail not included in this guide)
- ■ **Topographic Quadrangle** Rainbow Springs NC
- ■ **Blaze** Blue
- ■ **RD/NF** Wayah/Nantahala
- ■ **Features** Nantahala River; spring and early summer wildflower display; Standing Indian; AT approach

S**TARTING AT THE** N**ANTAHALA** R**IVER,** this route leads southward along Lower Trail Ridge to within 0.1 mile of Standing Indian's high point. Whoever gave this trail its name, Lower Ridge Trail, wisely avoided the obvious awkwardness of Lower Trail Ridge Trail. This route is one of three blue-blazed trails (Beech Gap and Timber Ridge are the other two) leading generally southward to the short segment of the AT from Standing Indian to Carter Gap. Of those three well-maintained paths, Lower Ridge ranks first in both length and difficulty. Botanically, it is by far the richest of the three; in fact, Lower

Ridge boasts more fern and herbaceous wildflower species than any other trail under 7 miles in length included in this guide.

The beginning of this walkway leads you in a few strides from blacktop down the wide, railroad-tie entrance to the cool shade beneath riverside rhododendron. The route is heavily used here because it closely parallels the shallow, cobble-bedded Nantahala upstream beside the activity areas of Standing Indian Campground. Sheltered and well watered from heavy annual rainfall, the riparian forest features rhododendron (usually blooming by the end of June), hemlock, and cool-country hardwoods such as sugar maple, yellow buckeye, basswood, northern red oak, and sweet and yellow birch. To the right at 0.1 mile, flush-toilet bathrooms offer a last chance, full-service pit stop before you head up the mountain.

The track pulls away from the Nantahala and crosses a paved campground road at its bridge over Kimsey Creek at 0.2 mile. Here at the road you have three options. The easiest, safest, and driest way is to turn left onto the road, cross the bridge over the creek, then re-enter the woods on the path to the right immediately after the bridge. The other two options lead you straight ahead across the pavement, as blazed, toward either a too-short wooden bridge or a feet-wet crossing. After reaching the far side of Kimsey Creek one way or another, follow the footpath through a dense colony of New York fern and a grassy opening before crossing another campground road, this one dirt-gravel, at 0.3 mile. One-tenth mile beyond the road, the treadway begins its first upgrade—a slow, steady rise that quickly parallels a small branch notched in its ravine.

After traversing the rocky bed of the often barely spilling branch, Lower Ridge crosses its last dirt-gravel road at 0.6 mile and enters big, unbroken woods. The wide, well-worn walkway ascends steadily and gently through rich, moist-slope forest. Far below the canopy, a lush tangle of ferns and herbaceous wildflowers flanks the trail. The flowering-stem tips of the tallest black cohoshes sometimes reach a height of 7 feet by late June. As the trail rises above Whiteoak Bottoms, now only a nameplace reminder of the virgin stand that formerly grew in the flat of the Nantahala's floodplain, the second-growth forest becomes larger and increasingly deciduous. Yellow poplar, white ash, black cherry, silverbell, yellow buckeye, red and sugar maple, sweet birch, yellow birch, and beech add their collective beauty to the green mosaic. The large leaves of the Dutchman's-pipe vine, sapling basswood, Fraser magnolia, cucumbertree, and striped maple give the slopes a look of near-rainforest fecundity. Easily recognized by its large diameter, an old-growth sugar maple (if it still holds heartwood and bole together) catches the eye to the left at 0.8 mile. Most of the occasional old-growth trees, northern red oaks, are further up the ridge.

The now single-file footpath heads uphill on two short, easy-to-moderate grades before making the first in a series of switchbacks at mile 1.1. Although Lower Ridge gains 2,000 feet of elevation, all of its more-difficult-than-easy grades are short, most between 30 and 120 yards, until near the end. The switchbacks wind the treadway up a steep, moist, north-facing slope now supporting a totally deciduous forest. Tall, dark-barked black cherries are easy to distinguish downslope. At mile 1.5 the predominantly undemanding walking enters the Southern Nantahala Wilderness at the customary large gray sign. One-tenth mile further, the final switchback curls left onto the crest of Lower Trail Ridge.

Heading south on the rising ridgeline, the track works its way up, occasionally in short bursts of easy to moderate or moderate difficulty, through a drier forest dominated by oaks—northern red, chestnut, and white. Now common in the mix are red maple, sassafras, soon-to-die chestnut saplings, and flame azalea. The route continues, dipping several times, on or near the broad keel of the ridge. Beyond the slight saddle of John Gap (4,420 feet), the course swings around the sunset side of an unnamed knob well below its high point. Although easy up overall, the next 0.5 mile follows a narrow, crooked, and often rocky path that undulates where needed to traverse the steep-slope terrain. The high, west-facing forest is similar to the north-slope hardwoods below, only here you will see fewer yellow poplars and more yellow birch. At mile 2.7 the walkway pops back up to ridgetop at the next gap (4,540 feet), this one unnamed.

Proceeding from gap to gap toward Standing Indian, this segment gains elevation (a short, moderate-to-strenuous pitch is the most difficult) with the ridgecrest for 0.3 mile before slabbing onto the upper-west slope of Frog Mountain. Like the last end run, the track traverses mild but rocky grades as it skirts below the high point of a knob. The walkway comes back to the top of Lower Trail Ridge where it passes through Frank Gap (4,820 feet) at mile 3.3.

The remainder of the route ascends on the wide ridgeline through an open, moist, and moderately rich forest. Here the combination of two moisture-adding factors—high elevation and northern exposure—create habitat for lush fern colonies (New York and hay-scented), wildflowers (tassel rue and assorted asters), grassy patches, and of course, briers. Clump after clump of flame azalea light up the woods in late spring and early summer. Above the 5,000-foot contour, oaks and birches increasingly dominate the forest.

The uppermost 0.8 mile gains 620 feet of elevation. Although not tough enough to meet the standard of hard hiking—a sustained 100-foot elevation rise per 0.1 mile of run—this upridge ascent at least gives you an idea of how rigorous a long 20 percent grade could be if you were carrying a heavy pack on a hot day.

Occasionally snaking from side to side, this final segment is relatively effortless for 0.2 mile past the gap. It then climbs an overall easy-to-moderate grade for slightly more than 0.2 mile before becoming easy again. At mile 3.9 the track rises sharply, eases to moderate, then surges once again before finishing with a mild grade. With 50 yards remaining, the wilderness path enters the belt of Catawba rhododendron that darkens Standing Indian's crown. Lower Ridge ends at its signed T-junction with the white-blazed Appalachian Trail.

To complete the hike to the top of Standing Indian, cross the AT and follow the signed (Standing Indian), blue-blazed sidepath that begins exactly opposite the end of Lower Ridge Trail. The wide, well-trodden treadway leads 0.1 mile past campsites and more chunks of white quartz to the grass and rock-slab opening atop the mountain's summit—5,499 feet at high point. The rock outcrop overlook open to the south provides good views when the weather is clear. (See Section 2 of the Appalachian Trail on page 88 for more information concerning the vista.)

The last easily obtained water along Lower Ridge Trail is located where the route crosses a small branch at 0.5 mile. A wet-weather spring is located off the AT very near the Lower Ridge–Appalachian junction. Turn right onto the white-blazed AT from the end of Lower Ridge, then walk 20 or 30 yards to the prominent sidepath leading downhill and to the right off the AT. This sidepath leads to the spring, which is intermittent. During October of a recent drought year, a friend and I searched the seepage run far below the spring for water, but brought our canteens back up the steep slope empty. The nearest reliable dry-weather water flows downslope from the Standing Indian Shelter. From the Lower Ridge–AT connection, turn right onto the Appalachian Trail and walk 1.6 miles toward Deep Gap. The shelter is uphill to the left; the water is downhill to the right.

Nature Notes

Lower Ridge rises through a rich, often north-facing forest that nourishes the most diverse spring wildflower community—the most species per mile—of all the trails detailed in this guide. Without making a special effort for a high count, I recorded thirty-seven spring-blossoming wildflowers while walking this trail on two separate occasions, both times in early summer after the herbaceous layer had hidden many of the small early bloomers. A short list of species found here—but either absent or uncommon along many of the trails in this guide—includes Vasey's and wake robin trilliums, firepink, Canada mayflower, hepatica, speckled wood lily, sweet cicely, yellow mandarin, and bloodroot. Dutchman's-pipe, a large-leafed vine bearing odd, pipe-shaped (sort of) blossoms, frequently spirals around trailside trees and shrubs.

The bloom beauty along Lower Ridge continues beyond Memorial Day—the traditional end of spring in the South—and often reaches flowering-shrub peak after the summer solstice. Many hikers, especially those from large heat-island cities, hang up their boots from Memorial Day to after Labor Day. They can't quite envision the relative coolness high in the green forest. Instead, they can picture only an oppressive heat that has them sloshing in their socks after the first climb. While lowland heat is often stifling, this trail's high elevations, ranging from 3,380 to 5,440 feet, significantly reduce summertime discomfort. If you pick a day when moderate temperatures are predicted and start early, you can be standing atop Standing Indian before the heat settles in down below.

Why hike in summer? Several reasons come to mind. Novelty for one. The forest has a different look and feel when the herbaceous layer reaches its peak of lushness and height. Beauty for another. Summer's tall wildflowers—crimson bee balm, black cohosh, and turk's-cap

crimson bee balm

lily—bloom in the warm weather after the canopy closes. The Southern Nantahala's biggest and best wildflower show of the year takes place during the last two weeks of June, when thousands of Catawba rhododendrons and flame azaleas color Standing Indian's ridgelines and upper slopes.

The crimson bee balm, one of Southern Appalachia's most colorful wildflowers, begins blooming by the end of June and continues into September. Dense colonies of these 2- to 4-foot-tall perennials grow beside spring runs and in the constantly wet soil of seepage flows. Occasionally, a long, linear swath of blooms forms a red vein all the way down a seep.

Like all members of the Mint family, this native herb has a square stem and opposite leaves that are pleasantly aromatic when rubbed. Bee balm leaves are 3 to 6 inches long, prominently toothed, and ovate-lanceolate in shape. When in bloom, this species cannot be mistaken for any other plant in the Southern Highlands. Numerous bright scarlet flowers crowd a ragged, crownlike head, 1½ to 3 inches in diameter. Thin and tubular, the two-lipped, five-lobed individual corollas are 1 to 1½ inches long. As you might guess from their size, shape, and color, these blossoms attract hummingbirds.

While negotiating a treaty with the Oswego tribe in the 1740s, botanist John Bartram (William Bartram's father) learned that these

Native Americans brewed a tea from the leaves of bee balm that relieved the muscle aches associated with fevers and chills. The colonists were soon drinking Oswego tea (another common name for this mint) as a substitute for imported tea.

If you walk this route from late June through July, you can't help noticing the long, wandlike spikes of the black cohosh, also known as mountain bugbane and black snakeroot. This giant member of the Buttercup family is one of the tallest (usually 4 to 8 feet high) herbaceous plants in the Southern Blue Ridge; its tapering flower clusters often reach 10 to 14 inches in length. Exceptionally long stems hold these graceful terminal racemes, sometimes called candles, high above their foliage and that of neighboring herbs. From a distance, the skinny stems blend with the background green, and the candles appear as disembodied wands of white floating well above the forest floor.

black cohosh

The longer flower cluster is held higher than the lateral ones, which usually number four or fewer. The tiny individual blossoms lack petals; the four or five white sepals often fall soon after blooming, leaving bushy tufts of stamens to provide the splash of white. Since the corollas open in succession upward from the bottom, the longer candles may remain lit for two weeks or more.

Cimicifuga, the Latin genus name for this perennial, means "to drive away bugs." Black cohosh blossoms, which emit a very strong, unpleasant odor, do drive away most of the usual pollinators. Attracted by the rotting-flesh scent, carrion beetles fly in from long distances to fertilize the flowers. Another quite similar, though not so smelly, *Cimicifuga* species called American bugbane (also known as black cohosh and black snakeroot) often shares the same rich

Southern Appalachian habitat. Native American herbalists and their students, the early settlers, used both plants to treat snakebites.

Directions

The Lower Ridge Trailhead can be most easily reached from Access Point 1. (See the detailed description of the Access Points on page 40.)

Access Point 1: From the US 64–West Old Murphy Road intersection, travel West Old Murphy Road for approximately 1.9 miles before turning right onto paved FS 67 at the prominent Standing Indian Campground sign. Proceed 1.8 miles on FS 67, then follow the right fork, the one marked with another large campground sign, down into Standing Indian Campground. After slightly more than 0.1 mile, the road passes a camp store and fee-pay station on the right. A fee-pay, day-use parking area is located to the left of the road just beyond the camp store. Noncamping hikers are expected to park in this lot—and pay.

A little more than 0.1 mile beyond the day-use parking area, the road crosses a bridge over the Nantahala River. To the right just across the bridge, a large sign lists four trails (Kimsey Creek, Park Creek, and Park Ridge are the other three). Lower Ridge is the only trail of the four that begins to the left across the road from the sign.

Notes

Beech Gap Trail

Length 2.9 miles

- **Dayhiking In** Easy to Moderate
- **Dayhiking Out** Easy
- **Backpacking In** Moderate
- **Backpacking Out** Easy to Moderate
- **Start** Beech Gap Trailhead, 3,750 feet
- **End** Appalachian Trail (Section 2) at Beech Gap, 4,420 feet
- **Trail Junctions** Big Indian Loop (horse trail, not described in this guide), Appalachian (Section 2)
- **Topographic Quadrangle** Rainbow Springs NC
- **Blazes** Blue for Beech Gap, orange for Big Indian Loop
- **RD/NF** Wayah/Nantahala
- **Features** Mooney Creek; flame azalea display; AT approach

BEECH GAP IS ONE OF THREE blue-blazed trails leading generally southward to the short section of the AT from Standing Indian to Carter Gap. Of those three well-maintained routes (Timber Ridge and Lower Ridge are the others), Beech Gap ranks second in length and third in difficulty. Unlike the other two, however, Beech Gap shares its treadway with a horse trail, Big Indian Loop, for 1.2 miles.

Dipping from the trailhead, the cut-in path quickly descends 0.1 mile through rhododendron, hemlock, and hardwoods to the wooden bridge over 30-foot-wide Mooney Creek. Once across, the track turns right at the double blue blaze and ducks through a hole in the rhododendron. It parallels the creek with the current a short distance before swinging up and away from the stream into skinny, third-growth broadleafs dominated by sweet and yellow birch. Here the hiking follows an easy upgrade on east- and northeast-facing slopes rich with ferns and herbaceous wildflowers. The trees—scattered hemlocks mixed with second-growth hardwoods including sugar and striped maple, black cherry, Fraser magnolia, and cucumbertree—soon become larger, more widely spaced, and more diverse than those in the early succession forest below.

A few rods above the second switchback, Beech Gap rises to the crest of Indian Ridge and its signed connection with orange-blazed Big Indian Loop at 0.6 mile. From here, the two-trail treadway works its way up (easy to moderate) the narrow ridgeline to the south. The path bisects a drier forest of northern red and chestnut oak, red maple, sourwood, and hickory. An understory of mountain laurel, deciduous heath, and galax frequently lines the walkway. At 0.9 mile the trail begins to follow the wilderness boundary, marked with black-and-white signs. From this point until it enters the Southern Nantahala at Kilby Gap, the footpath divides designated wilderness to the left (east) from nonwilderness on the right.

Continuing southward atop Indian Ridge, the walking gently undulates with the spine until mile 1.2, where it slabs onto the uppermost sunset slope and dips 0.1 mile—part of the way through a darkening rhododendron tunnel—to Kilby Gap (4,180 feet). The route passes through the gap onto south-facing slope and ascends (no harder than easy to moderate) into a moister forest of sugar maple, white ash, black cherry, yellow birch, northern red oak, and, as usual, hemlock. The lush forest floor along this segment is often covered by dense fern colonies. The track crosses the notch of a hollow, then switchbacks right and left through sloping swards of New York fern and beautiful open woods with flame azalea and two species of rhododendron in the undergrowth. Still angling higher, the treadway crests a spur before continuing the easy upgrade to mile 1.8, where it reaches the usually signed split with the horse trail at an old woods road.

On its own again, blue-blazed Beech Gap follows the roadbed to the left and down from the junction. The forest remains much the same—the evergreen of mountain laurel, rhododendron, and scattered hemlocks amidst the deciduous hardwoods, largely composed of oaks and yellow birch. Flame azalea becomes increasingly common near trail's end. The wide walkway proceeds as easy as mountain hiking gets to the crossing of a permanent water rivulet, a Kilby Creek feeder, at mile 2.4. Beyond the short, moderate descent to a smaller rivulet, the remainder of the route follows the contour of the slope to Beech Gap's loafing spot (4,420 feet) on the Appalachian Trail.

If you turn right onto the white-blazed AT and walk to the northwest, you will reach the Lower Ridge junction at Standing Indian after 2.9 miles, and Deep Gap after 5.4 miles. If you hike the AT to the left (generally east then north), you will come to the Timber Ridge junction after 2.8 miles, and Mooney Gap after 7.8 miles.

Nature Notes

Listen closely to the forest, and you will hear the nasal *yank-yank-yank* call note of the white-breasted nuthatch. Unlike most birds, whose songs are louder, longer, and more distinctive than their call notes, this small bird's call note is much more noticeable than its song—a rapid series of low, nasal notes with a slightly rising inflection. You will hear the nuthatches' call note not only because it is unusual and fairly loud, but also because this passerine is a common year-round resident and because it breeds at all elevations within the Southern Appalachians. Voiced by both sexes, this *yank-yank* call note is often one of the few bird sounds you will hear during a winter hike in the Southern Nantahala Wilderness.

The nuthatch's foraging behavior is unique among North American avifauna. Unlike most bark-gleaning birds, which move up trees as they search for food, nuthatches move downward head-first. This adaptation allows them to look into crevices missed by the upwardly mobile birds. A foraging nuthatch follows a high-low, low-high pattern as it feeds, flying high into a tree, often spiraling around the trunk as it walks down the bole, then flying high into the next tree.

Your best opportunity to observe this sparrow-sized (5 to 6 inches long) songbird is from mid-November through April when their downward movement is easily seen through the bare branches. The black cap, blue-gray back, and white face, neck, and breast of the white-breasted nuthatch are diagnostic. Extending back from the base of the upper bill, the cap makes a black Mohawk swath across the head before widening at its stopping point on the nape of the neck. Below the cap, the back is solid blue-gray; the feathers on the wings and tail are blended blue and black and edged in white. The clear bright white on the bird's face includes thin strips above the eyes. Lower flanks and undertail coverts are washed with variable amounts of chestnut rust. In the South the sexes look essentially the same.

This species' range spans from coast to coast in the United States, across parts of southern Canada, and far down into the mountains of Mexico. East of the Great Plains, the white-breasted occurs in suitable habitat throughout most of every state except Florida.

This perching bird's common name is a corruption of "nuthack," a word that describes one of its feeding behaviors. The nuthatch often wedges nuts and other large seeds into tree-bark crannies, then hacks them open with its long, sharp-pointed bill.

While flame azalea is often common atop Standing Indian's crest and upper spurs, it is absolutely profuse beside most of Beech Gap's uppermost 0.3 mile. This stretch is an azalea lover's dream; during peak of a good year the upslope near the end of the trail lights up orange. Although William Bartram's eighteenth-century "forest on fire" image may be too exaggerated by today's less romantic standards, at times this grove does flare into gaudy clumps of color. The first year I walked through these woods, the flames were still freshly lit on June 23. The next year, on June 25, the display was scarcely flickering.

A tall heath in the same genus as rhododendron, the flame azalea is almost as inconspicuous without its flowers as it is conspicuous with them. In prime bloom this woody wildflower is the most strikingly colored deciduous shrub in the Southern Highlands, and is immediately recognized by all who know its name. Particularly large and showy clumps are justifiably admired and photographed. But as soon as the fire has faded and fallen, the small, light green leaves blend in with the rest of the undergrowth, and the plants go largely unnoticed until the following spring.

Known to many old-timers as wild honeysuckle, mature azaleas are usually only 3 to 10 feet tall. Occasionally, in rich habitats, the shrub attains a treelike height of 15 to 18 feet. The blossoms appear before the leaves are fully grown. Clusters of five to seven corollas near branch ends range from light orangish yellow to dark orangish red. Most of Standing Indian's azaleas vary from light to dark orange.

Directions

The Beech Gap Trailhead can be most easily reached from Access Points 1 and 2. (See the detailed description of the Access Points on page 40.)

Access Point 1: From the US 64 –West Old Murphy Road intersection, travel West Old Murphy Road for approximately 1.9 miles before

flame azalea

turning right onto paved FS 67 at the large Standing Indian Campground sign. Continue straight ahead on FS 67 (do not take the right fork down into the campground) for approximately 6.5 miles (the road changes to dirt-gravel after 2.2 miles) to the signed Beech Gap Trailhead on the right side of the road.

Access Point 2: From the US 441–Coweeta Lab Road intersection, travel Coweeta Lab Road and FS 83 (Ball Creek Road) approximately 10.0 miles to the signed, three-way FS 83–FS 67 intersection. Coweeta Lab Road doesn't turn onto FS 83; the road becomes FS 83 where the route switches to dirt-gravel after 3.2 miles. After proceeding approximately 7.3 miles from the highway, follow the sometimes steep main road (FS 83) up and to the right at the junction.

At the FS 83–FS 67 intersection, FS 67 turns sharply up and to the right (traveling in this direction) toward Albert Mountain. Follow FS 67 straight ahead toward Standing Indian Campground for approximately 3.3 miles to the signed trailhead on the left side of the road.

Notes

Big Laurel Falls Trail

Length 0.6 mile

- **Dayhiking** Easy
- **Backpacking** Easy but not suitable
- **Start** Big Laurel Falls–Timber Ridge Trailhead, 3,750 feet
- **End** Big Laurel Falls, 3,820 feet
- **Trail Junction** Timber Ridge (see description)
- **Topographic Quadrangle** Rainbow Springs NC
- **Blaze** Blue
- **RD/NF** Wayah/Nantahala
- **Features** Three streams; Big Laurel Falls

BIG LAUREL FALLS, THE THIRD SHORTEST ROUTE described in this guide, quickly descends past yellow poplar, rhododendron, and hemlock to the wooden bridge spanning Mooney Creek. Once over the bouldery stream, the track forks at its usually signed junction. Timber Ridge leads to the left; Big Laurel Falls continues to the right. The trail follows the creek downstream on the wide walkway of a former railroad grade (several sections of rail still lie in Kilby Creek not far below the falls) through thin hardwoods and hemlock. Yellow and sweet birch dominate the dense, third-growth forest beside the creek. Serviceberry blossoms whiten the woods and treadway during the last half of April.

At slightly less than 0.2 mile, the route enters the signed Southern Nantahala Wilderness, curls to the south, then parallels cascading Kilby Creek upstream high above the clear water. The rocky, rhododendron-lined path, now cut into slope, ends at its namesake falls on Big Laurel Branch. Big Laurel splashes down a 25- to 30-foot-high double-ledge drop to a wading-depth plunge pool. Swirlholes pock the narrow, shelflike run below the shorter upper ledge. The branch is a small-volume stream; not much water flies white over the falls during summer drought.

If you bushwhack up and around the falls on the left slope and then boulder-hop up the streambed, you will reach—after a short but strenuous distance—a long slide that is less than 45 degrees but is still significantly higher than the falls. Another shorter bushwhack up and to the left will take you to the rock-slab top of the slide.

yellow birch

Nature Notes

Classified as a northern hardwood, the yellow birch abounds throughout much of the Southern Nantahala Wilderness, especially at the higher elevations. Here along Mooney Creek above the 3,700-foot mark, pole-timber birches—yellow and sweet—account for the majority of the boles in the young, successional, streamside forest. These yellow birch, only a few miles north of the Georgia border, are rooted near the southern limit of their huge range, which stretches from southeastern Canada down to northernmost Georgia. Like the many other trees that require cool, moist conditions, this hardwood enters the hot South only on the narrow peninsula of the higher mountains. Even within this restricted habitat, the yellow birch seeks the coolest, moistest conditions—streamsides at lower elevations, north-facing slopes at middle elevations, and north-facing ridges and all but the south-facing slopes at the high elevations.

This broadleaf's curling bark identifies it from sapling size to maturity. The yellowish silver to yellowish bronze bark peels into long, thin-layered, vertical strips. This papery bark works well as a fire starter even when wet. No other species in the Southern Nantahala Wilderness, nor any other Southern Blue Ridge tree found above 1,800 feet, can be mistaken for yellow birch. Mature specimens, those over the century mark, lose their youthful curls except on their upper branches.

Paired at the end of short branchlets, the leaves of the yellow birch turn bright butter yellow in autumn. The wonderful aroma of wintergreen emanates from cracked twigs, though not as strong as the nose-full wafting from sweet birch.

Over most of its extensive range, this species is a small- to medium-sized tree. In the Southern Highlands, however, it reaches fairly large dimensions. North Carolina's big tree register lists two co-champion yellow birches. The taller of the two measures 124 feet in height and the thicker one tapes 13 feet 4 inches in circumference.

Yellow birch seedlings often germinate on mossy, deadfall logs. If the log is moist enough, the seedling continues to grow, sending straddling roots downward over the log. Eventually, its "nurse log" decays, leaving the tree, propped up on its own roots, looking like a rider without a horse.

Directions

The Big Laurel Falls Trailhead can most easily be reached from Access Points 1 and 2. (See the detailed description of the Access Points on page 40.)

Access Point 1: From the US 441–West Old Murphy Road inter-section, travel West Old Murphy Road for approximately 1.9 miles before turning right onto paved FS 67 at the prominent Standing Indian Campground sign. Continue straight ahead on FS 67 (do not take the right fork down into the campground) for approximately 7.0 miles (the road changes to dirt-gravel after 2.2 miles) to the signed Big Laurel Falls–Timber Ridge Trailhead on the right side of the road.

Access Point 2: From the US 441–Coweeta Lab Road intersection, travel Coweeta Lab Road and FS 83 (Ball Creek Road) approximately 10.0 miles to the signed, three-way FS 83–FS 67 intersection. Coweeta Lab Road does not turn onto FS 83; the road becomes FS 83 where the route changes to dirt-gravel after approximately 3.2 miles. After pro-ceeding approximately 7.3 miles from the highway, follow the some-times steep main road (FS 83) up and to the right at the junction.

At the FS 83–FS 67 intersection, FS 67 turns sharply up and to the right (traveling in this direction) toward Albert Mountain. Follow FS 67 straight ahead toward Standing Indian Campground for approximately 2.8 miles to the signed Big Laurel Falls–Timber Ridge Trailhead on the left side of the road.

Notes

Timber Ridge Trail

Length 2.3 miles

- **Dayhiking In** Easy to Moderate
- **Dayhiking Out** Easy
- **Backpacking In** Moderate
- **Backpacking Out** Easy to Moderate
- **Start** Timber Ridge–Big Laurel Falls Trailhead, 3,750 feet
- **End** Appalachian Trail (Section 2), 4,660 feet
- **Trail Junctions** Big Laurel Falls (see description), Appalachian (Section 2)
- **Topographic Quadrangles** Rainbow Springs NC, Prentiss NC
- **Blaze** Blue
- **RD/NF** Wayah/Nantahala
- **Features** Streams; old-growth trees; winter views; AT approach

HREE BLUE-BLAZED APPROACH TRAILS—Beech Gap, Lower Ridge, and Timber Ridge—lead generally southward to the short section of the Appalachian Trail from Standing Indian to Carter Gap. Of these well-maintained routes, Timber Ridge ranks third in length and a distant second in difficulty. Walked to the AT and back, or in combination with various AT sections, this trail is especially scenic in the springtime. Warm sunny weather, rich wildflower slopes, and still-winter views of surrounding ridges combine to make mid-April through early May a particularly enjoyable time for a hike.

The track quickly switchbacks down through rhododendron, hemlock, yellow poplar, and birch before dipping to and crossing the wooden bridge over mossy-bouldered Mooney Creek. Across the bridge, the two-trail treadway splits at the usually signed fork. Big Laurel Falls heads to the right, downstream; Timber Ridge turns left and follows the fast-flowing stream a few rods to a low-ledged shoals, then curves up and away from the brook toward the AT. (Less than two miles away, Mooney and Bearpen Creeks rush together to beget the Nantahala River.)

Switchbacking and curling around rich hollows, the sidehill path rises steadily on a generally easy upgrade through a forest of rhododendron, hemlock, and moist-site hardwoods. On the way up, the route enters an older and more open forest of black cherry, yellow buckeye, basswood, sweet and yellow birch, beech, sugar maple, Fraser magnolia, and northern red oak. Old-growth yellow birch and sugar maple, some over 10 feet in circumference, stand conspicuously beside the trail. Several of the hollows hold mossy-barked, old-growth yellow buckeyes. The northeast-facing slopes often support lush undergrowths of herbaceous wildflowers, ferns, and striped maple saplings.

At 0.8 mile the gradual ascent tops out in the saddle of a Scream Ridge gap (4,160 feet). The trail enters the Southern Nantahala Wilderness at the gap's black-and-white signs, crosses over the saddle, then immediately slabs onto drier, south-facing slope. Here the easy hiking descends gradually beneath mountain laurel, hemlock, and such drier slope hardwoods as chestnut oak, red maple, and sassafras. Colonies of evergreen galax flank the footpath. After tunneling through rhododendron, the treadway dips a little sharper to a switchback veering onto old roadbed before it crosses the wooden bridge over Big Laurel Branch (4,100 feet) at mile 1.1.

The next 0.6 mile, from the branch to the backbone of Timber Ridge, makes an ascending half circle to the west. The first few tenths of a mile slant up a north-facing slope beneath hemlock and the same broadleaf species found beside the trail's first upgrade. The walkway again traverses open wildflower and fern slopes between rhododendron patches. The route rounds the first hollow on the rise, past more wildflowers and several mature silverbell trees, before heading uphill slightly harder. Beyond this short, easy-to-moderate stretch, the trail gains elevation steadily, through the shade of hemlock and rhododendron, on gentle grades to the wide backbone of Timber Ridge.

The remaining 0.6 mile heads due south, following the open, occasionally grassy ridgetop as it rises toward Ridgepole Mountain's 4,780-foot western peak. Wide and often nearly flat to either side, the crest allows nearly continuous bare-branch views to your left, to the east and southeast. One mile away to the east, the high roller-coastering keel of Little Ridgepole Mountain parallels the trail. Ridgepole Mountain's higher northern peak (5,060 feet) fills the southeastern horizon.

The ridgetop forest is unusually open and predominantly deciduous. Old-growth northern red oaks, some 8 to 10 feet around, have grown the thickest. Hemlock and rhododendron occasionally clump together in apparent association. Following the wide crest, the treadway heads up on an easy gradient to its usually signed junction with the white-blazed Appalachian Trail.

If you turn right onto the AT and walk the long green tunnel generally west then northwest, you will arrive at the Beech Gap junction after 2.8 miles, the Lower Ridge junction at Standing Indian after 5.7 miles, and Deep Gap after 8.2 miles. If you walk the AT to the left, generally east then north, you will reach Mooney Gap after 5.0 miles.

Nature Notes

From mile 0.4 to 0.7, Timber Ridge traverses a series of moist hardwood slopes and hollows. Wildflowers flourish in this rich, north-to-east-facing habitat. Here the mottled leaves of the trout lily cover patches of the forest floor in early spring before larger herbs overtop them. The trout lily belongs to the first wave of vernal beauties, the relatively small ones that must leaf out and break bud before the taller second-wave wildflowers steal their sun. Depending upon elevation and exposure, the trout lily usually blooms from late March down low to mid-May up high near the top of Standing

Indian. The colonies along lower Timber Ridge Trail typically peak between April 10 and April 25.

It is impossible to confuse this native perennial with any other Southern Appalachian wildflower. Like the mayapple and umbrella-leaf, this species requires the energy from two larger leaves to produce a blossom. The trout lily's paired basal leaves—shiny and prominently mottled with purple-brown—are usually 3 to 7 inches long when the plant blooms. The single leaves of the nonflowering lilies are smaller, less colorful, and much less conspicuous across a colony.

trout lily

The solitary yellow flowers of the trout lily nod from 4- to 8-inch stems. The 1- to 1½-inch-wide corollas consist of three petals and three sepals that bend gracefully backward toward each other until their tips often almost touch. Short rust-colored washes or speckled streaks often flare up from the center onto the lowermost third of the sepals and petals. Long, reddish brown anthers complete the easy identification.

This herbaceous perennial's most widely accepted common name arose from the fancied resemblance of its mottled leaves to the speckled sides of Southern Appalachia's only native trout (actually a char)—the now beleaguered brook trout. The Cherokee also associated the plant with the fish; they regarded this wildflower's blooming season as the best time to catch trout. Other common names for the trout lily include fawn lily, adder's tongue, and dogtooth violet.

Locally abundant in rich, moist, predominantly deciduous woods, this diminutive member of the Lily family often occurs in dense colonies covering large patches of the forest floor. Trout lilies grow and reproduce slowly. Because it takes individual plants seven or more years to produce blooms, flowering specimens (the ones with two large leaves) are often somewhat scarce across a colony. In some high-elevation locations, most notably the upper end of the road to Deep Gap and the moist slopes along the Appalachian Trail from Deep Gap to Standing Indian, colonies have spread and grown together to cover acres upon acres. These extensive beds of slow-growing plants make you wonder how many hundreds or thousands of years a colony may have occupied a particular site.

A few tenths mile before this trail reaches the wilderness boundary ridge, it passes a small stand of beeches to the left. Beneath the beech trees grows a colony of beechdrops—small, slender plants that appear stiff and skeletal, as if they had died and turned brown just before leafing out. A member of the Broomrape family (and a cousin of the squaw-root), the beechdrop parasitizes the roots of beech trees. This unusual plant lacks green pigment and bears leaves reduced to vestigial brown scales. Although this species occurs occasionally throughout the Southern Nantahala, it is locally abundant. Beech groves, its sole food source, are easy to find and fairly common at moist, high elevations within the wilderness.

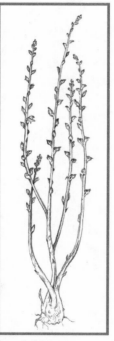

Ranging in height from 6 to 20 inches, this parasitic wildflower's slender, brownish tan stems are vertically streaked with dark purplish red. The shorter plants often remain unbranched; the taller ones branch alternately along a single plane. The dead, darker brown stalks persist beneath the gray-barked beeches all winter and into spring.

beechdrops

Beechdrops bloom during late summer. Even the larger, upper flowers measure only ⅜ of an inch long. The tubular corollas range in color from yellowish brown to reddish purple. Budlike and much smaller (⅛ inch long), the self-fertilized lower flowers never open, but they produce numerous seeds.

Directions

Timber Ridge Trail, which shares its treadway with Big Laurel Falls Trail for a short distance, begins at the same signed trailhead as Big Laurel Falls Trail. Both trails are listed on the sign. (See Big Laurel Falls on page 113 for directions to the Timber Ridge Trail-head.)

Notes

Betty Creek Gap Trail

Length 0.2 mile

- ■ **Dayhiking** Easy
- ■ **Backpacking** Easy
- ■ **Start** Betty Creek Gap Trailhead, 4,280 feet
- ■ **End** Appalachian Trail (Section 2) at Betty Creek Gap, 4,300 feet
- ■ **Trail Junction** Appalachian (Section 2)
- ■ **Topographic Quadrangle** Prentiss NC
- ■ **Blaze** Blue
- ■ **RD/NF** Wayah/Nantahala
- ■ **Features** Mooney Branch; AT approach

AN APPALACHIAN TRAIL APPROACH, Betty Creek Gap is a very short means to a very long end. It is not only the shortest and easiest trail in this guide, but it is also the only route described in the Southern Nantahala Section that remains completely outside of the wilderness.

The first 60 yards of this easily walked connector descend gently toward Mooney Branch on old road. Immediately after entering the woods, you will see blue blazes heading down and to the right away from the roadbed. This blazed path appears to be a high-water route leading to the rickety bridge spanning the narrowed branch. During low water, though, it seems easier and safer to follow the wide treadway to the shallow, stepping-stone crossing of Mooney Branch.

Once across the stream, the track quickly comes to a large, bare-ground camping spot where the blue-blazed alternate path ties back into the old road. The remainder of the route follows the wide walkway straight ahead from the camp through rhododendron and moist-site hardwoods. The trail ends at its T-junction with the AT in

Betty Creek Gap, an open loafing and camping area on the edge of the wilderness.

If you turn left (east) onto the Appalachian Trail and walk northeast, you will reach FS 83 in Mooney Gap after 0.8 mile. If you turn right (west) onto the AT and hike in that general direction, you will arrive at the AT–Timber Ridge intersection after 4.2 miles, the AT–Beech Gap tie-in after 7.0 miles, the AT–Lower Ridge connection just below the summit of Standing Indian Mountain after 9.9 miles, and the trailhead at Deep Gap after 12.4 miles.

Directions

The Betty Creek Gap Trailhead can be most easily reached from Access Points 1 and 2. (See the detailed description of the Access Points on page 40.)

Access Point 1: From the US 64–West Old Murphy Road intersection, travel West Old Murphy Road for approximately 1.9 miles before turning right onto paved FS 67 at the prominent Standing Indian Campground sign. Continue straight ahead on FS 67 (do not take the right fork down into the campground) for approximately 9.0 miles (the road changes to dirt-gravel after 2.2 miles) to the usually unsigned trailhead on the right side of the road. After approximately 8.6 miles on FS 67, you will see an open car-camping area to the right side of the road. Continue another 0.4 mile past the first opening to the Betty Creek Gap Trailhead—an open, grassy, downward-sloping, car-camping area. Near the road, a thin line of trees divides the opening; along the left edge, a pickup-truck track drops down to the lower opening. The trail begins at the gap of an old road 35 yards down from FS 67 along the left margin of the woods.

Access Point 2: From the US 441–Coweeta Lab Road intersection, travel Coweeta Lab Road and FS 83 (Ball Creek Road) approximately 10.0 miles to the signed, three-way FS 83–FS 67 intersection. Coweeta Lab Road does not turn onto FS 83; the road becomes FS 83 where the route switches to dirt-gravel after approximately 3.2 miles. After proceeding approximately 7.3 miles from the highway, follow the sometimes steep main road (FS 83) up and to the right at the junction.

At the FS 83–FS 67 intersection, FS 67 turns sharply up and to the right (traveling in this direction) toward Albert Mountain. Follow FS 67 straight ahead toward Standing Indian Campground for approximately 0.7 mile to the usually unsigned Betty Creek Gap Trailhead—an open, grassy, car-camping area on the left side of the road. A thin line of trees divides the downward-sloping opening near the road; along the left edge, a pickup-truck track drops down to the lower opening. The trail begins at the gap of an old road 35 yards down from FS 67 along the left margin of the woods.

Notes

Pickens Nose Trail

Length 0.7 mile

- ▪ **Dayhiking** Easy
- ▪ **Backpacking** Easy to Moderate
- ▪ **Start** Pickens Nose Trailhead, 4,680 feet
- ▪ **End** Rock outcrop overlook, 4,820 feet
- ▪ **Trail Junctions** None
- ▪ **Topographic Quadrangle** Prentiss NC
- ▪ **Blaze** No trail blazes; horizontal orange blazes mark border of the Standing Indian Bear Sanctuary
- ▪ **RD/NF** Wayah/Nantahala
- ▪ **Features** Rock outcrops, including Pickens Nose; vistas

IF **PICKENS NOSE WERE READILY ACCESSIBLE** by paved road, this treadway would be a bustling, blacktopped cavalcade. But thanks to the long dirt-gravel drive from either direction, this short, easy trail featuring three scenic overlooks receives only moderate use.

A former road, Pickens Nose Trail follows the wilderness boundary atop the crest of Brushy Ridge. The land to the right (west) of the trail is wilderness; the land to the left is nonwilderness Nantahala National Forest. The boundary of the Standing Indian Bear Sanctuary, marked with signs and blazes, coincides with the wilderness perimeter along much of the path.

The wide, well-used walkway rises steadily through rosebay rhododendron archways and cool-weather hardwoods—striped and sugar maple, white and northern red oak, yellow birch, and serviceberry. The track is often rocky and rutted, especially where it ascends a little harder on the two short, easy-to-moderate grades. Mountain laurel and flame azalea flank the trail where the rhododendron gives them room. Short northern red oaks, bent and pruned by ice storms and ridgetop winds, comprise the majority of the larger boles.

At 0.3 mile a bend-back sidepath to the left leads a short distance to a rock slab overlook open to the east. Spanning from 30 degrees to nearly 180 degrees, the view encompasses rank after rank of ridges fading into the hazy horizon. Eight to 10 miles out, a series of prominent, rock-faced ridges and knobs catch the eye at 60 degrees. The Cowee Mountains stand folded in the distance beyond them. At 80 degrees you can easily spot the high cliff face and mesalike crown of 4,900-foot Whiteside Mountain, a little over 18 miles away. Further south at 120 degrees, the broad hump of Rabun Bald—a 4,696-foot peak topped with an observation tower—rises rounded and worn, only 10 miles away in Georgia.

Continuing to the south on Brushy Ridge, the route ascends easily on narrow crest to the trail's high point (approximately 4,910 feet) before descending a generally easy downgrade slightly to the right of the exact ridgetop. The treadway occasionally tunnels through evergreen heath—mountain laurel and rhododendron—especially dark and shady after the hardwoods close the canopy overhead. At slightly less than 0.7 mile, the second and wider of two sidepaths to the right leads to another rock outcrop overlook: Pickens Nose. The slanting layers of undercut, upthrust rock were named for the famous snout of General Andrew Pickens, Revolutionary War hero and Indian fighter from South Carolina. He obviously had a big, bold, sharp-ridged schnozz.

The wide walkway continues another 100 yards to its end at open outcrop rock. Here the forest is all heath, including Catawba rhododendron, and stunted, wind-blasted broadleafs. The views from Pickens Nose and the rock at trail's end are similar. While the formation at the nose is more interesting, the final outcrop provides a more encompassing vista. Here, before leaf-out, you can see smooth outcropping way down and to the right and Pickens Nose nearby. You can also see more of the settled Betty Creek valley to the left and further into the wilderness toward the upper end of Betty Creek to the right.

From approximately 200 to 330 degrees, your eyes sweep over Betty Creek's deep trough to the largely hardwood forests and ridges across the steep-sided valley. (Due south the land falls 2,300 feet in elevation to the creek only a mile and a quarter away.) From nearly south to west, the outlook includes Wolf Knob at 200 degrees, Grassy Ridge at 220 degrees, and 5,060-foot Ridgepole Mountain at 230 degrees. The nearest low mountain across the unseen creek, Little Ridgepole, spans from 235 degrees to almost due west. Standing Indian, the long high wall at 290 degrees, rises to 5,499 feet.

Nature Notes

serviceberry

Widespread throughout the Southern Appalachians, the serviceberry is particularly common in the highcountry of the Southern Nantahala Wilderness. Many springtime hikers are familiar with this tree's flowers; especially from a distance, the white serviceberry petals stand out against the wintry-looking hardwood slopes. But few know the tree's name, and fewer still recognize it after it has finished blooming and blended into the ubiquitous green. Most people assume the serviceberry is a species of wild cherry—a good guess since both cherries and serviceberries belong to the Rose family.

Even the experts can't make up their minds about the number of serviceberry species attaining tree size in the Southern Highlands. Older guides usually describe two tree-sized serviceberries. Newer ones, however, usually lump the two into one species, or into one species with two varieties. Most recent field guides list it as downy serviceberry or just plain serviceberry. (Since the lumpers seem to be winning the battle with the splitters, I shall use the common name of serviceberry for the one tree-sized species inhabiting the wilderness.)

This broadleaf blooms earlier than any other white-flowering tree in the Southern Blue Ridge. During a recent year, the serviceberry bloomed from late April through early May along Pickens Nose

Trail at just below 5,000 feet. Earlier in the spring you can easily spot serviceberries from the trail's outcrops—look for the white splashes against the brown woods down below. The corollas appear on slender stalks in terminal clusters before the leaves have broken bud or just after the reddish leaves unfurl. Each blossom has five narrow, strap-shaped petals from ½ to 1 inch long.

The dark purplish red fruits, tiny applelike pomes from ¼ to nearly ½ inch in diameter, ripen from June through early August, depending upon elevation. Sweet and tasty, these juicy fruits attract a wide array of wildlife—fox, skunk, squirrel, deer, bear, and raccoon, as well as turkey, grouse, and smaller birds. Mountain people once harvested these wild fruits and cooked them into puddings, pies, and preserves.

Ranging from the lowlands to approximately 6,200 feet in the southern mountains, this small hardwood usually achieves a height of only 15 to 40 feet and a diameter of only 6 to 16 inches. Especially on young boles, the serviceberry's smooth gray bark is distinctively patterned with dark vertical streaks gradually twisting around the trunk. Its ovate, alternate leaves—pointed at the tip and finely saw-toothed on the margin—display a purplish red cast in spring and fall. The leaves resemble a wider and more rounded version of the black cherry leaf.

This tree has several common names. Up North, people often call this species Juneberry. Many mid-Atlantic residents still refer to it as shadbush or shadblow, because it blooms when shad make their spawning runs up the region's rivers. Old time Southern mountaineers know this tree as just plain service and pronounce the word as "sarvis." The name serviceberry originated during the days of circuit-riding preachers. Come the new year, traveling preachers made their first spiritual runs into the highcountry when these trees flowered white along their paths.

Directions

The Pickens Nose Trailhead can be most easily reached from Access Points 1 and 2. (See the detailed description of the Access Points on page 40.)

Access Point 1: From the US 64–West Old Murphy Road intersection, travel West Old Murphy Road for approximately 1.9 miles before turning right onto paved FS 67 at the large Standing Indian Campground sign. Continue straight ahead on FS 67 (do not take the right fork down into the campground) for approximately 9.7 miles (the road changes to dirt-gravel after 2.2 miles) to its three-way junction with FS 83. Here where FS 67 turns up and to the left (north) toward Albert Mountain, proceed straight ahead on FS 83 for approximately 1.2 miles to the signed trailhead and pull-in parking on the right side of the road.

Access Point 2: From the US 441–Coweeta Lab Road intersection, travel Coweeta Lab Road and FS 83 (Ball Creek Road) approximately 8.8 miles to the signed trailhead and pull-in parking on the left side of FS 83.

Coweeta Lab Road does not turn onto FS 83; the road becomes FS 83 where the route switches to dirt-gravel after approximately 3.2 miles. After proceeding approximately 7.3 miles from the highway, follow the sometimes steep main road (FS 83) up and to the right at the junction.

Notes

Part II

Chattooga National
Wild and Scenic River
and
Ellicott Rock
Wilderness

Regional Directions and Access Points

IMMEDIATELY TO THE EAST of Highway 107, the Ellicott Rock Wilderness surrounds the exact point where North Carolina, Georgia, and South Carolina meet. North of the wilderness, a 22-mile-around combination of NC 107 and two county roads completes a circuit—three sided and three cornered. This roughly triangular loop is defined by its three sides and three intersections. North Carolina 107, the eastern segment of the loop, stretches a little more than 5.0 miles from its southern Bull Pen Road intersection to its northern Whiteside Cove Road intersection. Bull Pen Road, the southern leg, runs slightly less than 9.0 miles from its eastern NC 107 intersection to its western Whiteside Cove Road-Horse Cove Road intersection. Whiteside Cove Road, the northwestern and final link, spans nearly 8.0 miles from its southwestern Bull Pen Road-Horse Cove Road intersection to its northeastern NC 107 intersection.

Like the Southern Nantahala section, this section utilizes a two-tiered system of directions, but does so for only three trails—Bad Creek, Ellicott Rock, and Chattooga Cliffs. This arrangement is designed to avoid repetition when trailheads are accessible from several combinations of roads coming from different directions. The following introductory directions are those to the three access points: the trailhead approach road intersections. The numbers of the access points correspond to the numbers on the map (page 133). The directions to the access points start from one or two major intersections away from the triangle—one from the south and the other from the north, for example.

The second tier of directions for those three trails, the instructions following the trail descriptions, begins at one or two of the closest access points. Final directions steer you from the access points to the exact trailheads.

Access Point 1

This access point is the three-way NC 107–Bull Pen Road intersection located along that stretch of Highway 107 between Cashiers, North Carolina, to the north, and the SC 28–SC 107 intersection north of Walhalla, South Carolina, to the south.

Approach from the south: From the SC 28–SC 107 intersection north of Walhalla, South Carolina, travel SC 107 North then NC 107 North for approximately 16.5 miles to the left turn onto dirt-gravel Bull Pen Road. A road sign and "SR 1100" on the back of Bull Pen's stop-sign post mark the turn. Opposite light industry, the entrance to Bull Pen Road dips toward a stream.

Approach from the north: From the US 64–NC 107 intersection in Cashiers, North Carolina, travel NC 107 South for approximately 7.0 miles to the right turn onto dirt-gravel Bull Pen Road. A road sign and "SR 1100" on the back of Bull Pen's stop-sign post mark the turn. Opposite light industry, the entrance to Bull Pen Road dips toward a stream.

Access Point 2

This access point is the three-way NC 107– Whiteside Cove Road intersection just south of Cashiers, North Carolina.

Approach from the south: From the SC 28–SC 107 intersection north of Walhalla, South Carolina, travel SC 107 North then NC 107 North for approximately 21.5 miles to the signed left turn onto paved Whiteside Cove Road (SR 1107).

Approach from the north: From the US 64–NC 107 intersection in Cashiers, North Carolina, travel NC 107 South for approximately 1.8 miles to the signed right turn onto paved Whiteside Cove Road (SR 1107).

Access Point 3

This access point is the three-way Horse Cove Road–Whiteside Cove Road–Bull Pen Road intersection located a few miles southeast of Highlands, North Carolina.

Approach from the northwest: This approach begins at the four-way US 64–NC 28 intersection in downtown Highlands, North Carolina. US 64 makes a 90-degree turn at this junction, which is also the site of The Old Edwards Inn. From this intersection, follow the only road—Main Street—that is neither US 64 nor NC 28 through the shopping area to the intersection of Main and 5th Streets. Proceed straight ahead on Main; it quickly becomes Horse Cove Road (SR 1603).

Starting at the US 64–NC 28 junction, travel Main Street then paved Horse Cove Road approximately 4.6 miles to its signed end at the three-way intersection with Whiteside Cove and Bull Pen Roads, both dirt-gravel for now.

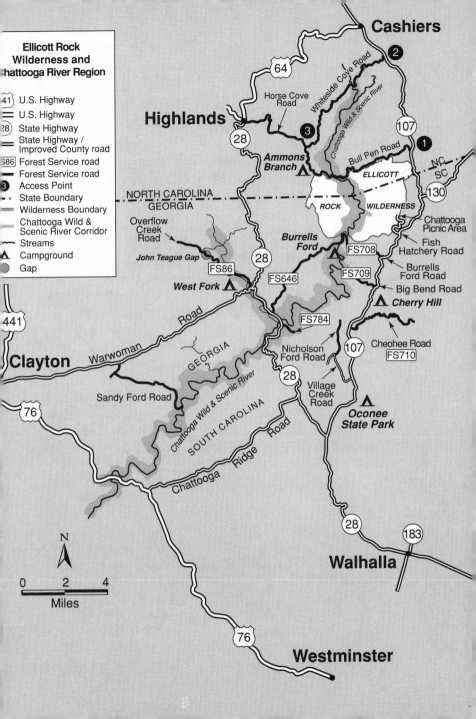

Ellicott Rock Wilderness and Chattooga River Region

Legend

- 41 U.S. Highway
- 28 U.S. Highway
- 28 State Highway
- State Highway / Improved County road
- 686 Forest Service road
- Forest Service road
- 3 Access Point
- State Boundary
- Wilderness Boundary
- Chattooga Wild & Scenic River Corridor
- Streams
- Campground
- Gap

Cashiers

Highlands

Horse Cove Road

Whiteside Cove Road

Chattooga Wild & Scenic River

64

3

2

107

1

28

Bull Pen Road

Ammons Branch

ELLICOTT

NC SC

ROCK

WILDERNESS

130

Chattooga Picnic Area

NORTH CAROLINA
GEORGIA

Overflow Creek Road

Burrells Ford

FS708

Fish Hatchery Road

John Teague Gap

FS86

28

FS646

FS709

Burrells Ford Road

Big Bend Road

West Fork

Cherry Hill

Road

GEORGIA

FS784

Nicholson Ford Road

107

Cheohee Road

FS710

441

Warwoman

Chattooga Wild & Scenic River

28

Clayton

Sandy Ford Road

SOUTH CAROLINA

Village Creek Road

Oconee State Park

76

Ridge

Road

Chattooga

28

183

Walhalla

N

0   2   4
Miles

76

Westminster

Awoke drenched with mountain mist, which made a grand show as it moved away before the hot sun. Crossed a wide, cool stream. There is nothing more eloquent in Nature than a mountain stream—its banks are luxuriantly peopled with rare and lovely flowers and overarching trees, making one of Nature's coolest and most hospitable places. Every tree, every flower, every ripple and body of this lovely stream seems solemnly to feel the presence of the great Creator.

—John Muir

Chattooga National Wild and Scenic River, *Southern Section*

Three Forks—
Holcomb Creek's last leap

Trails

Chattooga River, Section 1

Chattooga River, Section 2

Chattooga River, Section 3

Foothills National Recreation,
   Lick Log Section

Big Bend

Three Forks

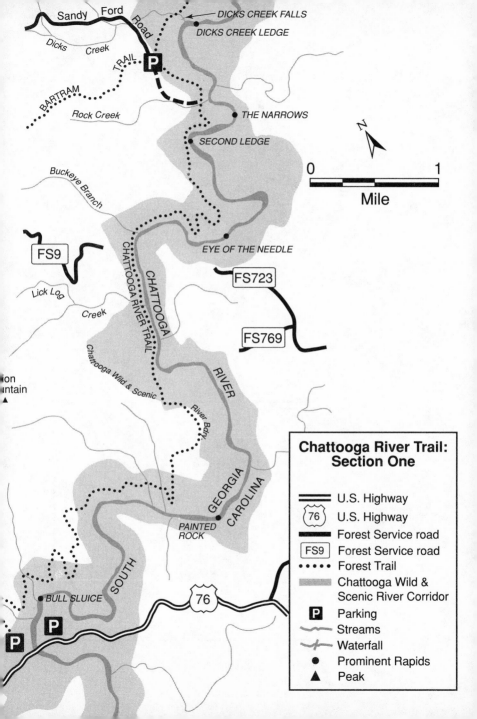

Sandy Ford Road

Dicks Creek

BARTRAM TRAIL

Rock Creek

P

DICKS CREEK FALLS
DICKS CREEK LEDGE

THE NARROWS

SECOND LEDGE

N

0   1

Mile

Buckeye Branch

FS9

Lick Log Creek

CHATTOOGA RIVER TRAIL

Chattooga Wild & Scenic

EYE OF THE NEEDLE

FS723

FS769

CHATTOOGA

RIVER

ion
untain
▲

River Bdy.

GEORGIA

CAROLINA

PAINTED
ROCK

SOUTH

BULL SLUICE

P

P

76

Chattooga River Trail:
Section One

═══	U.S. Highway
〔76〕	U.S. Highway
▬▬▬	Forest Service road
〔FS9〕	Forest Service road
••••	Forest Trail
▓▓▓	Chattooga Wild & Scenic River Corridor
P	Parking
∿	Streams
⌇	Waterfall
●	Prominent Rapids
▲	Peak

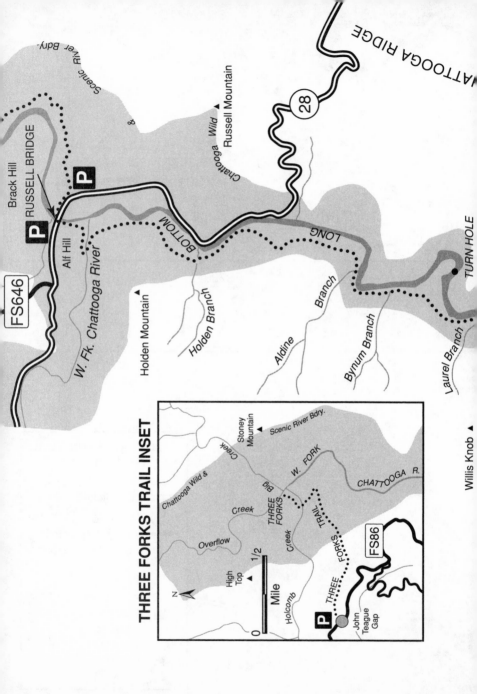

CHATTOOGA RIDGE

28

Russell Mountain ▲
Chattooga Wild &
Russell Mountain

Scenic River Bdry.
Brack Hill
RUSSELL BRIDGE
P
P
Alf Hill
FS646
W. Fk. Chattooga River

BOTTOM
LONG
Branch

TURN HOLE

Holden Mountain ▲
Holden Branch
Aldine
Bynum Branch
Laurel Branch

THREE FORKS TRAIL INSET

Stoney Mountain ▲
Scenic River Bdry.
Chattooga Wild &
Creek
W. FORK
CHATTOOGA R.
Big
Creek
THREE FORKS
Overflow
Creek
THREE FORKS TRAIL
High Top ▲
N
Mile
1/2
0
Holcomb
P
THREE FORKS
John Teague Gap
FS86

Willis Knob ▲

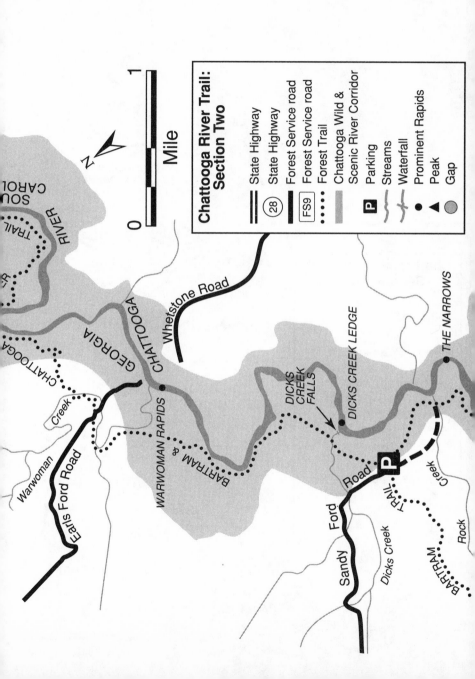

Chattooga River Trail: Section Two

- State Highway
- (28) State Highway
- FS9 Forest Service road
- Forest Service road
- Forest Trail
- Chattooga Wild & Scenic River Corridor
- P Parking
- Streams
- Waterfall
- Prominent Rapids
- Peak
- Gap

Mile

N

SOUTH CAROLINA

RIVER

TRAIL

CHATTOOGA

Warwoman Creek

GEORGIA

CHATTOOGA

Whetstone Road

Earls Ford Road

WARWOMAN RAPIDS

BARTRAM &

DICKS CREEK FALLS

DICKS CREEK LEDGE

THE NARROWS

Sandy

Ford

Road

Dicks Creek

BARTRAM

TRAIL

P

Rock

Creek

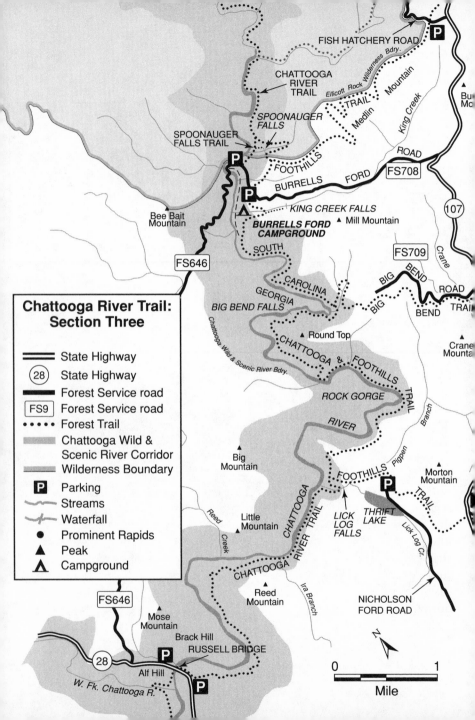

Chattooga River Trail:
Section Three

Legend

State Highway	
(28)	State Highway
	Forest Service road
FS9	Forest Service road
•••••	Forest Trail
	Chattooga Wild & Scenic River Corridor
	Wilderness Boundary
P	Parking
⌇	Streams
⊬	Waterfall
●	Prominent Rapids
▲	Peak
⛺	Campground

FISH HATCHERY ROAD

CHATTOOGA RIVER TRAIL

SPOONAUGER FALLS

SPOONAUGER FALLS TRAIL

Ellicott Rock Wilderness Bdry.

Medlin Mountain

King Creek

TRAIL

FOOTHILLS

BURRELLS FORD

ROAD

FS708

107

Bee Bait Mountain

KING CREEK FALLS

BURRELLS FORD CAMPGROUND

▲ Mill Mountain

FS646

SOUTH

CAROLINA

GEORGIA

BIG BEND FALLS

FS709

BIG BEND

ROAD

BIG

BEND

TRAIL

Crane

Chattooga Wild & Scenic River Bdry.

CHATTOOGA & FOOTHILLS

▲ Round Top

▲ Crane Mountain

ROCK GORGE

RIVER

TRAIL

Branch

FOOTHILLS

Pigpen

Big Mountain

▲ Morton Mountain

CHATTOOGA RIVER TRAIL

LICK LOG FALLS

THRIFT LAKE

TRAIL

Reed Creek

Little Mountain

Lick Log Cr.

CHATTOOGA

NICHOLSON FORD ROAD

CHATTOOGA RIVER TRAIL

Ira Branch

Reed Mountain

FS646

Mose Mountain

Brack Hill
RUSSELL BRIDGE

28

Alf Hill

W. Fk. Chattooga R.

N

0   1

Mile

Chattooga River Trail, Section 1

(US 76 to Bartram Trail junction beyond Sandy Ford Road)

Length 10.7 miles

- **Dayhiking** Easy in either direction
- **Backpacking** Easy to Moderate in either direction
- **Vehicular Access At Either End** Southwestern (lower elevation) terminus off US 76, 1,190 feet; northeastern (higher elevation) terminus off Sandy Ford Road, 1,640 feet
- **Trail Junctions** Bartram, Chattooga River (Section 2)
- **Topographic Quadrangle** Rainy Mountain GA-SC
- **BLAZE** Aluminum diamonds
- **RD/NF** Tallulah/Chattahoochee
- **Features** Small streams; Chattooga River

BEGINNING BESIDE US 76 at the lowest elevation (1,190 feet) within the areas described in this guide, Section 1 of the Chattooga River Trail (CRT) heads northeast along the Georgia side of the national wild and scenic river. The first half frequently wanders outside of the blue-blazed river corridor; the last half, however, remains inside of the protected boundary. Except for the 1.6 miles that closely parallel the Chattooga, most of the rest of this route follows ridgelines or winds along the slopes and hollows in the narrow strip of land pitching to the river. Although the terrain is frequently steep and often cut by streams, Section 1's numerous grades are all easy or easy to moderate. Most of the easy-to-moderate ups and downs are short.

If you want to walk beside the scenic Chattooga in a matter of minutes, Section 1 is probably not the right hike for you. Starting from the US 76 trailhead, the safer of the two ends to leave your vehicle, the path does not closely follow the river until mile 6.3. A few side-trails drop down to campsites near the river before mile 6.3, but they tend to be overused, and at least one of them had ORV tracks leading to it.

Once beyond the trailhead boulder, the bulletin board, and the three vehicle-blocking rocks, the wide and well-used treadway rises gently on old roadbed into a broadleaf-conifer forest. Hemlock and three pines—white, shortleaf, and Virginia—make up the conifer component. At mile 0.1 and again a tenth of a mile further, highly erodable cheater trails run to the right and down to the river; please don't take them. The trail continues straight ahead or left both times.

The track quickly swings parallel to the Chattooga, way down but within easy earshot. Widening under the dense shade of rhodo-dendron, the walkway dips slightly as it rounds the first of many hollows at 0.4 mile. The route rock-steps a shallow branch two-tenths mile further, the first of many watercourse crossings. At mile 0.7 Section 1 crosses a wooden bridge over Pole Creek, then curls to the right to follow the creek downstream before turning up and away. This pattern of half-circling hollows and stream ravines is repeated over and over again throughout the hike. All this snaking and half-looping means the trail frequently changes exposure and forest composition. Now a path cut into slope, the CRT proceeds upstream as it undulates around hollows. The whitewater you hear high above the river at mile 1.0 is Bull Sluice, a class 5 rapid. Here you enter an oak-pine forest—a drier woods with mountain laurel, three species of pine and seven species of oak, including the post oak. At mile 1.4 the treadway descends to and crosses a wooden bridge over a rocky unnamed branch flowing fast down from the southern flank of nearby Lion Mountain.

The route, alternating between former road and constructed path, passes through laurel and over a Lion Mountain spur dropping southward toward the river at mile 1.7. Following a switchback off woods road, this segment loses elevation into rhododendron and hemlock, crosses bridges over two small watercourses in quick succession at mile 1.9, then ascends toward the next Lion Mountain spur. Here the no-sweat walking remains up high on slope under hickory, red maple, blackgum, sourwood, shortleaf pine, chestnut oak, and southern red oak. At mile 2.5 the track works its way up beside a shallow saddle before quickly heading south below ridgeline. Two-tenths mile further, the trail bends left onto the dry spur top, passes through open woods where low deciduous heath and bracken fern are conspicuous in the understory, and then angles down below the crest. This stretch affords occasional partial summer views of the low ridges and mountains across the river in South Carolina.

Section 1 continues its modus operandi of rounding ravines, crossing rivulets, and rising to the oak-pine forests on the upper slopes and ridgetops. At mile 3.5 the walkway gains the crest of a low spur and follows it for 0.2 mile (50 yards of moderate-to-strenuous downgrade) before switchbacking to the left and down onto a hemlock- and rhododendron-shaded roadbed. At mile 4.2 the CRT crosses a long bridge over a boulder-strewn branch, this one also draining the slopes of Lion Mountain. Forty yards beyond where it crosses a former (hopefully it will remain former) ORV route at mile 4.4, the trail turns 90 degrees to the right and down at the double blaze. You will quickly drop to an unbridged stream if you miss this turn.

After a short, easy-to-moderate downgrade toward the river, the treadway bridges a small feeder stream, allows a few fleeting glances at the green water, then slants up and away from the Chattooga. Here the walking, which climbs to the crest of a low, river-flanking ridge, advances steadily up an old jeep road. The elevation gain, easy to moderate at worst, remains on or near the dry oak-pine ridgeline. Much of the timber here is small; perhaps the forest was cut a second time or the area remained open after the first logging.

The road-cut treadway roller-coasters upward to mile 5.5, where it begins the steady descent all the way to the river. At mile 5.9 the course swerves down and to the right off the ridgecrest at the blazed fork (the wrong way is blocked with berms). It then heads downhill above a hollow sheltering tall shortleaf and white pines, steps over two more rivulets, and finally reaches the narrow floodplain at mile 6.3. Here the trail runs alongside the national wild and scenic river, often rocky and 35 to 45 yards wide, upstream past green pools, low white shoals, and clear sliding riffles. Stands of shading hemlock frequently darken the forest floor.

The route curves away from the Chattooga to cross bridged Lick Log Creek at mile 6.8 before returning to accompany the shining river. Along the way, as it travels upstream near the clear mountain water, the track crosses a bridge high over Buckeye Branch at mile 7.4. After passing beside a huge outcrop with an overhang high and deep enough to keep you dry in a thunderstorm, the CRT switchbacks up and to the left onto another road grade at mile 7.9. Here the trail doubles back on a steady, easy ascent through hemlock, white pine, and hardwoods to the last look at the Chattooga.

At mile 8.0 the walkway switchbacks to the right, downriver, onto path; one-tenth mile further it switchbacks to the left and up to pass over a spur fingering toward the Chattooga. Losing elevation from the spur, the cut-in, sidehill footpath half-circles a ravine through rhododendron and hemlock and crosses a small branch at a doghobble thicket (mile 8.3). Beyond another low spur and a hollow sheltering Fraser magnolia, the grade rises slowly to an oak-pine ridgetop at mile 8.7. The roadbed treadway gradually roller-coasters on or near the ridge's crest for the next 1.1 miles. This stretch affords occasional partial summer views to the east and wild-water music from the rapids below—Eye of the Needle, Second Ledge, Narrows.

After slabbing off the ridge at mile 9.8, the route ventures downhill to mile 10.0, where it crosses Rock Creek and Sandy Ford Road in quick succession. The final segment is effortless walking on low-elevation oak-pine slope. One-tenth mile before Section 1 ends, it closely approaches but does not cross Sandy Ford Road. At mile 10.7 the CRT ties into the Bartram Trail at a Y-shaped junction. This connection is usually marked with a Pack it in–Pack it out sign and is always designated with a trail-sign rock inside the wedge of the Y. Section 2 of the Chattooga River Trail, now sharing its treadway with the Bartram National Heritage Trail, continues straight ahead from the junction, upriver toward the bridge over Dicks Creek. To reach the trailhead parking area for the end of Section 1, make a hard, bend-back left turn onto the Bartram, walk 100 yards to Sandy Ford Road, then turn right onto the road and stroll another 60 yards to the parking area to the right of the road.

Nature Notes

Section 1's low elevations and dry ridges provide habitat for the post oak, a species much more common in the Piedmont of Georgia and the Carolinas than in the Southern Blue Ridge. Although a few scattered specimens have been found above 4,000 feet, this small oak usually occurs below the 3,000-foot contour line—in the foothills ringing the higher mountains. The post oak is intolerant: it cannot tolerate the shade of faster-growing competitors. Most intolerant trees grow fairly quickly so

post oak

they can have a shot at sunlight and the canopy, but the post oak is both intolerant and slow growing. So although all of the Southern Highlands below 3,000 feet technically lies within this hardwood's range, the post oak is rare or absent from nearly every site with even moderately moist or moderately rich soils. This slow-growing, shade intolerant tree prefers, or competes best, in dry, open habitat on rocky, poor-soiled ridges and upper slopes or along sunny, sandy-soiled riverbanks. The post oak does have one ace in the hole; it survives and reproduces in part because of its great resistance to drought.

A member of the white oak group (characterized by rounded lobes without bristles at the tips), the post is one of the easiest oaks to identify by leaf alone. Its thick, somewhat leathery leaves are deeply divided into 5 to 7 (usually 5) broad, rounded lobes. The uppermost, paired lobes are prominent and roughly squarish in outline; they form a cross in combination with the end lobe. Usually 3½ to 7½ inches long and 2½ to 4 inches wide, the post's deciduous leaves vary substantially in size and shape.

This member of the Beech family gradually becomes a small- to medium-sized tree; it gains height very slowly, even for an oak. On poor sites it often remains shrubby. But where conditions are favorable and growing room is available, this species usually produces stout, often twisted or gnarled branches that spread into a dense, round-topped crown. Most mature post oaks remain less than 2 feet in diameter and 65 feet in height. Only the extremely rare specimen attains either a diameter of 5 feet or a height of 100 feet. The current Georgia state record, a national co-champion, measured an impressive 19 feet 9 inches in circumference and 84 feet in height.

The post's close-grained heartwood is hard, heavy, and durable even when in contact with the earth. In the past its wood was utilized for construction timbers, for railroad ties, and for wagon hubs. But as is obvious from its name, its wood was used most frequently for fence posts.

Dense beds of partridgeberry, a creeping perennial, often blanket the ground beside many segments of Section 1. Sending down roots as they spread, the colonies are often bisected by the bare-dirt treadway. (The beds were well established before the trail was constructed.) This member of the Madder family is particularly abundant from mile 6.6 to 6.9, where the route closely parallels the river, frequently under the shade of hemlock.

Except for the size of its beds, which occasionally cover hundreds of square feet, everything else about the partridgeberry is diminutive. This recumbent herbaceous plant usually starts flowering during the middle of May and continues through much of June. The fragrant white or pinkish flowers—trumpet shaped and fringed inside—always occur in joined pairs. These small (only ½ to ⅔ of an inch long) blossoms share fused ovaries that produce a single berry-like fruit with closely set, eyelike indentations, one from each ovary.

The bright red partridgeberry fruits are especially noticeable from midsummer through autumn. As the common name implies, ruffed grouse eat the fruits. Grouse and turkey, however, eat these colorful but flavorless fruits only as a last resort. Because the berries are apparently of little importance to wildlife, many of these fruits last through the winter, and a few remain until the next blooming season.

Even without berry or bloom, clusters of partridgeberry are easy to identify by their small, shiny, dark green leaves—opposite and prominently veined. The ovate evergreen leaves are from ½ to ¾ of an inch long. Native American women brewed a tea from the leaves to drink as an aid in childbirth.

This native wildflower is most abundant at lower elevations along the larger streams within the Ellicott Rock Wilderness and the Chattooga National Wild and Scenic River corridor. It is especially prolific in the flat floodplain areas along streams and rivers, where white pine and hemlock mix with the hardwoods. Predominantly a northern species, partridgeberry is common in rich forests over

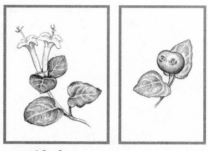

partridgeberry

much of the eastern United States and southeastern Canada. Only two species of the *Mitchella* genus are known to science. *Mitchella repens* is the North American species; the other one occurs in Asia.

Directions

Approach from the west: From the US 441–US 76 East intersection in Clayton, Georgia, travel US 76 East toward Westminster, South Carolina, for approximately 8.1 miles to the small (10 to 12 vehicles), paved, trailhead parking area to the left of the highway just before the bridge over the Chattooga River. This parking area is fee-pay, three dollars at present. A much larger parking lot, also fee-pay, is located to the left of the highway across the bridge in South Carolina. Chattooga River's unmistakable beginning is marked with a trail-sign boulder.

Approach from the southeast: From the US 76–US 123 intersection just west of Westminster, South Carolina, travel US 76 West for approximately 17.8 miles to the small (10 to 12 vehicles), paved, trailhead parking area to the right of the highway immediately after the bridge over the Chattooga River. This parking area is fee-pay, three dollars at present. A much larger parking lot, also fee-pay, is located to the left of the highway back across the bridge in South Carolina. Chattooga River's unmistakable beginning is marked with a trail-sign boulder.

(See Section 2 of the CRT on page 157 for directions to Section 1's northeastern terminus off Sandy Ford Road.)

Notes

Chattooga River Trail, Section 2
Bartram National Heritage Trail
(Bartram Trail junction off Sandy Ford Road to GA 28 at Russell Bridge)

Length 9.5 miles

- **Dayhiking** Easy in either direction
- **Backpacking** Easy to Moderate in either direction
- **Vehicular Access At Either End** Southwestern (slightly higher elevation) terminus off Sandy Ford Road, 1,640 feet; northeastern (slightly lower elevation) terminus at Russell Bridge (Highway 28) over Chattooga River, 1,580 feet
- **Trail Junctions** Bartram (see description), Willis Knob Horse, Chattooga River (Sections 1 and 3, see description to locate the beginning of Section 3)
- **Topographic Quadrangles** Rainy Mountain GA-SC, Whetstone SC-GA, Satolah GA-SC-NC
- **Blaze** Yellow plastic diamonds
- **RD/NF** Tallulah/Chattahoochee
- **Features** Dicks Creek Falls; small streams; Chattooga River; Warwoman Creek

S ECTION 2'S SOUTHWESTERN TERMINUS is located where the Bartram National Heritage Trail ties into the Chattooga River Trail just east of Sandy Ford Road. The two trails share the same treadway for the entire 9.5-mile distance to Highway 28. Along the way, the route crosses Willis Knob Horse Trail several times. Section 2 is described from southwest to northeast, traveling upriver and occasionally closely paralleling the green water and gray rock of the

Chattooga River and Warwoman Creek. Only one relatively short rise is difficult enough to be rated as moderate. Almost all of the other grades are nearly level or easy.

Starting where the two trails flow into one, the single path descends through a diverse, low-elevation, oak-pine forest dominated by a stand of tall white pine. A variety of trees—American holly, red maple, blackgum, Fraser magnolia, sourwood, yellow poplar, Virginia and shortleaf pine, and at least four species of oak—compete for sunlight below the white pines. The track curls beside Dicks Creek before crossing a bridge over the shallow stream at 0.3 mile. Forty-five yards beyond the bridge, a wide sidetrail to the right runs along the creek a short distance to Dicks Creek Falls—one of the most glorious sights in Georgia.

The upper portion of Dicks Creek Falls is a forest-framed blue aisle of sky above a white slide of water. The lower part of the falls splays out, its force dissipating as it sideslips into narrow runnels carrying the flow around the bedrock at its base. The 60-foot drop is the creek's final run; its catch basin is the Chattooga. From the end of the falls, the ribbon of fast water and rock extends, almost without break, for another 60 yards. Here the clear-water river is all brilliance and beauty and power as it churns through a bank-to-bank, state-to-state ledge—a Class 4 rapid known as Dicks Creek Ledge.

Beyond Dicks Creek, a turkey track of forking ridges forced the Chattooga into a half-loop to the east, to the north, then back to the west. Instead of following the meandering channel, the route gains elevation up to and over the ridge, taking the shortcut across the gap in the bend. The treadway follows a rivulet, crosses it, then ascends around hollow and over spur to mile 0.8, where it tops a spur and heads downhill. The dry oak-pine forest covering the upper slopes and spurs supports four species of pine and at least six species of oak, including southern red and post. An undemanding downgrade rounds several hollows, one full of ferns, before angling alongside the river. The first clear, unobstructed view of the Chattooga comes at mile 1.1.

For the next 0.5 mile the course treads an old road as it roller-coasters through a riverine forest with hemlock and basswood near the wild water. Occasionally this segment runs right beside the Chattooga and its long low slabs of streambed rock. At mile 1.6 the treadway slants up and away from the channel on an old jeep trail. The track rises slowly over a low spur into dry forest again. (Starting at mile 1.6, the Forest Service intends to reroute the trail away from at least two of the old road's most gullied sections.) Where the road is blocked at mile 1.9, the blazed reroute doglegs 90 degrees to the left and up onto higher slope. The wide footpath passes through even drier woods—mountain laurel, pitch and shortleaf pine, sassafras, and chestnut oak—as it heads up to a gap in the ridgeline at mile 2.1.

Once through the gap, the walkway loses elevation (easy to moderate at first), ties back into the jeep track, then works its way down to the slope above Warwoman Creek. The route continues level or slightly down as it descends to and then parallels the wide watercourse upstream. At mile 2.6 the treadway passes over a wooden bridge that spans a small, unnamed tributary. Beyond the bridge, the floodplain walking is mostly flat beside the usually shallow creek. The Chattooga River–Bartram Trail crosses Earls Ford Road, marked with a prominent rock sign on the first bank, at mile 2.9. A short stretch of trail to either side of the road is an often congested and messy car-camping area during dry, warm-weather weekends.

Across the road, the cakewalk continues as the path closely accompanies the slow stream through a largely evergreen forest of mountain laurel, rhododendron, hemlock, American holly, and tall shortleaf pine. At mile 3.1 the course crosses a long (nearly 70 feet), iron-rail bridge over Warwoman Creek, swings left, then proceeds upstream on road grade. The woods-road treadway gradually curves up and away from the creek. Two-tenths mile beyond the bridge, at a double blaze, the route turns up and to the right onto path. Here the hiking ascends parallel to a ravine, dips to and crosses its notch, then makes a moderate, 100-yard climb to the top of a spur off a Willis Knob ridge. Just over the crest the track trods across the signed horse trail at mile 3.5.

Continuing over another spur, the overall easy grade proceeds on a dry, oak-pine slope supporting a shrub layer of dense deciduous heath. The trail travels over a roadbed atop the long ridge running southward from Willis Knob at mile 3.9. Blue blazes on the crest mark the boundary of the Chattooga National Wild and Scenic River corridor. Once over the ridgeline, the treadway winds slowly downward—half-looping through hollows, ranging alongside ravines from above, and sweeping over spurs on cut-in path. At mile 4.5 the walkway crosses a bridge over a permanent-water rivulet. The mild grades meander around ravines to mile 4.8, where the route turns right onto another woods road.

The roadbed treadway follows an easy descent on or near the crest of a low ridge. Young, small-diameter trees to either side of the track are evidence of its former purpose. Mountain laurel thickets crowd the route in places. Section 2 veers off the spur and travels around several ravines before swerving down into dark rhododendron above a brook to the right. At mile 5.4 the course crosses a bridge over Laurel Branch, 8 to 10 feet wide at full flow. The gently undulating lower-slope hiking advances across the ridged gap of a thumblike river bend to the south known and labeled as Turn Hole. After switchbacking up and to the right at mile 5.8, the path doglegs left onto a road at the arrowed carsonite sign. The Chattooga River–Bartram Trail follows the road for 70 yards before continuing straight ahead on narrow treadway (second carsonite sign) where the road bears off to the left.

Back on footpath, the route heads downhill through a young, primarily pine forest striving for space in the canopy above a tangle of mountain laurel. Section 2 swings above a stream hollow, works its way down to water, then crosses over Bynum Branch just beyond a colony of New York fern at mile 6.2. The lower-slope traverse rises and falls through a forest where American holly thrives beneath a stand of tall shortleaf pine; most of the softwoods are mast straight and 16 to 20 inches in diameter. After passing over a road at mile 6.5 and gaining elevation for a short distance, the track descends through another young forest where American holly, even more abundant than before the road, dominates the understory. The trail curls to the left again, ventures up stream hollow again, then crosses the bridge over Adline Branch at mile 6.9.

A short distance beyond the brook, the old jeep-trail route turns right onto the signed horse trail and shares the treadway for 20 yards before splitting away to the left at the carsonite hiker sign. The nearly effortless walking continues as the old road slowly angles through young forest to the edge of an extensive floodplain known as Long Bottom, where the course becomes as flat as mountain hiking gets. A crop of white pine planted by Georgia Power in the 1960s stands to the right of the trail in the bottom. At mile 7.4 Section 2 comes to an open-grown, low-branched giant of a mulberry (if it is still alive) and an unbridged rivulet in quick succession. To the left, just beyond the drinking-water rivulet, the remains of the Holden homestead—an ice box, a piece of metal roofing, and the telltale stacked-rock chimney with largely intact chinking—are tucked fast against the toe of the slope.

The course proceeds flat as a flitter past a slowly rusting piece of farm equipment. To the right the pine plantation is now loblolly. At mile 7.6 the uniform rows of planted pines end, and the walkway now undulates slightly through a young, successional forest where pole-timber yellow poplars lead the charge toward light. Tall aster gardens bloom in late summer and early autumn in the moist, largely hardwood bottom to the right. After a wooden bridge over a rivulet at mile 8.0, the old-road treadway closely parallels the Chattooga again—finally. Beyond the one open viewing spot on the bank, much of the next 0.2 mile offers occasional looks through screening trees to the river below. Small American hornbeams, a Birch family species, are exceedingly numerous in the trailside woods.

The river-corridor route slants higher away from the Chattooga at mile 8.2, then quickly switches from former road to path at the double blaze. After dipping to and crossing Holden Branch at mile 8.3, the track rises slowly, ties back into roadbed, and passes a wall of kudzu to the left. Long Bottom widens away from the river again, and you can see another planting of loblolly, many of them dead or dying. Mother Nature seems to abhor a monoculture as much as a vacuum. Section 2 passes a young, south-facing oak–pine–red maple forest on the upslope as it heads back toward the Chattooga.

By mile 8.8 the trail is close enough to the channel for good partial views down through the trees. After following this quintessential mountain stream for 0.1 mile, the course ascends above the bottom onto the lowermost slope of Holden Mountain before dropping to the outer edge of the floodplain again and the 115-foot-long iron-rail bridge over the West Fork Chattooga River. Across the West Fork at mile 9.2, the final stretch curves right onto the roadbed constructed to bring in the bridge, then travels upstream along the main Chattooga on the lower slopes of Alf Hill. The route slabs off the road onto path and dips to its end at GA 28 next to Russell Bridge.

If you want to keep walking the Chattooga River Trail (Section 3) generally to the northeast, turn right onto Highway 28 and cross Russell Bridge over the Chattooga River into South Carolina. Follow the highway for 0.2 mile before turning left into the wide entrance of a gravel road (FS 784). Section 3 continues behind the road-blocking gate at the bottom of the parking area 75 yards in from the highway.

Nature Notes

The well-known American holly—the only evergreen hardwood inhabiting the Southern Highlands—is unusually prolific along much of Section 2. From just before Bynum Branch at mile 6.2 to several tenths of a mile beyond Adline Branch (mile 6.9), this small-to medium-sized tree occasionally dominates the understory. Glossy and thick, the American holly's leathery, wavy-edged, spiny-margined leaves are instantly recognizable. No other Southern Appalachian tree or shrub bears even remotely similar foliage. Each of the elliptical alternate leaves, usually 2 to 4 inches long and ¾ to 1½ inches wide, persists for three years. These leaves are so distinctive that you can even identify them at night, with your feet. Several times while backpacking, I have made painful and positive holly IDs during those too-often shoeless, late-night walks that could be delayed no longer.

This hardwood's bright red berries, which ripen in late autumn, decorate female trees only. Borne singly or in clusters of two or three, these fleshy berries, if not eaten, overwinter and may linger as late as May or June. Deer, turkey, and other birds, including pileated woodpeckers, eat the bitter berries. Flocks of turkey fly up into the crowns of larger female hollies to glean the berries. As you may have guessed, birds help propagate this species by dispersing the seeds far from the parent tree.

In the Southern Appalachians, the American holly is most numerous, though still usually only a minor component, in moist forests below 4,000 feet. It achieves its best growth and is most common on lower-elevation slopes and in the floodplains of larger streams such as the Chattooga. This species grows slowly even in the best of conditions, and takes 100 to 150 years to reach maturity. Largest of the native hollies, this tree commonly attains a height of 40 to 55 feet and a diameter of 1 to 2 feet on good sites. Alabama is home to the current national record—a monster of a holly 74 feet tall and 9 feet 11 inches around.

American holly

Once commonly known as Christmas holly, the berry-bearing females were cut as partially decorated Christmas trees. Today, people who live where this native species abounds still cut a few small branches for yuletide greenery. The Cherokee and early Appalachian settlers carved stirring spoons from this holly's nearly white, fine-textured wood. Later, the white wood was used for cabinetwork inlays and for piano and organ keys. Whether they know it or not, most people born before the age of plastic—baby-boomer vintage or older—have handled holly wood. Because of its light color and dye acceptance, this tree was once widely used to make rulers.

A small, stooped tree even at maturity, the American hornbeam thrives along Section 2's northernmost 2.0 miles. Saplings of this slow-growing species are much more difficult to recognize than the older trees. You may be able to identify young hornbeams by their clear gray bark and alternate, doubly saw-toothed, birchlike leaves. (The elliptical leaves, long pointed at the apex and rounded at the base, are usually 1½ to 4½ inches long and 1 to 2 inches wide.) As these hardwoods age, however, they are unmistakable. The trees thicken and stoop over; their short, crooked trunks become fluted with rounded, irregularly spaced vertical ridges, giving them the

American hornbeam

appearance of long, sinewy, deeply rippled muscles. You can immediately recognize a mature American hornbeam by its growth habit, smooth gray bark, serrated leaves, and "musclewood" trunk.

The American hornbeam also can be identified by its unusual seed-bearing bracts, conspicuous in late spring. These loose and leafy drooping clusters of bracts, usually from 2½ to 5 inches long, dangle from branches like miniature, winged Japanese lanterns. Grouse, turkey, songbirds, and squirrels eat the small nutlets located at the base of the three-pointed bracts.

This broadleaf is most common and achieves its best growth in the rich, moist soils of bottomlands and ravines. It becomes increasingly scarce in the Southern Appalachians above 2,800 feet, and its upper-elevation limit is probably between 3,200 and 3,400 feet. With the exception of most of Maine and most of Florida, this species grows throughout the eastern United States and extends into many of the forested states immediately west of the mighty Mississippi. But no matter where it is found, in northern New York or southern Georgia, the hornbeam remains a shade-tolerant understory tree, usually only 20 to 28 feet in height and 10 to 14 inches in diameter at maturity.

This Birch family species is also known as ironwood, blue beech, water beech, and musclewood. Renowned for its weight and strength, the hornbeam's heavy wood was once used for tool handles, levers, wedges, and the runners on pioneer land sleds. This broadleaf's accepted common name refers to the extreme toughness of its wood: "horn" connotes hardness, and "beam" is an old world word for tree.

Directions

Approach from the west: In Clayton, Georgia, where US 76 turns west at a traffic light, turn east (right if you are coming from the south) onto Rickman Street. Follow Rickman Street for approximately 0.5 mile to its end at signed Warwoman Road. Turn right onto Warwoman Road and follow it approximately 5.4 miles to the signed right turn onto paved Sandy Ford Road.

Approach from the north: From the US 64–NC 28 intersection in Highlands, North Carolina, travel NC 28 South then GA 28 South for approximately 12.0 miles to the signed right turn onto paved Warwoman Road. Follow Warwoman Road for approximately 8.2 miles to the signed left turn onto paved Sandy Ford Road.

Approach from the southeast: From the SC 28–SC 107 intersection north of Walhalla, South Carolina, travel SC 28 North then GA 28 North (cross Chattooga River into Georgia after approximately 8.4 miles) for approximately 10.6 miles before turning left onto signed and paved Warwoman Road. Proceed on Warwoman Road for approximately 8.2 miles to the signed left turn onto paved Sandy Ford Road.

From Sandy Ford Road: Follow Sandy Ford Road for approximately 0.7 mile before turning left across a road-level bridge. After this left turn, proceed approximately 3.7 dirt-gravel miles to an obvious pull-in parking area to the left of the road. Look for this parking spot approximately 0.3 mile beyond where the road fords Dicks Creek. (When the creek is running high, you may not want to risk the ford with a low-slung, conventional vehicle. A small opening to the left of the road offers limited parking just before the ford.)

From the parking area 0.3 mile beyond the ford, walk 60 yards further down the road to the Bartram Trail, marked with a prominent trail-sign boulder. Turn left off the road onto the Bartram Trail and continue 100 yards to the Bartram–Chattooga River Trail junction and its trail-sign rock. If you want to walk Section 1 of the Chattooga River Trail from north to south, turn sharply back to the right at the Y-shaped junction. Both the Bartram and Section 2 of the Chattooga River Trail share the same treadway straight ahead, upstream, toward Highway 28.

Near its northern end, Section 1 of the Chattooga River Trail (walked south to north) crosses Sandy Ford Road at trail mile 10.0. If you wish to end or begin the trail at this crossing, follow Sandy Ford Road another 0.6 mile beyond the Bartram Trail parking area to the trail-sign boulder on the right side of the road. With the exception of the overused car camping spot to the right of the road, there is little room for parking at this trail crossing. If you follow the Chattooga River Trail to the left side of the road (from the way you drove in), you will arrive at the Bartram–Chattooga River junction after 0.7 mile.

Section 2's northeastern terminus at GA 28 and Section 3's southwestern terminus off SC 28 are 0.2 mile apart. Section 2 ends on the downstream western side (the Georgia side) of Highway 28's Russell Bridge over the Chattooga River. You will find a parking area with a bulletin board across the highway from the end of Section 2. (See Section 3 of the CRT on page 167 for directions to Russell Bridge.)

Notes

Chattooga River Trail, Section 3
(SC 28 to Burrells Ford Road)

Length 12.8 miles

- **Dayhiking** Easy to Moderate in either direction
- **Backpacking** Moderate in either direction
- **Vehicular Access At Either End** Southwestern
  (lower elevation) terminus off SC 28, 1,585 feet;
  northeastern (higher elevation) terminus off
  Burrells Ford Road, 2,170 feet
- **Trail Junctions** Chattooga River (Sections 2 and 4),
  Foothills, Big Bend
- **Topographic Quadrangles** Satolah GA-SC-NC,
  Tamassee SC-GA
- **Blazes** White for Foothills; the old black blazes for
  Chattooga River are fading and will not be repainted
- **RD/NF** Andrew Pickens/Sumter
- **Features** Small streams; Lick Log Falls;
  Rock Gorge; Foothills Trail; Chattooga River cascades;
  King Creek Falls

SECTION 3 IS THE LONGEST, the most difficult, the most heavily used, and the most scenic of the first three Chattooga River Trail sections. While this South Carolina segment does not include a single sustained grade of even moderate difficulty, it does present many steady easy grades and numerous short rises and dips of easy-to-moderate or moderate difficulty. The footing, which is often rocky or rooty, is rougher than that of the first two sections. During warm-weather weekends, especially on three-day holidays, this trail is well trod and most of the riverside campsites are tented or tarped. The northeastern trailhead at Burrells Ford Road is much busier than the southwestern trailhead off Highway 28.

Section 3's popularity is not hard to explain: Burrells Ford Campground is right beside the northeastern trailhead, the river is stocked with trout below the Burrells Ford Bridge, access to the trail is easy, and this part of the CRT actually closely parallels its namesake river from time to time. Known as Section 0 to some, the stretch of river from Burrells Ford downstream to Highway 28 definitely lives up to its designated status of wild and scenic. The river here, especially from Lick Log Creek through Rock Gorge to Big Bend Falls, drops over high, bedrock ledges and crashes through boulder gardens. Dark green plunge pools—sanctuaries for frayed spirits and overheated bodies—beckon below several of the constricting cascades.

Section 3 is described from southwest to northeast, upstream from Highway 28 to Burrells Ford Road. Much of the route traverses lower slope. The only reasonable way to negotiate this steep-sided, cut-up terrain is to wriggle and wraggle side to side around ravines and hollows up high and to curl over spurs down low. And that is exactly what this well-constructed treadway does; it snakes back and forth, half-looping around ravines in one direction and half-looping over spurs in the other, all the while crossing those invisible contour lines as slowly as possible. Occasionally a couple of tight switchbacks lead up and around land too steep for a path. Because this section is long and demands description of cascades, waterfalls, swimming holes, junctions, and lunker pines, the lower-slope trail narrations will be short and to the point.

Twenty-five feet beyond the vehicle-blocking gate, the well-maintained trail heads up and to the right away from the road onto steps, then onto cut-in path. Here the first mild upgrade heads generally eastward on north-facing slope through a mixed broadleaf-conifer forest. Witch-hazel, silverbell, sweet birch, and hemlock attest to north-slope moisture. The walkway ducks to and crosses a small branch at 0.3 mile, the first of many tributary runs, rivulets, branches, and creeks. A short distance further, the track crosses the notch of the first rhododendron-filled ravine. Now the lower-slope walking is off and running around ravines beneath a two-tiered canopy—white pines towering over hardwoods, hemlocks, and other conifers. The treadway curves over the first well-defined spur at 0.8 mile. Several of the ravines support a shiny understory of rhododendron and moist-site broadleafs such as basswood. The footpath follows the river as it bends to the south around three sides of Brack Hill. After passing the southernmost point of the forced meander, Section 3 heads north on noticeably drier west-facing slope. The hike continues through a forest thick with deciduous heath and mountain laurel in the undergrowth and dry-site trees such as sourwood and three oaks—chestnut, post, and southern red. At mile 1.3, on the lower, westernmost slopes of Reed Mountain, the route ties into an old roadbed and proceeds through more oak-pine forest often dominated by white pine.

After working its way around Reed Mountain's narrow north slope, the course connects with another former road within eyesight of the river at mile 3.0. Here the walking gradually descends to the Chattooga—a clear riffling glide over rock and yellow sand bottom. The upriver run remains near water's edge until it pulls away to cross a long wooden bridge over Ira Branch at mile 3.4. The trail heads quickly back toward the Chattooga, makes a double switchback up and around rough terrain, then slowly descends from slope just above the river to the flat floodplain at mile 3.7. For the next 0.3 mile the route remains in the floodplain. Sometimes the river is barely out of sight; at other times the lively shoals and quieter pools are in plain view. The forest in the bottom is green year-round. Mountain laurel, rhododendron, and doghobble form the understory; hemlock, white pine, and American holly make up the taller tiers.

At mile 4.0 the grade crosses a small sidestream, turns away from the river, then swerves back toward the channel on cut-in path higher up the slope. At mile 4.3 the track swings away from the Chattooga again. This time it parallels Lick Log Creek past two cascades; the second, pouring down a ledge perhaps 15 feet high, is easier to see. Beyond a large colony of New York fern, the course crosses the bridge (mile 4.5) over Lick Log Creek just downstream from Lick Log Falls—a two-stage splash down widening rockface 20 to 25 feet high. The walkway doglegs left and heads downstream immediately after crossing the creek. One-tenth mile beyond the bridge, the CRT reaches its signed junction with the white-blazed Foothills National Recreation Trail. Straight ahead, the two trails share the same tread-way the rest of the way to Burrells Ford Road and beyond.

Past the junction, the river flows into a bend squared off on three sides to the northwest. Instead of following the Chattooga all the way around the crook, the track cuts across the dry-land gap through a saddle between a pair of 2,000-foot knobs. Here, as Section 3 gradually gains elevation farther from the river, the path affords long glimpses of the loud white way below. At mile 5.2 the course curls up to and over a saddle in the ridge along the blue-blazed river corridor. For the next mile the walkway, much of it on woods road, gently undulates on or near the crest of a spur.

The combined trail slips to the left of the ridgeline and begins its descent toward the Chattooga at mile 6.2. Along the way the route passes above Rock Gorge—a particularly rugged and steep-sided piece of river where huge cliff-fallen boulders and bedrock slabs routinely pinch the entire stream into powerful, log-wedged runs no more than 10 feet wide. A few of these cascading death traps are even narrower. At mile 6.6 two old-growth hemlocks (if they are still alive) stand close beside the footpath. Running along the river on high slope, the track roller-coasters downward toward better and better views of the rocks, rapids, sluices, pools, and cascades. A sidepath at mile 6.9 leads to another high-ledge cascade, commonplace and unnamed here in the Southern Appalachians, but beautiful enough to be the namesake centerpiece of a state park in flatter regions of our country. A final easy-to-moderate dip leads the CRT back down beside the river and to the beginning of effortless floodplain walking at mile 7.1.

One-tenth mile after entering the bottom, where the main path continues straight ahead to campsites, the treadway angles to the right with the blazes (the white Foothills blazes will remain). It quickly veers back near the national wild and scenic river and crosses a short wooden bridge over a small feeder branch at mile 7.3. Several sidepaths lead to open views of drops and pools. Beyond the first bridge, the pathway rises above the Chattooga through a tall stand of second-growth white pine before heading down on cut-in path to a second bridge, this one over a narrow, slightly entrenched branch at mile 7.4. Here the walking proceeds on lowermost slope above Rock Gorge–like scenery: the river pours over bedrock ledges and swirls around high, jagged boulders. After tying into road grade beside the channel, the trail skirts river-edge rock (a high-water alternate offers a bypass to the right), then quickly works its way onto low slope. Below, the river is patiently cutting through upward-tilted layers of bedrock, especially conspicuous during low-water drought.

At mile 7.7 a short sidepath leads to an open, heavily used beach opposite a narrow-based bluff 40 to 45 feet high. Two-tenths mile further, the route switchbacks to the right away from the river and up a ravine. Long ago Round Top (2,527 feet) forced the Chattooga into an entrenched, three-quarter-loop to the northwest. Instead of taking a shortcut across the gap in the bend east of the knob, the trail roughly follows the Chattooga around the southwestern and north-eastern slopes of the mountain high above the river. A steady, easy upgrade and three more switchbacks lead the CRT up and around a rhododendron-green ravine into dry-slope forest. The footpath ascends to and curves over the first Round Top spur at mile 8.6, descends, crosses over a second spur at mile 8.9, then loses elevation steadily toward the river.

At mile 9.2 the track passes close beside an old bluff 30 feet high. After proceeding past several sections of the bluff and heading up-slope, the trail comes to a sidepath slanting down and to the left under more bluff to a great view of Big Bend Falls. Here the Chat-tooga booms over a series of cascades 20 to 25 feet high, the last 15 feet dropping all at once over a broken ledge. Twenty yards beyond the sidepath, the trail switchbacks right, then left, as it rises higher above the river for 0.1 mile before venturing back down toward the Chattooga. For nearly 0.2 mile the walkway continues alongside the stream on slope above a series of wide whitewater shoals. At mile 9.6 the course switchbacks up and away from the Chattooga again through moist riverine forest— hemlock and sweet birch habitat.

After topping out high above a twist in the river, the treadway follows a gentle downgrade to its Big Bend Trail junction at mile 10.0.

You can't miss the approach to the Big Bend connection—bluff line to the right and an unnamed branch to the left, trail signs and wooden bridge over the branch. Big Bend Trail ends where it ties into the CRT above the bridge. The combined Chattooga River–Foothills Trail turns left, crosses the bridge above a low-volume spill, then heads back riverward. At mile 10.2 the route skirts the open rocky edge of the riverbed, no doubt underwater after heavy rain in the right season. Another high-water alternate bypasses the riverbank.

The next 0.6 mile roller-coasters beside the scenic river, from near bank level to perhaps 60 vertical feet above the wide ledges, pools, and chutes. Several impressive, second-growth white pine tower above this stretch. At mile 10.8 Section 3 again switchbacks up and away from the Chattooga around rough terrain. Passing beside outcrop rock, the grade heads uphill for 0.2 mile before descending more sharply toward the wild and scenic stream. The walkway crosses a wooden bridge (mile 11.3) over an intermittent rivulet that slides, when it's running, down rock above the bridge. Beyond the rivulet, the track undulates near the river until mile 11.7, where it makes a short, moderate climb up erosion-bar steps. A wide, signed path coming from the Burrells Ford Campground ties into the main trail at mile 11.9.

Continuing from this junction, the CRT swings to the right farther away from the floodplain, rounds a ravine, then dips to another signed sidetrail at mile 12.3. To the right, an orange-blazed path (blazes will not be repainted in the future) leads 0.3 mile upstream to King Creek Falls. What to say about the falls? Well, it's high and plenty wide enough to let the sun in. And its white-froth drapery narrows and funnels toward the middle, while the rockface widens toward the plunge pool. And in places, angel-hair patterns overlap each other in different directions. And when it's falling full bore, cool spindrift flies against your face. And…well, you'll see.

Section 3 follows King Creek downstream, makes a bridged crossing, then ascends into oak-pine forest. The final easy upgrade winds around ravines and switchbacks once before bearing toward Burrells Ford Road. At the road, you can either continue straight ahead to the campground parking lot or turn to the right and climb steps to the road. A Foothills Trail sign marks Section 4's beginning treadway across the road from the steps.

Back in the dim mists of the last millennium, a few decades ago, Section 3 of the Chattooga River Trail shared its treadway, all of it, with the Bartram National Heritage Trail. After the Foothills National Recreation Trail was established, however, three became a crowd and the Bartram Trail designation was dropped from the Forest Service's Chattooga National Wild and Scenic River map. Sumter National Forest's Andrew Pickens Ranger District does not recognize the Bartram Trail on the South Carolina side of the Chattooga River.

Nature Notes

The first time I hiked this section, in late May, I spotted one of the largest kingsnakes I had ever seen, winding through the branches of a mountain laurel thicket above the Chattooga. At least 5½ feet long, the boldly patterned reptile glided with ease through the Vs of forked branches until it came to a gap in the laurel nearly as wide as it was long. As I continued to watch, the snake paused only long enough to judge the distance and effort required. Then, like a living, rippling rope, the running end poked forward across the open space, slowly pushed ahead by the stationary yet unwinding coil at the anchoring end. Displaying incredible muscle control, the king stretched out horizontally through the air, body dipping lower than level and head held up, until it caught the far branch and reeled in its tail while pushing its head forward through the laurel.

The easily recognized common kingsnake is the longest thick-bodied nonpoisonous serpent found in the Southern Appalachians. The muscular kingsnake's length at maturity normally ranges from 36 to 60 inches; the longest on record spanned an impressive 82 inches. The black racer is as long as the king, and the black rat snake even longer, but both of these ophidians are solid black on the back and noticeably more slender. You won't be likely to mistake either of them for the king.

Scaled shiny and smooth, the common kingsnake is identified by the diamond pattern on its black back and sides. Distinct white or pale yellow spots on the scales form these crossbands, which vary from bold chain links to blotches and specks in a faint diamond configuration. The king is the only black snake with crossband diamond markings in the Southern Appalachians.

Most often encountered along the larger, low-elevation streams in the Southern Highlands, this predator usually hunts during the day, especially during early morning or near dusk. In the spring and fall when nights are cool, they often sun in the open near riverside trails. The hottest days of summer force these non-thermoregulating reptiles to become active at night. When first disturbed, kingsnakes often vibrate their tails at whirr speed. If the snake happens to be hidden on dry leaves, the resulting buzz really gets your attention.

This creature is our country's champion constrictor. It stuns its prey with a cat-quick jab of its head, then ropes the victim in a death knot of squeezing coils, clenched tighter and tighter until the animal suffocates. Like all snakes, this one can swallow a meal substantially thicker than its body.

The kingsnake eats lizards, rodents, small birds, all kinds of eggs—and other snakes. In the Southern Blue Ridge, this species frequently feeds on the northern water snake, which helps explain why they are often found along stream margins. Not only do kingsnakes kill northern water snakes—fairly large and formidable themselves at maturity—they also strike, squeeze, and eat coral snakes, copperheads, and rattlesnakes (they are immune to the poison). Any snake capable of killing a timber rattler with its bare coils and swallowing that pit viper whole and raw for breakfast, from fangs to rattles, is without a doubt the man.

Beyond where the Foothills Trail ties into the Chattooga River Trail at mile 4.6, a ridge on the South Carolina side of the river long ago forced the Chattooga into a half loop to the northwest. Rather than follow the river around the bend, the combined trails take a much shorter and straighter route up and over the ridge, across the gap in the meander. Along the way, on the higher and drier oak-pine slopes and crests, the trail passes beside several small colonies of pinesap that were in bloom during early September the last time I walked Section 3.

Like the more common Indian pipe, the pinesap is a nongreen saprophyte—a plant lacking chlorophyll and obtaining its nourishment from decaying wood buried in the soil or leaf mold, probably with the aid of fungi. These colorful perennials are reddish orange and usually only 3 to 8 inches high. And like other saprophytes, the pinesap's leaves have become nonfunctioning vestigial scales clasping the stem. A downward-nodding raceme at the top of the stem produces several tawny yellow to orangish red blooms. The urn-shaped, half-inch-long flowers normally open sometime between late June and mid-September.

Primarily a northern species, the pinesap is at best occasional within its preferred Southern Appalachian habitat, oak-pine forests below 4,000 feet. Although pinesap colonies occur in deciduous forest, they are much more common in the drier, acidic, upland soils where pines are a major component. No doubt its name originated from this association.

pinesap

Directions

Approach from the west: In Clayton, Georgia, where US 76 turns west at a traffic light, turn east (right if you are coming from the south) onto Rickman Street. Follow Rickman Street for approximately 0.5 mile to its end at signed Warwoman Road. Turn right onto Warwoman Road, follow it for approximately 13.5 miles to its eastern end at GA 28, then turn right onto GA 28 South. Proceed on Highway 28 for approximately 2.4 miles (cross the Chattooga River into South Carolina at mile 2.2) to the left turn onto a wide gravel road (FS 784). Section 3 begins behind the road-blocking gate 75 yards in from the highway.

Approach from the south: From the SC 28–SC 107 intersection north of Walhalla, South Carolina, travel SC 28 North for approximately 8.3 miles to the right turn onto a wide gravel road (FS 784). This gravel road is located 0.2 mile before SC 28 crosses the Chattooga

River. Section 3 begins behind the road-blocking gate 75 yards in from the highway.

Approach from the north: From the US 64–NC 28 intersection in Highlands, North Carolina, travel NC 28 South, GA 28 South, and SC 28 South for approximately 14.2 miles to the left turn onto a wide gravel road (FS 784). This turn is located 0.2 mile beyond the bridge over the Chattooga River. Section 3 begins behind the road-blocking gate 75 yards in from the highway.

(See Section 4 of the CRT on page 197 for directions to Section 3's northeastern terminus off Burrells Ford Road.)

Notes

Foothills National Recreation Trail
(Lick Log Section)

Length 2.3 miles

■ **Dayhiking** Easy in either direction
■ **Backpacking In** Easy
■ **Backpacking Out** Easy to Moderate
■ **Start** Foothills Trailhead at the junction
   of SC 107 and Cheohee Road, 2,210 feet
■ **End** Chattooga River Trail (Section 3)
   near Lick Log Falls, 1,690 feet
■ **Trail Junction** Chattooga River (Section 3)
■ **Topographic Quadrangles** Tamassee SC-GA,
   Satolah GA-SC-NC
■ **Blaze** White
■ **RD/NF** Andrew Pickens/Sumter
■ **Features** Lick Log Falls (see description);
   Chattooga River near end of trail section;
   CRT approach

THE **FOOTHILLS NATIONAL RECREATION TRAIL** spans 76 miles
   between South Carolina's Oconee and Table Rock State Parks.
Starting from its southwestern, Oconee State Park terminus, the
white-blazed trail crosses SC 107, then winds northwestward to its
junction with the Chattooga River Trail. From this connection, the
Foothills Trail shares the same treadway with the CRT for 8.8 miles,
generally northward and upstream within the national wild and
scenic river corridor. A short distance after the trails cross Burrells
Ford Road, they split; Chattooga River swings back toward its namesake stream and Foothills heads east then northeast before crossing

SC 107 again at Sloan Bridge Picnic Area.

For the purposes of this guide, I have described two short segments of the Foothills Trail from east to west, as access trails to the Chattooga and its namesake treadway. Both of these sections, well constructed and well maintained, are easily walked, cut-in paths. And as delineated, both of these short stretches end within the protected land along the national wild and scenic river. This section, Lick Log, is shorter and located further south than the other link, the Medlin Mountain section (see page 199). The Lick Log portion of the Foothills Trail, as described in this guide, begins at SC 107 and leads northwestward to its junction with the Chattooga River Trail near the falls on Lick Log Creek.

This Foothills segment begins on the west side of SC 107, across the highway from the entrance to Cheohee Road. Marked by various signs, including a wooden one with mileages a little further in, the path dips from the road into low-elevation oak-pine forest. The upslope to the right is the southern toe of Morton Mountain. At 0.3 mile the easy downgrade parallels the beginning run of a rivulet to the left. Here the forest becomes riparian; you'll see the familiar moist-site species—rhododendron, hemlock, and hardwoods such as sweet birch and yellow poplar.

With the lone exception of a very short, downhill pitch cross-tied with erosion-bar steps, the treadway follows gentle grades above the now-spilling branch. The Lick Log Creek feeder slips away to the west as the route descends slightly harder into a predominantly pine forest. By comparing the growth habit, the needle length and number, and the general size and shape of the cones, you can readily distinguish four pine species—white, pitch, shortleaf, and Virginia—along this route. Soon after the track swings close to Nicholson Ford Road, it enters a woods where broadleafs are more common and crosses its first wooden bridge, this one over a seasonal rivulet, at 0.7 mile.

Two-tenths mile farther, through dry oak-pine forest where deciduous heath (huckleberry and blueberry) often grows thick in the understory, the walkway dips slightly to the second bridge.

Immediately across this bridge, which spans a small dry ravine, a sign points to the path leading 115 yards to the Thrift Lake Parking Area off Nicholson Ford Road. This parking lot was developed for fishers who wanted quicker access to the river and for backpackers who wanted to leave their vehicles overnight in a spot safer than Highway 107. After another two-tenths mile and another undemanding downgrade, the trail crosses the third bridge over a beginning branch flowing year-round.

The route turns away from the stream and quickly enters a grove of mountain laurel, which blooms here beginning in late April or early May. At this low elevation the mountains provide habitat for six oak species—white and chestnut in the white oak group, and southern red, northern red, black, and scarlet in the red oak group. Red maple, Fraser magnolia, sassafras, sourwood, blackgum, and several species of hickory compete for light beneath the oaks.

After passing through a stand of tall white pine, the course comes to a dirt-gravel road (a short spur off Nicholson Ford Road) at its parking area/turnaround end. Here at mile 1.6 the Foothills Trail doglegs right onto road and quickly re-enters the woods at the back right corner of the dead end. The rest of the route gradually loses elevation as it works its way down toward water. By mile 2.0 the footpath follows fast-moving Pigpen Branch through hemlock and rhododendron. With 0.2 mile remaining, the track crosses a bridge over Lick Log Creek less than 100 feet upstream from its meeting with Pigpen. The next bridge crosses the same 12- to 15-foot-wide stream that ran parallel to the trail, only at this point it is called Lick Log Creek instead of Pigpen Branch. By mapmaker's convention, creeks trump branches, even branches much wider and longer than the creeks they join.

Beyond the second bridge over Lick Log Creek, the treadway enters the national wild and scenic river corridor, passes a confusing cheater path heading straight downhill to the left (don't take it), then ends at its signed junction with the Chattooga River Trail. To the right, the Foothills and Chattooga River Trails share the same winding tread upstream and to the north. A turn left onto the CRT leads slightly less than 0.1 mile to Lick Log Falls—a small, two-stage drop 20 to 25 feet high.

Nature Notes

This section of the aptly named Foothills Trail traverses the lower southern and western slopes of Morton Mountain—a 2,470-foot knob in the transition zone between the Piedmont a short distance to the south and the much higher mountains of the Blue Ridge a short

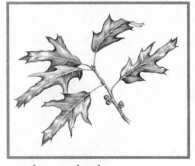

southern red oak

distance to the north. This zone of rapid transition harbors a flora that is neither strictly Piedmont nor Southern Appalachian, but rather a mix of the two. The low elevations and dry exposures of the foothills suit the southern red oak, a tree that is much more abundant and well known in the Piedmont of the South than in the Southern Blue Ridge. When you find this tree in the mountains, you are almost invariably walking on a dry, often poor-soiled ridge or slope below 2,500 feet.

Although highly variable in length and outline, the dark green leaves of the southern red oak are easy to identify. The bases of the 5- to 9-inch-long and 3- to 5-inch-wide leaves are strongly rounded into an upside-down bell-curve and usually have three, five, or seven sharply pointed and bristle-tipped lobes separated by rounded sinuses. The uppermost center lobe is the key: it is often considerably longer and narrower than the others. Occasionally, this bold middle finger is longer than the rest of the leaf. The ends of these prominent terminal lobes often have three to five much smaller bristle-tipped lobes.

This species ranges from Long Island and New Jersey southward to northern Florida, then west to eastern Texas and north to southern Missouri. It is generally absent from the high Southern Appalachian chains that finger down into the Deep South. In many areas of the South, it is still known as Spanish oak, a name probably suggested by the leaf's resemblance to a Spanish dagger.

A medium-sized tree, this Beech family member often matures to 1½ to 3 feet in diameter and 60 to 85 feet in height. The current South Carolina record—a short, squat, open-grown lunker located on lower and richer land further south—stands 73 feet high and measures 20 feet 4 inches around.

While it is usually easy to recognize a hickory, differentiating one species of the genus from another is often difficult. The mockernut hickory, another low-elevation hardwood found along the Foothills Trail, is the second easiest (shagbark is first) of the Southern Appalachian hickories to identify. Leaves alone are enough to verify the mockernut. Alternate and pinnately compound, the large leaves are usually 8 to 18 inches long and unfurl 7 to 9 (rarely 5, usually 7) finely saw-toothed and nearly stalkless leaflets. The sharp-pointed leaflets are 3 to 7 inches long; the terminal leaflet is noticeably larger than the lateral ones.

mockernut hickory

The leaf stems of this species are matted with a fine, hairy fuzz. If you rub the fuzzy stem or the leaflets, you will smell the strong and distinct hickory scent. While other trees of the *Carya* genus produce a similar odor, the mockernut's aroma is keenly pungent.

This member of the Walnut family has typical light gray hickory bark; low, irregular ridges—rounded, narrow, and forking—interlace with shallow furrows to form a netlike pattern on the bark's surface. The mockernut hickory is occasional to common throughout the Southern Highlands up to approximately 3,000 feet. It competes best on the drier soils of oak and oak-pine ridges and slopes. In the uplands of the Southern Blue Ridge, this slow-growing, heavy shade–intolerant broadleaf usually remains a small- to medium-sized tree—45 to 65 feet in height and 1 to 2 feet in diameter. On good sites it reaches 100 feet in height and 3 feet in diameter. The largest mockernut listed in South Carolina's big tree register has lifted the top of its crown to 132 feet and has slowly thickened to 9 feet 8 inches in circumference.

The Cherokee used hickory branches to make arrows and blowgun darts. Pioneers favored the wood for preserving pork and other meats in their smokehouses. They also used the incredibly tough wood for baskets, firewood, fences, axe handles, wagon wheels, and barrel hoops—and whipped their kids with hickory switches.

Directions

Approach from the south: From the SC 28–SC 107 intersection north of Walhalla, South Carolina, travel SC 107 North for approximately 6.2 miles to the right turn onto signed Cheohee Road (Forest Service 710, also marked with a Winding Stair Road sign further back from the highway). Pull-in and pull-off parking is to the left of Cheohee Road just beyond its paved entrance. The Lick Log section of the Foothills Trail, as described in this guide, begins across the highway from the entrance of Cheohee Road.

Approach from the north: From the US 64–NC 107 intersection in Cashiers, North Carolina, travel NC 107 South then SC 107 South for approximately 17.2 miles to the left turn onto signed Cheohee Road (Forest Service 710, also marked with a Winding Stair Road sign further back from the highway). Pull-in and pull-off parking is to the left of Cheohee Road just beyond its paved entrance. The Lick Log section of the Foothills Trail, as described in this guide, begins across the highway from the entrance of Cheohee Road.

Thrift Lake Parking Area: If you want to use the Thrift Lake Parking Area for overnight campers on the Foothills and Chattooga River Trails, start at the SC 107–Cheohee Road junction and travel SC 107 South for approximately 2.8 miles to the signed right turn onto paved Village Creek Road. Proceed approximately 1.8 miles on Village Creek to the stop, road, and dead-end signs that mark the turn to the right and down onto dirt-gravel Nicholson Ford Road. Follow this road for approximately 1.9 miles to the sign on the left that points to the parking lot just uphill and to the right of the road. Walk the path leading away from the back of the parking area 115 yards to the Foothills Trail—left to the river, right to Highway 107.

Big Bend Trail

Length 2.7 miles

- ■ **Dayhiking** Easy in either direction
- ■ **Backpacking** Easy to Moderate in either direction
- ■ **Start** Big Bend Trailhead off Highway 107, 2,210 feet
- ■ **End** Chattooga River (Section 3)–Foothills Trail near the Chattooga River, 2,010 feet
- ■ **Trail Junction** Chattooga River (Section 3)–Foothills (two trails sharing same treadway)
- ■ **Topographic Quadrangle** Tamassee SC-GA
- ■ **Blaze** Old orange blazes are fading and will not be repainted
- ■ **RD/NF** Andrew Pickens/Sumter
- ■ **Features** Small streams; diverse oak-pine forest; Chattooga River; Chattooga River–Foothills approach

BIG BEND IS ONE OF THE THREE nonwilderness, Chattooga River Trail approaches that begin at or near South Carolina's Highway 107. The other two lead-ins described in this guide are short sections of the 76-mile-long Foothills Trail. Of these three, all of which end just inside the Chattooga River's protected corridor, Big Bend ranks second in length and third in difficulty. Named for the river's three-quarter-loop bend it approaches, this well-constructed cut-in path, well-maintained and easily walked, remains on upper slope for most of its length.

The trail, which has no sustained grades more difficult than easy, winds west-northwest from the highway toward the Chattooga. The treadway descends into the conifer-broadleaf forest, past additional trail signs, then quickly enters the green Southern Appalachian thicket-growth of rhododendron, mountain laurel, and hemlock saplings. The track levels as it passes beside Big Bend Road to the right and the first set of ledges on Crane Creek to the left. Beyond the second set of low cascades, the effortless downgrade ends at a doghobble thicket where the path crosses the wooden bridge over the stream at mile 0.3.

After gradually rising from the first bridge, the route settles into the familiar pattern of upper-slope travel until mile 1.7. Here in the interlocking splay of spur and hollow, the trail half-loops around one or more steep-sided upper hollows before curling over the next spur ridge—then repeats the maneuver again and again. The path crosses bridges over narrow ravines at 0.7 mile and again at mile 1.6.

The upper-slope walkway winds through a diverse, low-elevation oak-pine forest. As you might expect, the pines—shortleaf, pitch, and white—and the oaks—chestnut, white, northern and southern red, scarlet, and perhaps black—make up the majority of the larger boles. Other common and easily identified trees include sourwood, sassafras, red maple, Fraser magnolia, and blackgum. Pines are more numerous on the drier west- and south-facing slopes. Yellow poplar and sweet birch join the other hardwoods on the moister east- and north-facing slopes. Deciduous heath shrubs (huckleberries and blueberries) often form solid colonies beneath the mountain laurel.

At mile 1.7 the footpath crosses straight over an old road atop a ridgecrest, and, after a short upgrade, begins the easy descent to trail's end above the Chattooga. The course follows the same upper-slope pattern as before, through a similar oak-pine forest. Blue blazes at mile 2.3 mark the boundary of the protected Chattooga National Wild and Scenic River corridor. With 0.2 mile remaining, the route rock-steps across a small branch, continues 15 yards, then turns sharply to the left and down before quickly recrossing the same narrow stream. The final stretch closely parallels the now-wider but still-unnamed watercourse through a riparian forest of hemlock, rhododendron, and doghobble. Sheltered by the narrow valley, tall, arrow-straight white pines flank the branch toward the river.

Big Bend ends where it ties into the white-blazed Chattooga River–Foothills Trail next to the bridge spanning the stream. Several signs mark the junction. Just down-flow from the bridge, the brook begins its final cascading run—dropping perhaps 80 vertical feet—to the shoaling river below. If you cross the bridge and follow the Chattooga River–Foothills Trail upstream and generally north, you will reach Burrells Ford Road after 2.8 miles. If you walk the other way, downriver and generally south, you will arrive at Big Bend Falls after 0.8 mile, the Chattooga River–Foothills junction (Lick Log section) after 5.4 miles, and SC 28 after 10.0 miles. (See Section 3 of the CRT on page 159 for more information concerning the falls.)

Nature Notes

If you hike Big Bend or any other trail leading to the Chattooga River corridor from mid-April through June, you probably will hear the ovenbird repeatedly as you walk through one nesting territory after another. You will hear these little warblers because they are numerous and loud and because the males persistently counter-sing, one bird chiming in immediately after the ending of its neighbor's song. Most bird guides describe its song as *teacher-teacher-teacher…*, repeated louder and faster, up to ten times in rapid succession. Ovenbirds do vocalize *teacher* in the northern part of their large range. Here in highland Dixie, however, they sing with a regional variation. Southern Appalachian ovenbirds drop the "-er", transform the noun into an imperative verb, and chant *teach-teach-teach…*, usually in an emphatic, ringing, slightly louder staccato. Early on cold mornings their songs often sound weak. But after the sun shines on the forest floor, they warm to the task and belt out their *teach* songs loud and clear. The ovenbird also sings a completely different flight song, rambling and bubbly, during late afternoon, at dusk, or even at night.

This sparrow-sized (6-inch) wood warbler breeds no farther south than the upper Piedmont of Georgia and Alabama. From mid-May through much of June, probably when there are young to feed and protect, this normally secretive passerine pops up and fusses at intruders. Sometimes it makes a complete circuit of short flights around you, steadily scolding with call-note *chips*.

Also known as the teacher-bird, the ovenbird lacks the tropical coloring and flashy flight patterns characteristic of most wood warblers. It is olive-brown above and white with prominent streaks of dark spots below. From the neck down it resembles a small thrush. For a positive visual identification, you must see the diagnostic band-striping color pattern on its head. The band is a mohawk brushstroke of bright orange-brown from the base of its bill back across the top of its crown. The stripe forms a thin black eyebrow, bordering the band and accentuating the white of the eye ring below.

This perching bird is named for the domed, ovenlike nest it builds on the ground. The ovenbird weaves leaves on top of its grass-lined nest to further camouflage its stoop-in entrance. I now have discovered a grand total of three ovenbird nests. Each time, an adult bird flushed from a trailside nest as I walked by with my bright orange and clicking measuring wheel. And each time, even though I had seen the exact spot where the bird had emerged, I had to squat down and look carefully before I found the nest.

Unlike some wood warblers, this species does not have stringent elevation or vegetation-type habitat requirements; it does, however, need extensive, unfragmented blocks of forest. You will hear them chant at all elevations in all but the moistest forests within the Chattooga River corridor and throughout the Ellicott Rock and Southern Nantahala Wildernesses. Listen for them in spring and early summer on low- and middle-elevation oak-pine ridges and upper slopes, where they are most common. Most have headed south by the end of September; all but a few genetically encoded stragglers are gone by the end of October.

Mainly a mountain tree of the Appalachians, the chestnut oak is one of the most common ridge and dry-slope hardwoods in the Ellicott Rock Wilderness and Chattooga River corridor. It greatly increased its share of the canopy after the chestnut blight and is now a major component of low- to middle-elevation oak-pine and oak-hickory forests. Another common name for this species is mountain oak. Scouts and other children are taught to remember this name by folding a leaf in half along the midrib to see the silhouette of the rolling mountains.

This tree received its given name because its leaves somewhat resemble those of the American chestnut, no longer able to survive beyond sapling stage in most of its range. The foliage of the two species, however, is easy to differentiate. Much narrower than those of the chestnut oak, American chestnut leaves have numerous sharp-pointed teeth. The chestnut oak's leaves—solar panels 4 to 9 inches long—have margins with noticeably rounded, wavy lobes, with no points and no bristles. No other large Southern Highland hardwood possesses this leaf shape.

Quercus montana averages 60 to 85 feet in height and 2 to 4 feet in diameter at maturity. Like many other eastern North American broadleafs, the chestnut oak attains its largest dimensions in the Southern Appalachians. The current South Carolina state record is an impressive specimen—13 feet 3 inches in circumference and 130 feet in height. Slow-growing even on good sites, this member of the white oak group is also long-lived—up to half a millennium.

chestnut oak

Directions

Approach from the south: From the SC 28–SC 107 intersection north of Walhalla, South Carolina, travel SC 107 North for approximately 8.5 miles to a parking area blocked by posts in the back to the right side of the highway. Big Bend Road and Cherry Hill Recreation Area are located 0.1 mile beyond the parking area.

Approach from the north: From the US 64–NC 107 intersection in Cashiers, North Carolina, travel NC 107 South then SC 107 South for approximately 15.0 miles to a parking area blocked by posts in the back to the left side of the highway. The entrances to Big Bend

Road and Cherry Hill Recreation Area are 0.1 mile before the parking area.

A brown, double-sided Hiking Trail sign stands in the woods on the south edge of the parking area. Big Bend Trail, marked with additional signs, begins 50 feet to the left across the highway from the parking area.

Notes

Three Forks Trail

Length 1.4 miles

- **Dayhiking or Backpacking** Easy to Moderate to end of designated trail at Holcomb Creek. The final 0.2 mile, an unmaintained path, is Strenuous. Short sections of this path are very steep and potentially dangerous when muddy.
- **Start** Three Forks Trailhead at John Teague Gap, 2,370 feet
- **End** Holcomb Creek at Three Forks, 1,830 feet
- **Trail Junctions** None
- **Topographic Quadrangle** Satolah GA-SC-NC
- **Blaze** Metal diamonds for first 1.0 mile
- **RD/NF** Tallulah/Chattahoochee
- **Features** Swirlhole waterfall on Holcomb Creek; three cascading mountain streams; bluff; West Fork Chattooga River; miniature gorge

THREE FORKS RECEIVED ITS NAME from the three mountain streams—Holcomb, Overflow, and Big Creeks—that tumble together at right angles to form a fourth: West Fork Chattooga River. Holcomb Creek, which originates in northernmost Georgia, falls into the forks from the west. Overflow, the middle stream, conveys its contribution from the north-northwest, from its headwaters in North Carolina's Nantahala National Forest. Also arising in the Nantahala National Forest, Big Creek cascades in from the northeast.

Beginning beside its nearly vandal-proof trailhead sign, a small boulder, the route rises gently into an oak-pine forest with a dense understory of deciduous heath (huckleberries and blueberries). Tall white pines and the oaks—chestnut, scarlet, northern red, and white—

have captured much of the canopy. Shaded by these taller trees, red maple, blackgum, and sourwood comprise much of the subcanopy. The mild upgrade continues to mile 0.3, where the steady descent to Holcomb Creek begins. Here the treadway works its way down the lower northwest-facing slope of Bent Ridge. At 0.7 mile the footpath crosses the boundary of the Chattooga National Wild and Scenic River. The immediate Three Forks area and a narrow corridor along both banks of the entire West Fork Chattooga River are protected as part of the national wild and scenic river.

As the walkway loses elevation toward the first fork, the forest becomes moister, and yellow poplar, sweet birch, hemlock, and rhododendron become more common. Following a 150-yard, easy-to-moderate dip, the track T's into an old roadbed at mile 1.0. Turn left and descend with the former woods road (the progressively sharper decline is moderate near the end) 0.2 mile to the rock overlooking the high, churning, swirlhole-carved cascade on Holcomb Creek. Below the narrow, water-worn falls, the stream makes its final rock-cutting run entrenched in a short, steep-walled gorge.

The cascade is the end of the official blazed trail. If you want to continue to Three Forks by the most direct route, you must cross Holcomb Creek and negotiate the steep trout-fisher's path that starts on the other side. During low-water drought days, you may be able to skirt the rock bank upstream and cross dry shod where the stream is pinched into a low shoals. Usually, however, you face a feet-wet wade of various depths, usually mid-thigh or lower after June 1. Even though the water is deeper, make your ford well back from the brink of the potentially dangerous cascade. Also, keep in mind that these steep-sided, small-watershed streams rise quickly after heavy rain. One time my fairly easy ford on the way in became nearly waist deep and uncomfortably fast on the way out.

The final 0.2 mile to Three Forks deserves and requires a disclaimer. Here the unmaintained goat path is steep, and it should be attempted only by hikers with decent knees and fairly sure feet. Though short, several of the sharpest pitches drop at more than a 45-degree angle. Hiking sticks come in handy. The first short segment of the often-narrow track snakes along the steep slope leading to the lip of Holcomb Creek's miniature gorge. Carelessness or lack of coordination here could result in trouble for you or your children. The path quickly angles away from potential danger. Disclaimer over. Back to hiking.

The treadway picks up nearly straight over from the ford. With slightly less than 0.1 mile remaining, the route plunges down a short pitch, well worn and often scuffed with recent traffic. (Don't take the cheater straight downslope to the right before the first lurch.) The second and final nosedive drops you at the alder-lined bank of Overflow Creek.

Rock-hopping and aqua-hiking upstream quickly leads you to Overflow's last fall—a narrow, sluicing cascade perhaps 7 or 8 feet high. Just downstream, two rock- and water-drilled swirlholes now share a vertical opening where they join near their bottoms. When I first hiked to Three Forks in 1975, these Siamese swirlholes were not connected. Just below the rock, an over-your-head deep pool lets you know you're alive even on the hottest of days.

Cinnamon ferns cap the dry tops of river rocks with green headdresses. Back downstream, the next fork on the tour is Big Creek, which finishes with a long white flourish to the left. (The topo sheet erroneously shows Holcomb Creek coming in slightly before Big.) Across from the tall sentinel bluff that marks the exact beginning of the West Fork Chattooga, Holcomb Creek's last leap pours over a low rock ledge. The right side of the ledge forces a freefall just high enough so that you can jump behind the discontinuous curtain of cold creek water. Every time I have ducked behind the falls I have found at least one unperturbed salamander.

By skirting up along Holcomb's left bank, you can work your way into the bottom end of its gorge. Slanting cliffs rise high over your head; rhododendron arches out over the light gap above. Straight ahead, a flowing wedge of whitewater is actively knifing into the bedrock.

Nature Notes

When you finally stop rolling at trail's end, you will be standing beside Overflow Creek's alder-lined bank. Usually a tall, spreading shrub with multiple stems, the common alder can form stream-flanking thickets where plentiful. This widespread species is the only native alder throughout the Southeast south of the Southern Appalachians. With the lone exception of one other alder species occurring on a single peak—North Carolina's Roan Mountain—the common is the only alder throughout the rest of the Southern Highlands.

Also known as hazel alder, this Birch family shrub is readily identified by its water-dependent habitat, its shrubby growth habit,

common alder

and its leaves and catkins. This alder is frequently found along the margins of watercourses wide enough to let the sun in, and around the edges of beaver ponds up to 3,000 feet in the Southern Blue Ridge. The common alder most often takes root in that narrow strip of bankside soil between the rhododendron and the water. Rarely becoming a small tree, this thicket-forming shrub usually stands less than 18 feet in height and measures less than 4 inches in diameter.

Its deciduous leaves are finely saw-toothed along the margins, broadest at or beyond the midpoint, and obovate to elliptical in shape. Most of these alternate leaves are 2½ to 4¾ inches long and 1½ to 3 inches wide. The tiny male flowers blossom on dangling, cylindrical catkins, conspicuous in winter and early spring before leaf-out. Present most of the year, the ⅜- to ⅝-inch-long female catkins resemble miniature pinecones. This species is one of the first woody plants to flower; in the Southern Appalachians, it often begins blooming in late February and early March.

Directions

Approach from the west: In Clayton, Georgia, where US 76 turns west at a traffic light, turn east (right if you are coming from the south) onto Rickman Street. Follow Rickman Street for approximately 0.5 mile to its end at signed Warwoman Road. Turn right onto Warwoman Road and proceed approximately 13.3 miles to the left turn onto signed Overflow Creek Road (FS 86) just after you cross the West Fork Chattooga River.

Approach from the north: From the US 64–NC 28 intersection in Highlands, North Carolina, travel NC 28 South then GA 28 South for approximately 12.0 miles to the signed right turn onto Warwoman Road. Follow paved Warwoman Road for approximately 0.2 mile before turning right onto signed Overflow Creek Road (FS 86) just before the bridge over the West Fork Chattooga River.

Approach from the south: From the SC 28–SC 107 intersection north of Walhalla, South Carolina, travel SC 28 North then GA 28 North (cross Chattooga River into Georgia after approximately 8.4 miles) for approximately 10.6 miles before turning left onto signed Warwoman Road. Follow paved Warwoman Road for approximately 0.2 mile, then turn right onto signed Overflow Creek Road (FS 86) just before the bridge over the West Fork Chattooga River.

From Overflow Creek Road: Follow dirt-gravel Overflow Creek Road for approximately 3.9 miles to the obvious trailhead on the right side of the road at signed John Teague Gap. The trailhead is further marked with a nearly vandal-proof trail-sign boulder. There is pull-in parking to the right and left of the road.

Notes

Wilderness is the raw material out of which man has hammered the artifact called civilization. Wilderness was never a homogenous raw material. It was very diverse, and the resulting artifacts are very diverse. These differences in the end-product are known as cultures. The rich diversity of the world's cultures reflects a corresponding diversity in the wilds that gave them birth.

—Aldo Leopold

Ellicott Rock Wilderness and Chattooga River, *Northern Section*

eft: Chattooga River from Bull Pen Bridge
Right: Bad Creek Trailhead

Trails

Chattooga River, Section 4

Foothills National Recreation, Medlin Mountain Section

Spoonauger Falls

East Fork

Ellicott Rock

Bad Creek

Fork Mountain

Chattooga Cliffs

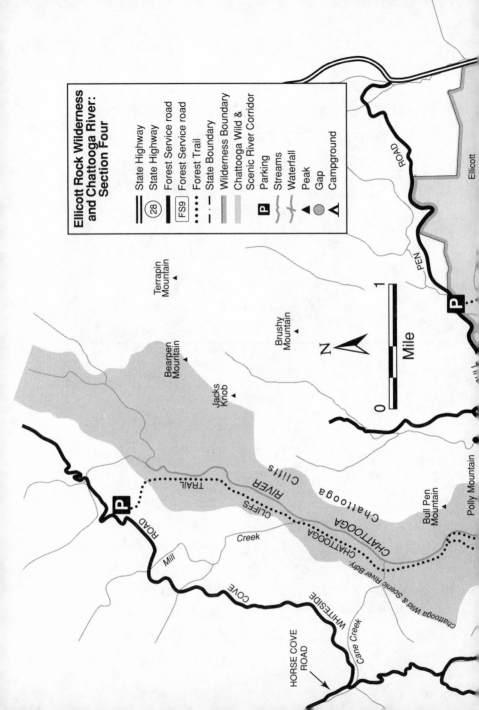

Ellicott Rock Wilderness and Chattooga River: Section Four

═══	State Highway
(28)	State Highway
▬▬	Forest Service road
FS9	Forest Service road
⋯⋯	Forest Trail
─·─	State Boundary
▬▬	Wilderness Boundary
	Chattooga Wild & Scenic River Corridor
P	Parking
≈	Streams
↟	Waterfall
▲	Peak
●	Gap
▲	Campground

N

0 ___ Mile ___ 1

Terrapin Mountain ▲

Bearpen Mountain ▲

Brushy Mountain ▲

Jacks Knob ▲

CHATTOOGA RIVER CLIFFS

CHATTOOGA RIVER CLIFFS

Chattooga Cliffs

TRAIL

Chattooga Wild & Scenic River Bdry.

Bull Pen Mountain ▲

Polly Mountain

Creek

Mill

ROAD

COVE

WHITESIDE

HORSE COVE ROAD

Cane Creek

PEN

ROAD

Ellicott

P

P

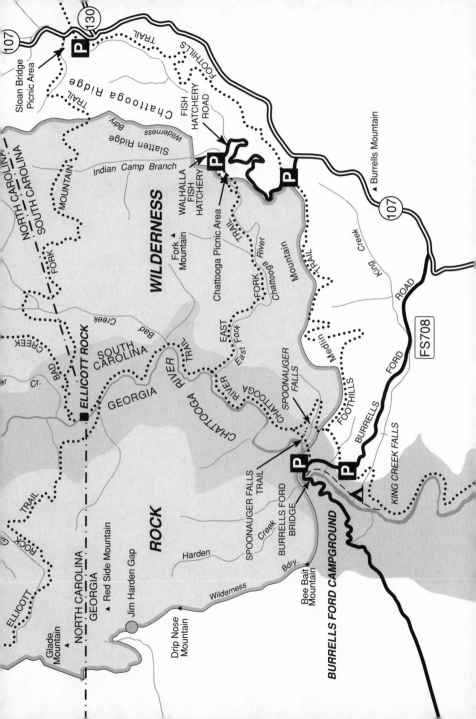

Chattooga River Trail, Section 4
(Burrells Ford Road to Bad Creek junction)

Length 4.5 miles

- **Dayhiking** Easy in either direction
- **Backpacking** Easy to Moderate in either direction
- **Start** Chattooga River–Foothills Trailhead off Burrells Ford Road, 2,170 feet
- **End** Bad Creek Trail beyond Ellicott Rock, 2,140 feet
- **Trail Junctions** Chattooga River (Section 3), Foothills, Spoonauger Falls, East Fork, Ellicott Rock, Bad Creek
- **Topographic Quadrangles** Tamassee SC-GA, Cashiers NC-SC-GA
- **Blazes** White for Foothills; the old black blazes for Chattooga River are fading and will not be repainted
- **RD/NF** Andrew Pickens/Sumter, Highlands/Nantahala
- **Features** Chattooga River; East Fork Chattooga; Ellicott and Commissioner's Rocks

THIS NORTHERNMOST SEGMENT OF THE CRT is the shortest, the easiest, and the most heavily used of the four Chattooga River Trail sections. Section 4 differs from the first three sections in several ways: it does not have vehicular access to both ends; it traverses wilderness in addition to protected river corridor; and, most importantly, it often remains close to the Chattooga, affording frequent views of the famous mountain stream. Section 4 shares the first 0.6 mile of its treadway with the 76-mile-long Foothills National Recreation Trail. After the paths split apart, the Chattooga River Trail quickly enters the Ellicott Rock Wilderness before looping down to floodplain at mile 1.6. From here the remainder of the route closely parallels its namesake stream generally northward. Beyond the East Fork junction, the track occasionally rises and dips to match riverside terrain, and short stretches have rocky and rooty footing. Although this final 1.8-mile segment is more difficult than the previous floodplain cakewalk, most of it is nearly level and easily hiked.

Angling east away from Burrells Ford Road, the narrow path ascends gently into a white and pitch pine forest shading a dense shrub layer of deciduous huckleberries and blueberries. Just beyond the first of several towering white pines, the course switchbacks to the left away from the road, then gains elevation steadily to a rhododendron thicket. At 0.3 mile the route rock-steps a short, unnamed Chattooga tributary just above where it tumbles down a long slide of slick rock face. Several old-growth hemlocks flank the small branch.

After passing through a backpacker's squeeze in the outcrop rock, the well-cut-in treadway leaves the rhododendron and continues on mild grades to the first signed connection. Here where the two trails split apart at 0.6 mile, the white-blazed Foothills Trail turns to the right and uphill onto ridgecrest, and the CRT continues straight ahead on slope. On its own now, the Chattooga River Trail enters the Ellicott Rock Wilderness and descends through an oak-pine forest high above and well away from the river. The steady downgrade crosses another unnamed Chattooga feeder at 0.9 mile and continues downhill above the rushing stream, which also shelters a few old-growth hemlocks in its steep-sided ravine.

As the branch drops faster toward Spoonauger Falls, the track pulls away from riparian habitat back into drier oak-pine woods. Fraser magnolia saplings (easy to identify by their whorls of five to eight large leaves, each prominently eared at the base) are frequently rooted at trail's edge. The easy walking continues as the footpath rounds an upper hollow at mile 1.3 before slanting down toward the river and the signed junction with the Spoonauger Falls Trail. Here on the far edge of the floodplain at mile 1.6, the Chattooga River Trail slants to the right and upstream onto the wide, heavily used treadway. Just beyond the intersection, a sign informs fishers that the river above Burrells Ford Bridge is not stocked with trout; it encourages catch and release fishing rather than filet and fry.

After the turn, the floodplain route remains flat until mile 1.7, where it swings beside the river—here less than 100 feet across. The quick current is calm for the Chattooga. From this first National Wild and Scenic River sighting to its end, Section 4 follows a familiar pattern as it closely parallels the Chattooga upstream. The treadway either heads up and away out of sight of the river before returning streamside, or it ascends steep-sided terrain right above the flow before returning to near bank level. Either way, the track offers frequent views of riffles, rapids, rocks, and pools.

From Burrells Ford Road northward to the East Fork, the Chattooga's floodplain is unusually wide in places. Although not particularly diverse, the relatively young, second-growth floodplain forest shelters a number of noticeably tall trees. White and pitch pine, hemlock, and yellow poplar lift their branches to the top of the canopy. These four species are joined by American holly, another evergreen, and the relatively few other hardwoods—red maple, northern red and white oak, sweet birch, basswood, Fraser magnolia, and witch-hazel—to make up the majority of single-boled trunks in the flat.

After passing through an extensive camping area, the course crosses an 80-foot-long wooden bridge over the swift East Fork Chattooga River. On the far bank at mile 2.7, the signed East Fork Trail ends where it ties into the Chattooga River Trail. Section 4 rapidly returns to the river on a high bank above a long green pool. It then continues to follow the channel closely, often near the bank where only a thin screen of rhododendron and mountain laurel separates trail from rippling water. Doghobble and galax flank the path. On the slope across the river, white pines spire several whorled tiers above the other trees.

Four-tenths mile beyond the bridge, the grade curves away from the Chattooga to cross normally shallow, branch-sized Bad Creek at an easy place. Ignore the first path down and to the left toward the watercourse, continue upstream through a flat camping area, and curl down to stream level; there you will find the intended rock-step crossing at mile 3.3. Once across, the walkway rises gradually, turns left onto former roadbed, then descends back to bankside, where it remains for the rest of its length. Now open or partial views of the relatively calm Chattooga are nearly constant. Except during high water, the river runs clear, shallow, shining, and fast over a cobble and yellow-beige sand bottom. Where the bigger riverbed rocks obstruct the flow, and where ledges force a fall, the gliding water shatters into low white shoals.

At mile 4.2, you will pass a prominent, 8- to 10-foot-high boulder sitting in your side of the river. One-tenth mile beyond this boulder, the treadway drops right beside the Chattooga at a gap in the bankside vegetation opposite a small branch entering on the other side of the river. This spot is the CRT's usually unsigned junction with the Ellicott Rock Trail, which fords to its end here in South Carolina. If you want to walk the Ellicott Rock Trail from this connection, ford the stream at a slight downriver angle to the steep bank just left of the branch. (If you walk Section 4 to the south from its northern end, you will find the CRT–Ellicott Rock junction 40 yards past a small wooden bridge.)

Slightly more than 0.1 mile beyond the short wooden bridge (the one a little over 0.1 mile past the riverbed boulder mentioned in the previous paragraph), you will reach the spot hikers are always looking for and asking about—the location of Ellicott Rock. The spot, as it turns out, is directly above two separate but remarkably close historical markers—Ellicott Rock and Commissioner's Rock. Few of the people who have searched for Ellicott Rock, however, have actually found it. Most of the searchers who have managed to drop down to the river in the right place have actually located the three short lines, inscribed in 3½-inch-high letters, on Commissioner's Rock:

LAT 35

AD 1813

NC + SC

Ellicott Rock, 15 feet further upstream and a little higher on the bank, is even more difficult to find. Andrew Ellicott finished his survey of the Georgia–North Carolina border, the thirty-fifth parallel, in 1811. And after all that work, Ellicott may have left posterity only two inconspicuous capital letters—NC—carved above the river. (Several written sources state that Ellicott carved 1811 and state abbreviations into rock as far as 500 feet upstream from Commissioner's Rock. I will search for more lettering and report back in the next edition.) Two years later, a commission convened to establish the North Carolina–South Carolina border to the thirty-fifth parallel. The commission's surveyors chiseled those three lines that most modern-day hikers have always assumed to be those of Ellicott Rock.

Over the years, the exact location of the two rocks has been marked by various combinations of sign, hemlock, and tattered scraps of flagging. When signs are absent, the most reliable way for a northbound hiker to locate the historical inscriptions is to start by finding a certain hemlock on the left margin of the trail. Slightly more than 0.1 mile beyond the short bridge, look for a wide, cut-in section of treadway, above but only a slight angle back from river's edge. Approximately 25 feet past the scramble down to Commissioner's Rock, you should find the medium-sized hemlock (provided it is still standing, of course) that bears a nail head from a former sign and a metal survey marker disk, roughly the same size and color as an old silver dollar.

Once you have found this short-needled conifer, backtrack the 25 feet or so until you find foot-worn bank and perhaps flagging. Climb down the steep, rhododendron-lined pitch to the water's edge. The unobtrusive three lines of Commissioner's Rock are usually only a few feet above the flow; high water regularly rises above the letters. You will find Ellicott Rock, with its modest NC inscription, 15 feet upstream, 3 or 4 feet higher than Commissioner's Rock and further back from the river.

One hundred and fifteen yards beyond Commissioner's Rock, Section 4 ends at its usually unsigned and unnoticed junction with Bad Creek Trail. As you continue northward, the path bends to the right up and away from the river near a campsite with several old-growth hemlocks. As soon as you start the ascent away from the Chattooga, you will be walking on Bad Creek.

Nature Notes

If you walk a trail alongside a large stream, you might be lucky enough to see one of Southern Appalachia's least-known and most strikingly colored creatures: the red eft. This amphibian is startlingly beautiful because of its bright orange or orange-red warning coloration. (The dozen or so I have seen over the years have all been bright orange.) The red eft is small, 1½ to 3½ inches long during its life stage on land. Though common, it is seldom seen during the dry weather hikers prefer.

An eft is actually a type of salamander; it is the terrestrial form of a newt, as in Shakespeare's "eye of newt." The eastern is the only newt inhabiting the eastern United States north of Georgia's fall line. Several subspecies occur within its extensive range; the common name for the subspecies crawling throughout most of the South is red-spotted newt.

Newts differ from other salamanders in two easily observable, nonscientific ways. Their life cycle often includes an extra, terrestrial stage known as the eft. Instead of feeling slimy or slippery to the touch like most salamanders, efts have drier, rougher skin that feels much like squirming latex. Most of the eastern newt's aquatic, olive-green larvae transform themselves into brightly colored efts, then leave the water for a one- to three-year walkabout on land. While in the forest, they often travel far up the slopes above their natal streams. Shortly before their woodland tour is finished, they change back to olive-green, enter the water again, grow a little larger, and complete the cycle as aquatic breeding adults.

Unlike other terrestrial salamanders, which are nocturnal, efts often ramble boldly about on the forest floor in broad daylight. They can roam around as they please because their skin glands secrete toxins or irritants that discourage even the hungriest of predators. Once seized and spit out, the eft has made a lasting impression on its enemy. Warm-weather rain stimulates efts into actively foraging for insects, worms, and young amphibians. Only then, during and right after rain while the forest floor remains wet, do you have a fair chance of spotting the eastern newt's orange-colored eft.

Along the floodplain segment beyond the Spoonauger Falls junction, the trail passes beside a large colony of New York fern (mostly on the upslope) at mile 2.1. The New York is not only the most common fern in the wilderness, but it is also one of the easiest of all ferns to identify. The mostly alternate pinnae (leafy foliage) of this species taper gradually to nearly nothing at either end. The lowermost pinnae of this deciduous, 12- to 24-inch-tall fern resemble tiny wings.

New York fern

This nonflowering plant frequently occurs in dense monocultural beds. Growing at even intervals beneath widely spaced trees, they are similar in uniformity to an agricultural crop. There are two reasons for this homogeneity. First, because many ferns grow from perennial underground rhizomes, they often form large, evenly spaced, cloned colonies. Second, New York ferns have a competitive edge: they produce a herbicide to poison other plants.

Directions

Approach from the southwest: In Clayton, Georgia, where US 76 turns west at a traffic light, turn east (right if you are coming from the south) onto Rickman Street. Follow Rickman Street for approximately 0.5 mile to its end at signed Warwoman Road. Turn right onto Warwoman Road, follow it for approximately 13.5 miles to its eastern end at GA 28, then turn right onto GA 28 South. Travel Highway 28 for approximately 1.8 miles before turning left onto signed Burrells Ford Road (FS 646). Proceed on dirt-gravel Burrells Ford Road for slightly less than 7.0 miles to the Burrells Ford Bridge over the Chattooga. Once across the river into South Carolina, continue 0.4 mile to the large Burrells Ford Campground-trailhead parking area to the right of the road. Section 4 begins to the left of the road 100 feet beyond the parking area. A post with a Foothills Trail emblem and white blazes marks the treadway.

Approach from the south: From the SC 28–SC 107 intersection north of Walhalla, South Carolina, travel SC 107 North for approximately 10.2 miles to the signed left turn onto paved Burrells Ford Road.

Approach from the north: From the US 64–NC 107 intersection in Cashiers, North Carolina, travel NC 107 South then SC 107 South for approximately 13.0 miles to the signed right turn onto paved Burrells Ford Road.

From Burrells Ford Road: Follow Burrells Ford Road (pavement ends after 0.3 mile) for approximately 2.4 miles to the large Burrells Ford Campground–trailhead parking area to the left side of the road. Section 4 begins on the right side of the road 100 feet before the parking area. A post with a Foothills Trail emblem and white blazes marks the treadway.

Notes

Foothills National Recreation Trail
(Medlin Mountain Section)

Length 3.2 miles

- **Dayhiking In** Easy
- **Dayhiking Out** Easy to Moderate
- **Backpacking In** Easy
- **Backpacking Out** Easy to Moderate
- **Start** Foothills Trailhead off Fish Hatchery Road,
  2,960 feet
- **End** Chattooga River Trail (Section 4) near
  Burrells Ford Road, 2,380 feet
- **Trail Junction** Chattooga River (Section 4)
- **Topographic Quadrangle** Tamassee SC-GA
- **Blaze** White
- **RD/NF** Andrew Pickens/Sumter
- **Features** Medlin Mountain; winter views;
  CRT approach

TWO SHORT SEGMENTS of the white-blazed Foothills National Recreation Trail can be walked westward from SC 107 as approach paths leading toward the Chattooga River and its trail. This Foothills section, Medlin Mountain, is longer and located further north than the other link, Lick Log. (See the Lick Log section, page 169, for additional information concerning the Foothills Trail and its route.) As detailed in this guide, Medlin Mountain starts to the left side of Fish Hatchery Road and heads west toward its meeting with the Chattooga River Trail near Burrells Ford Road.

Beginning at the back of the parking area beside a Foothills Trail sign with mileages, the path enters the dry oak-pine forest on the upper-south slope of Medlin Mountain. The treadway rises gradually through white and pitch pine, sassafras, sourwood, red maple, and this habitat's customary oaks—chestnut, scarlet, northern red, and even a few whites. Here near the 3,000-foot contour, the southern red oak approaches its upper-elevation limit in the Southern Appalachians. Look-offs to the left, to the south and southwest across the King Creek valley, afford winter views of a line of nearby low ridges. Just over 3,000 feet in elevation, Burrells, the closest mountain, heaves up to high point slightly more than half a mile away to the south.

At 0.3 mile the route angles to the right onto Medlin Mountain's crest and continues on effortless grades through an open ridgetop forest. Good winter and partial summer prospects to the right provide a peek at another line of ridges, this one collectively known as Chattooga Ridge. Four and one-half miles distant at 30 degrees, broad-topped Flat Mountain lifts the land across the border in North Carolina to a respectable 3,931 feet.

The lightly used footpath slabs onto upper-south slope at 0.5 mile. Here the track begins a pattern that lasts for the next 1.2 miles. Each time Medlin's ridgeline heads higher toward a knob, the walkway slips onto the upper southern slope and makes an end run around the uplift on easy or nearly level grades. The oak-pine forest remains generally open. The larger pitch pines are readily identified by their dense crowns of thick, contorted branches. In the understory, mountain laurel and deciduous heath (blueberries and huckleberries) are common and rhododendron clumps occasional.

The narrow path ducks below the crest to the other side, the north side, at mile 1.7 before switchbacking down and to the right away from the ridge. Now the trail descends the steep, west-facing slope above the river by long, looping switchbacks, the grades all level or slightly down. To the west, winter vistas stretch away to the farthest rolling swell on the horizon. Bee Bait Mountain (3,045 feet) shoulders up due west across the Chattooga; Drip Nose Mountain (3,310 feet) sweeps up to the next crown north of Bee Bait. The steep slope's largely oak canopy stands over a tangle of mountain laurel.

After rounding the narrow crease of an upper hollow, the route switches from slope back to Medlin Mountain ridgeline at mile 2.5.

The rest of this pleasant, deep-woods walk follows the keel on mostly gentle grades, a few uphill, beneath an oak-pine canopy shading a dense deciduous heath understory. With 0.1 mile remaining, the course skirts the edge of Ellicott Rock Wilderness, then makes a short, moderate descent to its signed junction, well away from and high above the river. To the left, the Foothills and Chattooga River Trails share the same treadway for 0.6 mile to Burrells Ford Road. To the right, Section 4 of the Chattooga River Trail continues generally northward 2.1 miles to its connection with the East Fork Trail, 3.8 miles to Ellicott and Commissioner's Rocks, and 3.9 miles to its northern terminus, where it ties into Bad Creek Trail.

The Medlin Mountain section of the Foothills Trail can be walked as the first or last leg of a four-trail, no-backtrack, 17.9-mile loop. If you want to travel this loop in a clockwise direction, hike this stretch of the white-blazed Foothills Trail as described for 3.2 miles to its junction with the Chattooga River Trail. Turn right onto the signed Chattooga River Trail and follow its treadway, northeast then north, upriver 3.9 miles into the Ellicott Rock Wilderness. Just beyond the two inconspicuous but historic carvings known as Ellicott and Commissioner's Rocks, the route gains elevation away from the river after tying into Bad Creek Trail. Proceed eastward for 1.1 miles on Bad Creek before veering uphill and to the right onto Fork Mountain Trail.

Walk all of Fork Mountain's 6.4 miles to the east, to SC 107 and the Sloan Bridge Picnic Area. Once you have reached the highway, turn right and head toward the nearby picnic area parking lot. A path leads 25 yards beyond the far side of the parking area to a Hiking Trail sign marking the Foothills Trail. To the left of the sign, the Foothills Trail crosses Highway 107. To complete the circuit, follow the track straight ahead from the sign (do not cross the highway) and cruise the final 3.3 miles southwestward back to the beginning trailhead on Fish Hatchery Road.

With the exception of the last 3.3 miles, all of the loop's trails and turns are detailed within this guide. The undescribed 3.3-mile segment of the Foothills Trail, from the picnic area off Highway 107 to Fish Hatchery Road, is easily walked and surprisingly scenic where it closely parallels the cascades and plunge pools of the East Fork Chattooga River.

Nature Notes

Medlin Mountain's dry, oak-pine forest provides habitat for a pine—the pitch—near the southern limit of its range, which stretches northeast to southwest from southern Maine all the way to the eastern half of northernmost Georgia. The pitch pine is more abundant

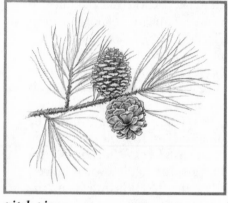

pitch pine

and better known up North. It is Cape Cod's pine; it is the pine in New Jersey's Pine Barrens. In the mountains of the South, however, this conifer is relatively unknown and usually remains only a minor component even within its restricted habitat.

A medium-sized tree in the Southern Highlands, the mature pitch pine has distinctive needles, cones, bark, and growth habit. The stiff, somewhat twisted needles—2½ to 5½ inches long and spraying out at nearly right angles to the twigs—are dark yellowish green. This species is the only Southern Appalachian pine that always bears three needles to the sheath (shortleaf pine has two or three). Stubby branches or tufts of needles occasionally sprout from the lower trunk, an unusual identifying feature.

One and a half to 3½ inches long, the oval cones are tipped with rigid, curved spines. The cones are persistent; they remain on the branches long after the seeds, an important wildlife food, have been released. The orangish brown bark on mature boles is broken into large, irregular platelike scales (the shortleaf pine has somewhat regular rectangular scales).

Pitch pine branches spoke away from their boles in whorls. (The whorls are not an indication of age; there can be more than one per year.) These branches, unusually thick for a pine, often grow into contorted, pendulous shapes, giving mature specimens particularly large and picturesque crowns. Shortleaf pines usually exhibit smaller crowns of thinner branches.

Southern Appalachian pitch pines often attain a height of 50 to 70 feet and a diameter of 1½ to 2½ feet. The current South Carolina state record measures 90 feet tall and 9 feet 3 inches in circumference. Height growth essentially ceases by age 90, but mature specimens can live another 110 years after attaining their highest point in the canopy. In the Southern Appalachians, these pines are often restricted to the less fertile soils of dry, acidic ridges and slopes below 5,000 feet. Because the pitch pine is fire resistant and markedly intolerant of shade from competing trees, it has evolved into a fire- or disturbance-dependent species. It thrives only in habitats dry enough for cyclical fires and poor soiled enough to discourage fast-growing successional hardwoods, such as the yellow poplar, from stealing their sun. As you will notice, most of the pitch pines along this route are mature, having sprouted after the heyday of logging and slash fires during the last century.

This conifer's common name refers to the high resin content of its knotty wood. Before the Southern pinelands were tapped, colonists collected the resin from the pitch pine to produce turpentine and to make tar for axle grease. Mountaineers called this tree candlewood because its knots made good torches; they often carried the flaming knots as they roamed the woods at night, occasionally using them to "shine" deer.

One of the oak-pine forest's most beautiful spring wildflowers, the dwarf iris, blooms in good numbers along three trails in this guide— Bad Creek, Big Bend, and this section of the Foothills. Like other early spring wildflowers in the dry woods along this path, the dwarf iris begins blooming well before the canopy closes. This fragrant herb usually starts flowering in this area from April 12 to April 17 and finishes, except for a few stragglers, by May 1. The colorful blossoms, which have three sepals and three petals, appear singly atop 3- to 4½-inch-high stems. The flame-hued honey guides—landing strips for pollinating insects—lick outward from the center of each sepal. Two to 2¾ inches wide, the corollas range in color from washed-out violet and pale yellow-orange to a vibrant blue that becomes deep purple near the fiery streaks down the center.

Even after the blossoms disappear, you can probably recognize these small rhizomatous perennials by their colony size, most often a few to twenty plants, and by their essentially straight, swordlike leaves—more or less 12 inches tall and less than ½ inch wide. But if you see these thin, grasslike leaves in combination with the distinctive flowers in dry habitat, you can be sure you're looking at a dwarf iris.

dwarf iris

Directions

Approach from the south: From the SC 28–SC 107 intersection north of Walhalla, South Carolina, travel SC 107 North for approximately 11.8 miles to the left turn onto Fish Hatchery Road—the paved road leading to the Walhalla Fish Hatchery. If the road sign is missing, use the large brown-and-white Walhalla State Fish Hatchery–Chattooga Picnic Area sign to mark your turn.

Approach from the north: From the US 64–NC 107 intersection in Cashiers, North Carolina, travel NC 107 South then SC 107 South for approximately 11.5 miles to the right turn onto Fish Hatchery Road—the paved road leading to the Walhalla Fish Hatchery. If the road sign is missing, use the large brown-and-white Walhalla State Fish Hatchery–Chattooga Picnic Area sign to mark your turn.

After turning onto Fish Hatchery Road, continue 0.1 mile to the Foothills Trail parking area on the left side of the road. The white-blazed trail crosses the road at the parking area. The Medlin Mountain section of the Foothills Trail, as described in this guide, enters the woods at the back of the parking area.

Spoonauger Falls Trail

Length 0.5 mile

- **Dayhiking** Easy in either direction
- **Backpacking** Easy in either direction (no camping within one-quarter mile of Burrells Ford Road)
- **Start** Spoonauger Falls Trailhead off Burrells Ford Road near the Chattooga River, 2,050 feet
- **End** Chattooga River Trail (Section 4), 2,065 feet
- **Trail Junction** Chattooga River (Section 4)
- **Topographic Quadrangle** Tamassee SC-GA
- **Blaze** Old blazes fading and will not be repainted
- **RD/NF** Andrew Pickens/Sumter
- **Features** Floodplain forest; Chattooga River; Spoonauger Falls; CRT approach

THE COMBINED **C**HATTOOGA **R**IVER–**F**OOTHILLS **T**RAIL crosses Burrells Ford Road close to the large parking area for Burrells Ford Campground. Three-tenths mile further down the road toward the river, another trail begins to the right behind its bulletin board and three vehicle-blocking boulders. Neither drawn nor labeled on the Chattooga National Wild and Scenic River Map, this wide walkway is usually referred to as the Chattooga River or Spoonauger Falls Trail. To avoid nomenclatural confusion, I chose to describe this short, heavily used route as the Spoonauger Falls Trail.

The flat treadway parallels the river through a floodplain forest featuring tall conifers—white and pitch pines plus hemlock—and the year-round, riverine green of rhododendron, mountain laurel, and, closer to the water, doghobble. Blooming profusely where rooted in the riverside sun, mountain laurel flowers during May; rhododendron opens later, in late June and July. At 0.1 mile the old roadbed track comes close to the river and enters Ellicott Rock Wilderness at the prominent sign. Here the Chattooga glides swift and shallow and clear between riffles and low shoals.

Just beyond where the trail rock-steps across a small, unnamed branch at mile 0.2, it reaches the sign marking the sidepath to Spoonauger Falls, located further up the branch. A moderate, switch-backing grade leads 250 yards to the small-volume falls—a white spill widening as it drops from one narrow ledge to the next. The sheerest pitch of bare rock is wider than it is high. After hard rain, the 40- to 45-foot fall leaps away from its bottommost lip, but during the dog days, the water scarcely dribbles away from the rock.

The nearly flat walking continues close beside the Chattooga, occasionally offering long upstream views. Where the flow slackens and the water darkens into pool, trout often hold in the slow current, mouths facing upstream awaiting a meal. The large-leaved whorls of the Fraser magnolia saplings are conspicuous beneath the tall flood-plain pines. A dense colony of New York fern crowds the forest floor to the right of the footpath. After the river curves away to the north, Spoonauger Falls Trail ends where it ties into the Chattooga River Trail at the signed junction. The CRT angles down to the floodplain before continuing upriver straight ahead from the junction.

If you continue hiking straight ahead, upstream, from the Spoonauger Falls–Chattooga River connection, you will reach the Chattooga River–East Fork intersection after 1.0 mile, Ellicott and Commissioner's Rocks after 2.8 miles, and the CRT's northern ter-minus where it ties into Bad Creek Trail after 2.9 miles. If you want to walk the loop back to the Spoonauger Falls Trailhead, make a bend-back right turn uphill onto the Chattooga River Trail at its Spoon-auger Falls junction, follow that route for 1.6 miles to Burrells Ford Road, then turn right onto the road and head downhill for a little more than 0.3 mile to the three boulders. (See Section 4 of the CRT on page 191 for more information.)

Directions

This wide walkway begins off South Carolina's segment of Bur-rells Ford Road 0.3 mile from the beginning of Chattooga River

Trail's Section 4. All but the final directions to Spoonauger Falls are exactly the same as those for Section 4 of the Chattooga River Trail. (See Section 4 of the CRT on page 197 for directions to its trailhead beside the Burrells Ford Campground parking area.)

If you turn onto Burrells Ford Road from its Highway 107 intersection in South Carolina, the Spoonauger Falls Trailhead (pull-off parking, three vehicle-blocking boulders, small bulletin board, several signs) will be on the right side of the road 0.3 mile beyond the large parking area for Burrells Ford Campground.

If you turn onto Burrells Ford Road (FS 646) from its Highway 28 intersection in Georgia, the Spoonauger Falls Trailhead (pull-off parking, three vehicle-blocking boulders, small bulletin board, several signs) will be on the left side of the road 0.1 mile beyond the Burrells Ford Bridge over the Chattooga River.

Notes

East Fork Trail

Length 2.4 miles

- **Dayhiking In** Easy
- **Dayhiking Out** Easy to Moderate
- **Backpacking In** Easy
- **Backpacking Out** Easy to Moderate
- **Start** East Fork Trailhead at the Walhalla Fish Hatchery, 2,500 feet
- **End** Chattooga River Trail (Section 4), 2,080 feet
- **Trail Junction** Chattooga River (Section 4)
- **Topographic Quadrangle** Tamassee SC-GA
- **Blaze** Old blazes are fading and will not be repainted
- **RD/NF** Andrew Pickens/Sumter
- **Features** Pocket of old-growth forest; East Fork Chattooga River; bluff; Chattooga River; CRT approach

SHORT AND SCENIC, THIS TRAIL closely parallels the East Fork Chattooga River from the Walhalla Fish Hatchery to a few yards shy of the Chattooga River. Except where it rises higher above the stream onto drier, sunnier, south-facing slope, the treadway usually remains within the riparian zone of evergreen rhododendron, hemlock, and doghobble. At first, East Fork's paved approach road, relatively large parking area, stone bathrooms, and boardwalked beginning make you think you're headed for a four-foot-wide macadamed walkway instead of a wilderness footpath. But you quickly discover that most of the folks here are fishing, visiting the hatchery, or cooking hamburgers in the Chattooga Picnic Area. Although this route is heavily used, it does not show major signs of wear and tear, primarily because backpackers do not camp along its length.

East Fork's boardwalked beginning immediately enters the picnic area's small but impressive pocket of old-growth hemlock and white pine. A hemlock 10 feet 1 inch in circumference stands to the left of the boardwalk a few yards into the forest. To the left of the path just before the pavilion, look for a pair of towering white pines. You'll have to crane your neck way back to see their tapering tips. The thicker of the two, the state record until somebody tapes a larger one (or until it dies), spires 156 feet and measures 11 feet in circumference. This relatively puny new record, nominated by a hiker, is champion by default: the former record holder—168 feet tall and 12 feet 9 inches around in its prime—crashed to the ground not far from the pavilion.

A few paces past the pavilion, the effortless walking proceeds to the left at the signed turn, passes into a less imposing conifer-broadleaf forest, then enters the designated wilderness before reaching the river. At 0.3 mile the course crosses the wooden bridge over the East Fork of the Chattooga, here a fast-footed, creek-sized stream about 30 feet wide. Immediately beyond the bridge, at the usually signed connection, a nature walk completes the loop back toward the fish hatchery.

Once across this major Chattooga tributary, the rest of the route remains on the north side of the stream, closely following the frequently cascading East Fork to the west. The trail parallels the river at various distances and heights. Sometimes the flashing whitewater is within sight, sometimes not, but it is always within earshot. The fast-dropping fork roars especially loud after heavy rain. The flat hiking continues on old roadbed through a second-growth forest. Two-tenths mile after the first bridge, the track crosses a smaller one over a steep-sided ravine. When there is water enough, the ravine's rivulet makes a slanting, 6- to 8-foot-high spill over rockface beside the bridge.

Following the first downgrade worth mentioning, short and easy to moderate, the treadway descends gently to a slick-bottomed branch at mile 1.0. Concrete stepping stones a stride apart allow safe crossing of the unnamed stream during high water. The trail passes through short sections of predominantly deciduous forest. Views between dormant hardwoods extend to the ridges across the East Fork.

At mile 1.6 the path, now close to river's edge, passes beside a bluff perhaps 45 feet high at its peak. Both swirling and parallel striations line the rock face. A lush rock garden of saxifrage, Jack-in-the-pulpit, umbrella-leaf, and mountain meadow rue grows along the base of the often wet and dripping bluff.

The remainder of the route undulates with the steepness of the streamside terrain. Occasional old-growth hemlock flank the East Fork; across the water on the south bank, several impressive specimens

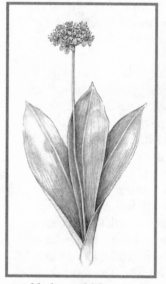

rise arrow straight with little taper. Extensive doghobble thickets line several stretches along the trail's lower end. The overall easy downgrade becomes progressively flatter and closer to the pools and shoals below. Ending near the long wooden bridge spanning the East Fork, the footpath loses its proper noun status where it ties into the usually signed Chattooga River Trail.

If you want to extend your hike to Ellicott and Commissioner's Rocks, turn right onto Chattooga River Trail and follow its easily walked treadway to the northwest, upstream, 1.7 miles to the carved rocks. (See Section 4 of the CRT, page 194, for further information concerning the rocks and their location.)

speckled wood lily

Nature Notes

A small colony of speckled wood lily resides to the left of this path along the short stretch from the pavilion to the bridge over the East Fork. When you see either berries or blooms in combination with the dark and glossy leaves, you will not be likely to mistake this native rhizomatous perennial for any other low- to middle-elevation Southern Appalachian wildflower.

Usually two to five in number, the wood lily's basal leaves are elliptically shaped, prominently midribbed, and most often 5 to 9 inches long. A rounded umbel of five to twenty (rarely more) fragrant white flowers caps a largely leafless stalk rising 6 to 14 inches above the leaves. Each small corolla (approximately ½ inch wide) has six identical petals and sepals (three of each) speckled with purple and green. During a recent year this wood lily colony was blooming on May 15. The blossoms are quickly replaced by an upright cluster of shiny dark blue to nearly black poisonous berries. Native Americans gathered the large round berries to produce a vivid dye.

Also known as white clintonia, this herb is much more widespread and common further north. The range of this species narrows as it fingers deep into the South along with the Appalachians. The southern limit of the plant's habitat—one of nature's many unseen boundaries—runs across northern Georgia and northwestern South Carolina. In the Southern Appalachians, the speckled wood lily is occasional but locally common in moist, rich forests at low and middle elevations.

umbrella-leaf

The base of the often-dripping bluff at mile 1.6 nurtures a natural rock garden, diverse and lush where the soil is deep enough. Easily identified even when not in flower, the umbrella-leaf bears the largest herbaceous-plant leaf throughout Southern Appalachia. The nonflowering stems produce a single giant and jagged leaf 1 to 2 feet across. The flowering stems send forth two somewhat smaller leaves held aloft at slightly different levels because of their alternate arrangement along the stem. All of the umbrellalike leaves are deeply cleft in the middle, and each half has five to seven toothed lobes. No other Southern Appalachian plant produces leaves that closely resemble those of this species.

This rhizomatous perennial puts much more of its biomass into foliage than into flower. A long-stemmed cyme, 2 to 3 feet above the ground at its apex, rises well above the two broad leaves. Blooming in a cluster atop the flowering stem, the blossoms—white and ½- to

¼-inch wide—have six petals, six sepals, and six stamens. Fleshy blue fruits appear after the petals fade and fall. A second-wave spring wildflower, the umbrella-leaf blooms at the bluff sometime between May 5 and May 25.

A member of the Barberry family, which also includes the may-apple, the umbrella-leaf is a Southern Appalachian endemic. Its genus is represented by only two species, this one and an almost identical plant in the mountains of Japan. Because of its stringent habitat requirements, this herb is occasional to uncommon throughout its restricted range. The umbrella-leaf needs to keep its feet wet, and it needs to keep its feet wet in rich, cool mountain forests. While it some-times grows beside rivulets or seeps, it is most common and conspic-uous where large colonies stretch into lush, tropical-looking linear swaths down rocky seepage runs. The umbrella-leaf's upper elevation limit is approximately 6,000 feet.

Directions

Approach from the south: From the SC 28–SC 107 intersection north of Walhalla, South Carolina, travel SC 107 North for approxi-mately 11.8 miles to the left turn onto Fish Hatchery Road—the paved road leading to the Walhalla Fish Hatchery. If the road sign is missing, use the large brown-and-white Walhalla State Fish Hatch-ery-Chattooga Picnic Area sign to mark your turn.

Approach from the north: From the US 64–NC 107 intersection in Cashiers, North Carolina, travel NC 107 South then SC 107 South for approximately 11.5 miles to the right turn onto Fish Hatchery Road—the paved road leading to the Walhalla Fish Hatchery. If the road sign is missing, use the large brown-and-white Walhalla State Fish Hatchery-Chattooga Picnic Area sign to mark your turn.

Follow Fish Hatchery Road for slightly less than 2.0 miles (all paved, take the left fork over the river near the end) to the large parking area. East Fork's boardwalked beginning is located past the restrooms at the far end of the pavement.

Ellicott Rock Trail

Length 4.3 miles

- **Dayhiking In** Easy
- **Dayhiking Out** Easy to Moderate
- **Backpacking In** Easy to Moderate
- **Backpacking Out** Easy to Moderate
- **Start** Ellicott Rock Trailhead, 2,820 feet
- **End** Chattooga River Trail (Section 4), 2,135 feet
- **Trail Junction** Chattooga River (Section 4)
- **Topographic Quadrangles** Highlands NC-GA,
  Cashiers NC-SC-GA, Tamassee SC-GA
- **Blaze** None
- **RD/NF** Highlands/Nantahala, Tallulah/Chattahoochee
- **Features** Small streams; Chattooga River;
  Ellicott and Commissioner's Rocks (see description);
  CRT approach

THREE WELL-MAINTAINED TRAILS—Chattooga River, Bad Creek, and this one—converge close to Commissioner's Rock and Ellicott Rock near the center of the wilderness. Of these three, this route ranks second in both length and difficulty, and is by far the least traveled. If seeing the two rocks is part of your plan, keep in mind that this trail will force you to ford the Chattooga River to reach the rocks. You probably won't want to hike this route to the rocks from November through April, or after substantial rainfall during warm weather. But if you have already seen the markers, their unpretentious lettering more historical symbol than impressive monument, this trail is an excellent site for a cold-weather walk through winter greenery— hemlock and white pine, mountain laurel and rosebay rhododendron, galax and evergreen fern.

Winding to the east, Ellicott Rock Trail follows the bed of a former road for all but its final few yards. The wide walkway rises gently for 0.3 mile through a forest of conifer, heath, and mixed hardwoods. In the ravine to the right, a small prong of Ammons Branch flows back toward the trailhead road. The track levels through a wide, shallow saddle between low knobs before descending into another watershed. By 0.5 mile you will see another ravine to your right, only now the water, the beginning of Glade Creek, is running deeper into the wilderness toward the Chattooga. Where rhododendron and mountain laurel allow them light, Virginia creeper's five leaflets and poison ivy's three often cover the trailside floor.

The overall easy downgrade loses elevation to a series of rivulets, some dry in summer, that cross over and under the treadway starting at mile 1.3. Along the way, at mile 1.1, Glade Creek flows under the woods road and turns to the northeast toward the wild river. Beyond where the branch-sized stream switches sides, the route traverses the lower northeastern slopes of Glade Mountain (second highest peak in the wilderness at 3,672 feet). Here the forest becomes moister and more deciduous. Fraser magnolia, silverbell, black cherry, and sweet birch share sunlight with red maple, yellow poplar, and at least three species of oak.

Starting at mile 1.4, the footpath undulates slightly as it winds to the east and rounds a pair of hollows to a normally summer-dry rivulet at mile 1.8. It then follows a gentle upgrade into drier forest where galax is often common on the high-side slope and evergreen fern occasionally flanks the road cut. The gradual elevation gain ends after 0.3 mile at a shallow, nearly level saddle atop a spur. Another roadbed forks to the left and down from the treadway at the gap. The track the trail follows continues straight ahead, bending to the left back onto slope and rising slowly a short distance to the top of an almost imperceptible spur. Across the spur, the descent to the scenic river begins. While occasional short ups and a few easy-to-moderate downs break the pattern, most of the remainder of the route is somewhere between level and easy down. At mile 2.4 the track enters third growth—small diameter trees, some still in the sapling stage, numerically dominated by yellow poplar, white pine, and stump-sprout red maple. After 0.4 mile, just beyond a prominent colony of New York fern (deciduous), the path leaves the cut and travels beneath tall white pine again.

At mile 3.1 the small branch to the left drops into a ravine slotted toward the Chattooga. Four-tenths mile further, beyond the rotting bridge logs, you can see the narrow ribbon of a cascade to the left after heavy rain during the bare-broadleaf season. As the last segment of the route angles steadily lower and closer to the Chattooga, the trail roughly parallels the river downstream, often through rhododendron. After rounding several steep-sided hollows, the course comes close enough for good looks at the wide water gliding swift and clear through calm shallows, breaking white around rocks or in a line of froth over a ledge. With less than 120 yards remaining, the route rock-steps across an unnamed tributary branch, doglegs left onto path, enters a belt of old-growth hemlock, and dips to the river-bank. The trail fords the Chattooga, usually shallow and easily waded in the summer, at a slight upstream angle, then ends at its usually unsigned junction with the Chattooga River Trail.

The ford at this trail's end spans the Chattooga River from Georgia to South Carolina, not from North Carolina to North Carolina. Since Ellicott Rock Trail ties into the Chattooga River Trail south of the surveyor's chiseled inscriptions, you must turn left onto Chattooga River Trail and follow that path for slightly more than 0.1 mile upstream to reach Ellicott and Commissioner's Rocks. (See Section 4 of the Chattooga River Trail on page 194 for directions to both historic boundary markers.)

Nature Notes

Fortunately, the snake most frequently encountered by Southern Appalachian hikers—the common garter snake—is nonpoisonous, docile, and easily identified. Normally 18 to 30 inches long at maturity, this medium-sized serpent is lined with three yellow stripes running the length of its slender, brownish green body. One thin band marks the centerline of the back; the other two run along the sides of the snake's body. These streaks, which resembled the striped garters once worn to hold up men's socks, account for this reptile's common name.

Able to survive at surprisingly high latitudes, this species is the most widely distributed snake in North America, ranging south to north all the way from the Everglades to Hudson Bay, and east to west across southern Canada. The garter inhabits all of the eastern half of the United States, but this moisture-loving ophidian is missing from the driest sections of our country west of the hundredth meridian—the deserts, the southern Great Plains, the southern Rocky Mountains. This snake's adaptation to cold weather allows it to live at the highest elevations in the Southern Blue Ridge, and to remain active much of the year at the lowest elevations. When winter comes to the high-country, large, slithering numbers of these reptiles hibernate in communal dens called hibernaculums.

While this cold-blooded creature occupies a variety of habitats, it is most abundant in moist forest and near streams. Its prey-species menu—insects, worms, toads, frogs, salamanders, mice, and even small fish—explains its preference for rich woods. During the summer this diurnal species gives live birth to a writhing litter of twelve to seventy snakelets. Though the garter is generally unaggressive, if you grab one it will slime you with a foul-smelling musk.

Leathery, evergreen ferns occasionally flank both sides of the Ellicott Rock Trail. Especially near the middle of the route, from mile 2.0 to 2.2, the distinctively shaped Christmas fern is particularly numerous on the high side of the former roadbed. Abundant in suitable habitat throughout eastern United States and southeastern Canada, the Christmas is one of the most common ferns in the Ellicott Rock Wilderness. Most often found on shaded slopes and in ravines, this nonflowering plant can tolerate drier and more disturbed soils than other mesophytic (medium moisture) ferns; it often thrives on the low-elevation, dry-exposure cut-banks left over from former logging operations.

Also known as the evergreen fern, this dark green pteridophyte is easily recognized by its clusters of linear fronds, which gradually taper to their pointed tips. Fern guides define the frond (leaf) as both the stem and the green pinnae (leaflets). Christmas fern fronds usually measure between 10 and 24 inches in length. The fertile fronds (those with sporangia) are noticeably longer than the sterile ones.

The oblong-to-lanceolate leaflets appear alternately up the frond and, especially in the middle, spread away from the stem at right angles. The small, pointed thumbs on the upper base of the leaflets often make them appear to be attached by more than a short, thin stalk. Occurring only on the upper one-half to one-third of the fertile fronds, the fertile pinnae are much shorter and narrower than the sterile pinnae further down the frond.

Christmas fern

Late in autumn, the tissue at the base of the stem weakens and the evergreen fronds slump to the ground, becoming even more conspicuous in the winter woods. Early New England settlers gathered this plant as a Christmas decoration.

Directions

The Ellicott Rock Trailhead can be most easily reached from Access Points 1, 2, and 3. (See the detailed description of the Access Points on page 130.)

Access Point 1: From the NC 107–Bull Pen Road intersection, travel dirt-gravel Bull Pen Road approximately 6.7 miles (cross Bull Pen Bridge over the Chattooga River at mile 5.4) to the Ellicott Rock Wilderness sign, wooden steps, bulletin boards, and pull-in parking to the left side of Bull Pen Road.

Access Point 2: From the NC 107–Whiteside Cove Road intersection, travel paved Whiteside Cove Road (turns to dirt-gravel after approximately 6.0 miles) for approximately 7.5 miles to its end at the three-way intersection with Bull Pen and Horse Cove Roads. Turn left onto dirt-gravel Bull Pen Road and continue approximately 1.8 miles to the Ellicott Rock Wilderness sign, wooden steps, bulletin boards, and pull-in parking to the right side of the road.

Access Point 3: From the Horse Cove–Whiteside Cove–Bull Pen intersection, travel straight ahead on dirt-gravel Bull Pen Road for approximately 1.8 miles to the Ellicott Rock Wilderness sign, wooden steps, bulletin boards, and pull-in parking to the right side of the road.

Bad Creek Trail

Length 3.0 miles

- **Dayhiking In** Easy
- **Dayhiking Out** Easy to Moderate
- **Backpacking In** Easy to Moderate
- **Backpacking Out** Moderate
- **Start** Bad Creek Trailhead, 2,700 feet
- **End** Chattooga River Trail (Section 4), 2,140 feet
- **Trail Junctions** Fork Mountain, Chattooga River (Section 4)
- **Topographic Quadrangle** Cashiers NC-SC-GA
- **Blaze** None
- **RD/NF** Highlands/Nantahala
- **Features** Winter views; Chattooga River; Ellicott and Commissioner's Rocks (see description); CRT approach

EASILY FOUND AND EASILY FOLLOWED, lightly used and surprisingly scenic during early spring, Bad Creek is an excellent choice for your first warm-up walk of the New Year. Its through-the-bare-branch views and nearly ubiquitous green of galax, rhododendron, mountain laurel, hemlock, and white pine make this trail a good winter hike. During most of April the drama of distance remains while the close-up wildflower beauty begins. Ellicott Rock, Chattooga River, and Bad Creek Trails converge near Ellicott Rock in the heart of the wilderness. Of these three, Bad Creek ranks last in length and first in difficulty.

The trail starts, and continues for nearly half of its length, on an old woods road, often still wide between banks of rhododendron and mountain laurel. The forest along this easily walked first section is a rich tangle of second-growth hemlock and tall white pine mixed with hardwoods, including many mature red maples. At 0.3 mile the treadway dips to its step-over crossing of a branch, an unnamed Fowler Creek feeder. This small stream is the first and only permanent source of water all the way to trail's end at the Chattooga. Rising from the watercourse, the track gradually ascends—occasionally on deep-cut roadbed where rhododendron archways fill in the light gap overhead—to a shallow gap at mile 0.6.

Once through the gap, the wide walkway maintains its generally southern course on the upper, east-facing slope of a spur ridge. The gentle upgrade proceeds toward an unnamed knob (3,103 feet, bench mark on top) under the canopy of white pine and diverse deciduous species. A glance to the left gives you an excellent winter view of 3,740-foot Ellicott Mountain, the highest in the wilderness, only 1½ miles due east. Shortly after gaining the crest of the spur, the route makes an end run around the eastern flank of the knob. A look back over your left shoulder along the way provides another winter prospect—sharp-peaked, 4,460-foot Terrapin Mountain to the north outside of the wilderness.

Bad Creek maintains its steady, nearly effortless elevation gain to the trail's high point (approximately 2,980 feet), the ridgetop south of the knob's crown, at mile 1.2. Staying on or near the oak-pine ridgeline, it slowly descends 0.4 mile to a shallow saddle, where the course leaves the road cut and crosses the ridge onto narrow path. Now on northwest-facing slope, the level treadway affords several partial winter views of Whiteside Mountain to the right and nearly north. At mile 1.9 Fork Mountain Trail ties into Bad Creek at its usually signed junction. Fork Mountain's western end is up and to the left; Bad Creek Trail continues straight ahead.

Two-tenths mile beyond the connection, the footpath curls to the right over a spur and begins the winding, switchbacking, downhill run to the river. Here on the upper, west-facing slope high above the Chattooga, the forest—white pine, chestnut oak, red maple, sassafras, sourwood, and mountain laurel—is drier. Large colonies of galax often line the well-maintained walkway. The bare-branch looks now feature a series of low ridges and white pine slopes to the south and to the west across the wild river. At mile 2.6 the steady downgrade rounds an upper-hollow notch, then parallels the steep-sided hollow from above. Further below, where you can clearly hear the whitewater, the route enters the sheltered belt of rhododendron, hemlock, and white pine.

This trail officially ends as soon as it drops to the narrow floodplain and its usually unsigned meeting with the Chattooga River Trail. Both trails end at this inconspicuous junction next to a campsite with two old-growth hemlocks and one hollowed out, soon-to-die beech. Approached from either direction, the trails flow into one another seamlessly without sharp angle or differing treadway.

If you want to extend your walk to the two historical inscriptions—Commissioner's Rock and Ellicott Rock—follow the Chattooga River Trail downstream for approximately 115 yards to the wide, cut-in section of treadway, above but only a slight angle back from river's edge. The exact spot where you descend to the river is often marked with flagging and occasionally marked with a sign of some sort. You will know you are in the right location when you find a certain hemlock (provided it is still standing)—the one with a black blaze (blazes will not be repainted in the future) and a round, silver-dollar-sized metal survey marker on the downstream side of its trunk just to the right of the trail coming from Bad Creek. (See Section 4 of the Chattooga River Trail, page 194, for directions to both rocks.)

Bad Creek can be backpacked as the first and last leg of a four-trail, 21.7-mile loop, with only 1.9 miles of backtrack. Walking this loop in a counterclockwise direction, you start with Bad Creek's generally southwestward 3.0 miles to its ending junction with Chattooga River Trail. Follow that treadway downriver, to the south then southwest, for 3.9 miles to the left turn onto the signed and white-blazed Foothills Trail. Hike to the east on Foothills for 3.2 miles to paved Fish Hatchery Road. Cross the road and continue to the northeast on the Foothills Trail for another 3.3 miles to the Sloan Bridge Picnic Area beside Highway 107.

The Foothills Trail crosses the highway at the south end of the picnic area. To complete the circuit, leave the Foothills Trail and remain on the picnic area side of the highway. Skirt the highway for 75 yards beyond the far side of the paved picnic area parking lot, curve to the left away from the road, then follow Fork Mountain Trail generally westward 6.4 miles to its Bad Creek connection. Turn right onto Bad Creek and backtrack 1.9 miles to the trailhead.

With the exception of the Foothill Trail's 3.3 miles between Fish Hatchery Road and Highway 107, all of this loop's turns and trails are detailed in this guide. The undescribed 3.3-mile segment of the Foothills Trail is easily walked and surprisingly scenic where it closely parallels the East Fork Chattooga River.

red maple

Nature Notes

Maturing red maples are noticeably common along the first mile of Bad Creek Trail. Not only are these maples plentiful along this trail, but they also thrive throughout the Ellicott Rock Wilderness and the entire Southern Appalachian region except at the highest elevations. In fact, this hardwood—with its vivid red leaf stems, flowers, early fruit, and fall foliage—is the most numerous and widespread tree in eastern North America. Its north-south range, from Newfoundland to southern Florida, is the most far-reaching of any tree in the eastern forest; the western limit of its huge range stretches to the Great Plains.

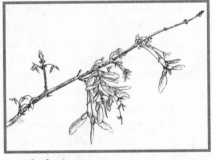

maple fruit

The red maple is at least a minor component in nearly every forest east of the Mississippi. In the South, its elevational reach extends from sea level to slightly over 6,000 feet. With a push from global warming and a pull from the recent devastation of the high-elevation spruce-fir forests, red maples probably will ascend to the crowns of eastern North America's highest peaks (which we all know are in the South) in the next century or two.

Foresters call the highly successful red maple a "super generalist" because it now prospers in nearly every forested habitat within its range. Once considered chiefly a swampland species, the red maple has adapted so well to current forest conditions over much of the East— logging, heavy deer browsing, wildfire suppression, and gypsy moth defoliation—that it has aggressively spread into uplands where it was rare a century ago. The numbers of this resilient, stump-sprouting broadleaf have increased most dramatically in disturbed woodlands, where it has displaced oaks in the process. In some northern forests, red maple saplings accounted for up to 90 percent of new growth after gypsy moths stripped the oak forests clean. Red maple foliage contains chemicals that discourage deer and some insect pests. And, to further ensure its survival, this hardwood sends its whirlygig seeds, too small to offer the larger mammals much food, spinning to the forest floor in spring, when they are not in great demand by wildlife.

You can often spot this species from a distance in spring as well as in fall. During late winter and early spring, its numerous red flowers appear before the leaves break bud. The red blush of its blooms sweeps up to the high slopes from mid-March to early April. Where these trees occur in large, sunlit stands, the color is almost as dazzling as their bright red fall foliage.

Red maple leaves are readily identified, even though they vary somewhat in size and shape. The opposite leaves have three prominent, short-pointed lobes and coarsely toothed margins (the sugar maple leaf has a smooth margin). Often two smaller lobes (for a total of five) point outward near the base of the 2½- to 5½-inch-long leaves.

Like other trees that inhabit a wide range of sites, the red maple's size depends upon where it is rooted. On dry, thin-soiled ridges, where many hardwoods don't grow at all, this maple usually remains a stunted understory tree beneath the pines and oaks. But in coves and along stream corridors, the red maple grows into the canopy tall and straight. In good habitats many second-growth specimens are already 70 to 90 feet in height and 2 to 3 feet in diameter. The maximum size for a Southern Appalachian red maple is approximately 120 feet in height and 4½ feet in diameter.

If you walk this trail on a warm sunny day during mid- to late-April, before the trees leaf out, you will probably notice a violet blooming bright yellow along the edge of the treadway. It will most likely be the halberd-leaved violet, one of the few native violets hikers can pin-

halberd-leaved violet

point to the species level without resorting to a hand lens and identification key. Just look for the yellow petals, the typical violet flower shape and the distinctive, atypical leaves. These low (usually only 3 to 8 inches tall) rhizomatous perennials bloom early with the first wave of spring wildflowers and prefer the light gaps of old roads. Occasional to common throughout the Southern Highlands in the right habitat, the halberd-leaved violet makes its home in moist deciduous or mixed broadleaf-conifer forests at low and middle elevations.

True to form, the ½- to 1-inch-wide flowers display five petals; the lowest two are prominently veined with purple honey guides. The leaves of this *Viola* species, however, are noticeably different in coloration (mottled silver on their upper surfaces) and shape (long and pointed) from the violet leaves we are all familiar with. Instead of the classic Valentine's-heart shape, this plant's two to four toothed leaves are widest at the base and about twice as long as they are wide. A protruding lobe at each side of the base gives the leaves an elongated triangle or arrowhead outline.

This violet's common name stems from the unusual shape of its leaves, which reminded someone—probably a man well-versed in warfare—of the head of a halberd, a weapon from the fifteenth and sixteenth centuries. The halberd—a combination short bayonet and axe-blade head mounted to the end of a long staff—was a murderously efficient weapon, especially used by cavalrymen. DeSoto's men used swords and halberds to slay Native Americans by the thousands during their long murderous raid across the Southeast.

Directions

The Bad Creek Trailhead can be most easily reached from Access Points 1 and 3. (See the detailed description of the Access Points on page 130.)

Access Point 1: From the NC 107–Bull Pen Road intersection, travel dirt-gravel Bull Pen Road for approximately 2.6 miles to the Ellicott Rock Wilderness sign, bulletin board, and very small pull-in parking spot to the left of the road. If trailhead parking is full, continue straight ahead less than 0.1 mile to the open area on the right across Fowler Creek. Please don't block access through the gate.

Access Point 3: From the Horse Cove–Whiteside Cove–Bull Pen intersection, travel straight ahead on dirt-gravel Bull Pen Road (cross the Chattooga River and keep going) for approximately 5.9 miles to the very small pull-in parking spot, Ellicott Rock Wilderness sign, and bulletin board at the Bad Creek Trailhead. Begin looking for the trailhead, which is to the right of the road, after crossing Fowler Creek at mile 5.8.

Notes

Fork Mountain Trail

Length 6.4 miles

- **Dayhiking** Easy in either direction
- **Backpacking** Easy to Moderate in either direction
- **Start** Fork Mountain Trailhead at Sloan Bridge Picnic Area off SC 107, 2,760 feet
- **End** Bad Creek Trail, 2,720 feet
- **Trail Junctions** Foothills (at trailhead, see description of loop), Bad Creek
- **Topographic Quadrangle** Cashiers NC-SC-GA
- **Blaze** None
- **RD/NF** Andrew Pickens/Sumter, Highlands/Nantahala
- **Features** Small streams; occasional old-growth white and pitch pine

FORK MOUNTAIN WINDS TO THE WEST at a right angle to the general north-south grain of the land, following the practical and familiar pattern for traversing slope. The well-constructed track curls over a ridgecrest, then frequently rounds a series of hollows or ravines, some large enough for a stream, before rising to the next ridge. At 6.4 miles, Fork Mountain is the longest route in the Ellicott Rock Wilderness trail system. This footpath, usually cut into slope, has no sustained grades more difficult than easy. In fact, its elevation changes are so steady and mild that it breaks form with only one very short, easy-to-moderate ascent.

Entering the woods from Highway 107, the treadway slowly ascends through a diverse broadleaf-conifer forest, a low-elevation mix from the drier slope above and the moister riparian zone below. A colony of New York fern flanks the way at 0.1 mile, and large-leaved

Fraser magnolias are unusually numerous along this first stretch. At 0.4 mile the route parallels Slatten Branch, flowing east away from the wilderness toward the highway and the East Fork Chattooga River. After pulling away from the stream, the course enters the signed wilderness at 0.6 mile, crosses narrow Slatten Branch 0.1 mile further, then passes over the first low spur ridge at 0.9 mile. Here a dry, oak-pine forest shades a dense thicket-growth of mountain laurel and deciduous heath on the upper slopes and ridges. You can recognize the older pitch pines by their numerous thick (for a pine) and twisting limbs.

Dipping slightly from the first crest, the wilderness pathway snakes around two shallow hollows full of American holly and New York fern (in season) before heading up to the next spur top at mile 1.1. It then angles downslope through an oak-pine forest—including blackgum, sourwood, white pine, and chestnut oak—curls around several narrow ravines, and passes over another pine-capped finger ridge (mile 1.8) splaying southward from Ellicott Mountain. The familiar pattern of rounding moist, often ferny hollows and crossing dry, often piney spurs continues.

At mile 2.1 the trail descends to and crosses small Indian Camp Branch, which flows through a forest of rhododendron, hemlock, white pine, and such moist-site hardwoods as sweet birch and yellow poplar. The undemanding walkway advances on slope past several lunker white pines, swings around a running-water hollow at mile 2.4, then gradually gains elevation into drier oak-pine forest again. After passing through extensive fields of New York and hay-scented ferns, the track crests the top of a Fork Mountain spur at mile 3.0. It soon drops below ridgeline, slips southward around the sunrise side of a low knob, then crosses over the same spur through a shallow saddle at mile 3.4.

The path continues its meandering course west through a series of narrow upper hollows, often steep-sided and ravinelike. At mile 4.3 the course passes beside the trail's largest tree (if it's still alive)—a yellow poplar with a girth of approximately 12 to 13 feet. Beyond the poplar, the route half-loops into North Carolina, crosses both forks of Bad Creek, then bends back into South Carolina. Along the way, before crossing the eastern fork at mile 5.0, the treadway parallels the branch as it slides down water-worn rock and tumbles out of sight.

Two-tenths mile past the first crossing, the wilderness walkway rock-steps across the western fork. To avoid the steep bank straight across, the trail swerves sharply to the left and downstream while crossing. Please follow the trail rather than climbing straight up and eroding the opposite bank. Forty yards beyond the real route's exit from the stream, the track turns left onto a rhododendron-lined former logging road and passes beside an abandoned engine block and through a stand of yellow poplar still in the pole timber stage. At mile 5.4 the walking slants up and away from the roadbed onto erosion-bar steps.

The final mile, mostly gentle upgrade, continues the hollow-spur pattern of slope trail as it skirts around the southern flank of a low (2,900 feet) unnamed knob. Rock outcrops grace the first moist hollow. The east-facing slope beyond the outcrops supports a tall, open forest of hemlock and hardwoods—hickory, oak, and yellow poplar. Soon after you start to hear the river, the course heads up and angles to the right across a woods road at mile 5.9. Now higher and drier, the footpath passes through oak-pine forest featuring canopy-height pitch pine and tangles of mountain laurel. The first time I walked this route, on May 20, the laurel was at full bloom. With 0.1 mile remaining, the treadway re-enters North Carolina, then dips to its signed end where it ties into Bad Creek Trail.

Fork Mountain can be walked as the first or last leg of a four-trail, no-backtrack, 17.9-mile loop. Hiking the loop in a counterclockwise direction, you start with Fork Mountain's generally westward 6.4 miles to its ending junction with Bad Creek Trail. Turn left onto Bad Creek and continue westward for 1.1 miles to the Chattooga River Trail. Follow that treadway downriver, to the south then southwest, for 3.9 miles to the left turn onto the white-blazed Foothills Trail. To complete the circuit, hike Foothills to the east for 3.2 miles to paved Fish Hatchery Road. Cross the road and continue northeastward on the Foothills Trail for another 3.3 miles to the Sloan Bridge Picnic Area—Fork Mountain's trailhead.

With the exception of the final 3.3 miles, all of the loop's trails and turns are detailed in this guide. The undescribed 3.3-mile segment of the Foothills Trail, from Fish Hatchery Road back out to the picnic area off SC 107, is easy walking and surprisingly scenic where it closely parallels the cascades and plunge pools of the East Fork Chattooga River.

Nature Notes

If you hike this trail (or other trails that aren't constantly under the heavy shade of hemlock and rhododendron) during a warm, sunny spell in late winter or early spring, you may be fortunate enough to see at least one overwintering mourning cloak. Almost everything about this butterfly, including its name, is unusual or unique. It estivates in the summer, lives long enough to hibernate in the winter, and undertakes a partial migration during both spring and fall. It occupies an immense range, sucks tree sap for a living, lives to an incredibly old age for a butterfly, partakes in a distinctive, spiraling mating dance, and actually makes a noise. On top of all that, this winged insect is beautiful, common, and easy to identify.

The mourning cloak, wings spanning a moderately large 2⅞ to 3⅜ inches, is brownish black and cream yellow above. The yellow forms irregular outside bands, a bowl-shaped edge of color, extending from the tips of the forewings to the inside bottom of the hindwings. At close range, the dark color appears iridescent purple; the light-colored band is inwardly bordered by blue spots along both wings. Both sexes have the same markings.

When closed, the mourning cloak's wings offer potential predators a completely different and confusing appearance. Few butterflies exhibit such contrasting coloration from above to below. The upperwing pattern is repeated on the underwing, but the colors are drab and camouflaging. The undersides are mottled brown, the blue spots are absent, and the band is gray with dark smudging—the color and pattern of lichen blending into tree bark. If its camouflage fails, or if an unsuspecting predator pokes about too close, the mourning cloak simultaneously produces an audible click and takes flight. This quick click in combination with the sudden movement is meant to startle the predator.

One of the most conspicuous and widespread butterflies in North America, this species occupies a vast range, taking advantage of nearly every habitat that supports its hosts. It ranges almost everywhere throughout temperate and subarctic North America, from Alaska to the Okeefenokee, and extends southward to the highlands of central Mexico. This cosmopolitan insect also lives in temperate Eurasia.

The mourning cloak that flutters across your path in March is an old, overwintering individual. One of the very few butterfly hibernators, this species spends its winters in hollow tree trunks or branches for weeks or months at a time. During warm sunny spells in late winter, they leave their roosts to search for mates. Nightfall and colder weather drive them back to their dens.

Unlike most butterflies, the mourning cloak has only a single brood, or flight, per year. The year's remaining population mates in the late winter and early spring sun; the females lay eggs, then that generation dies. The eggs hatch, the larvae munch, and brand new butterflies emerge from their chrysalises in early summer. They feed hard in the early summer, estivate during the hottest days, eat again during late summer and fall, then go into hibernation. Although even a partial migration is unusual for butterflies, an unknown portion of each mourning cloak flight migrates southward with autumn and back north with spring.

Most butterfly species live only 2 to 21 days. Scientists believe that the mourning cloak, with a maximum lifespan of 10 to 11 months, is the longest-lived butterfly in North America. The monarch, which makes its incredible migration to Mexico each fall, has the second-longest maximum lifespan of North American butterflies—5 to 6 months.

For nourishment, mourning cloaks seek sap flows of trees, especially oaks. They are frequently attracted to trees with fresh sap ooze kept open by sapsuckers. These butterflies are also fond of fermenting fruit, flower nectar, and slimy fungus fluxes.

This insect received its name not only for its mourning color, but also because it flew during the first warm spells of late winter, when the ground over much of its range thawed enough for folks to bury those who had died during the dead of winter.

At mile 1.6 the track crosses a narrow ravine that looks much like many of the others at first glance. On closer inspection you will see that it supports a colony of broad beech fern, both upslope and down. Although it is not one of the most common ferns in the Ellicott Rock Wilderness, the distinctively shaped broad beech is both numerous and noticeable beside the next 0.1 mile of the trail beyond the ravine. This species thrives where the underwood on the southeast-facing slope is particularly open.

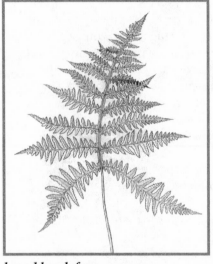

broad beech fern

This fern's dull green fronds (the entire leaf from the ground up), usually 12 to 24 inches in height, wither brown with the fall's first frosts. Their blades (the leafy part of the frond) are broadly triangular, often slightly wider than long, and widest at the base. Lanceolate and tapering to sharp points at their tips, the opposite pinnae (leaflets) are connected to each other by winglike webbing along the blade stem. The lowest pair of pinnae, larger and longer than those above, sweeps forward and downward at a different angle than all the rest.

Found throughout the Southern Appalachians, this nonflowering plant's range extends from eastern Texas up to southern Canada, eastward across southern Canada to the coast, then southward to northernmost Florida. Within its huge range, this species seeks humus-rich, well-drained woodlands and the cool, shaded slopes of ravines. Individual fronds, which lean back at an angle and are easily noticed, are well spaced within the colony by means of creeping underground rhizomes. This fern's name stems from its slight preference for beech-dominated forests.

Directions

Approach from the south: From the SC 28–SC 107 intersection north of Walhalla, South Carolina, travel SC 107 North for approximately 14.3 miles to the paved parking area for Sloan Bridge Picnic Area (unsigned) on the left side of the highway. The picnic area is 0.2 mile beyond the Highway 107–Highway 130 junction.

Approach from the north: From the US 64–NC 107 intersection in Cashiers, North Carolina, travel NC 107 South then SC 107 South for approximately 9.0 miles to the paved parking area for Sloan Bridge Picnic Area (unsigned) on the right side of the highway. The picnic area is 0.2 mile before the Highway 107–Highway 130 junction.

Fork Mountain Trail begins off Highway 107 on the same side of the road as the picnic area. From the northern edge of the picnic area parking lot, walk along the highway to the north (to the right facing the picnic area from the highway) for approximately 75 yards to the path leading to the first trail sign.

Notes

Chattooga Cliffs Trail

Length 5.1 miles

- **Dayhiking** Easy to Moderate in either direction
- **Backpacking** Moderate in either direction
- **Vehicular Access At Either End** Southern
  (lower elevation) terminus at Bull Pen Bridge,
  2,400 feet; northern (higher elevation) terminus
  near Whiteside Cove Cemetery, 2,720 feet
- **Trail Junction** Loop (see description)
- **Topographic Quadrangles** Highlands NC-GA,
  Cashiers NC-SC-GA
- **Blaze** None
- **RD/NF** Highlands/Nantahala
- **Features** Chattooga River; Chattooga Cliffs;
  winter views; Chattooga tributaries; rock outcrops

LOCATED NORTH OF THE ELLICOTT ROCK WILDERNESS, this highly scenic route is the northernmost trail within the Chattooga National Wild and Scenic River corridor. This footpath's northern end is located at the northern limit of publicly owned land within the river's protected corridor, and it is only 1¾ miles south of the federally designated river's northern boundary. Paralleling the western bank of the river, the walkway remains within the preserved strip of riverside land for all but its final 0.3 mile near Whiteside Cove Road.

Most hikers do not walk this entire trail. Instead, most start at Bull Pen Bridge and walk the loop back to the trailhead, or they continue upriver to the first or second iron bridge before turning back. Accordingly, this path is described as it is most often begun, from south to north, from Bull Pen's swirlhole cascades upstream to the calm and shallow water of the upper Chattooga. No matter which way you walk it, however, this trail's difficulty is greater than its 300-foot, end-to-end elevation differential might suggest. This route negotiates steep riverside slope. Some segments rise and fall while wriggling and wraggling side to side to traverse the precipitous terrain. Although all of the sustained grades are easy, the very short ups and downs, some of them sharp, are too numerous to count or describe.

The frequent undulations plus the tricky footing raised this trail's difficulty rating a notch. Hiking sticks come in handy here. Brief stretches of the beginning 1.6 miles to the first iron bridge are rocky, wet, narrow, and steep. Especially during winter and spring, rivulets and branches often intersect the footpath. Bridges span the slickest and steepest of the slanting waterslides. Though still occasionally rough, the footing beyond the first iron bridge is better and the grades are generally longer and gentler.

Starting close beside Bull Pen Bridge, the treadway enters the streamside green of Southern Appalachia—doghobble, rhododendron, and mountain laurel in the understory and hemlock, white pine, and mixed mesophytic hardwoods high overhead. Boulders and riverbed slabs squeeze the stream into sluices and shoals below. Many of the thick trailside mountain laurels are lunkers for their species. After traveling further up and away from the Chattooga, the track passes beside a huge, canted mass of outcrop rock, perhaps 15 feet high and 100 feet long. At 0.5 mile the course crosses a bridge over a descending slick of wet rock. After the right amount of rain, a thin curtain of water freefalls over the 8- to 10-foot-high ledge to the left. Normally, however, the spill is no more than a steady drip.

Two-tenths mile beyond the bridge, Chattooga Cliffs comes to its only signed junction—the loop trail heading up and to the left, doubling back on higher slope to the Bull Pen Trailhead. The main route continues to follow the Chattooga through a forest predominantly hemlock, hardwood, and rhododendron. Not far beyond this connection, the treadway becomes narrow, rocky, and steep while skirting below an overhang of upthrust rock. Looks toward the river range from glimpses of shining water to largely unobstructed upstream views. Boulder-choked runs launch a steady roar.

At mile 1.1 the walkway switchbacks left, then right, higher above the entrenched river. Here the forest is more white pine and hardwood, less hemlock and rhododendron. Winding around two narrow hollows along the way, the path slowly descends to the iron bridge over Cane Creek, a major Chattooga tributary, at mile 1.6. It then gradually rises from the stream on old roadbed far from the river. Slightly undulating, this segment's nearly effortless walking continues through a predominantly deciduous forest occasionally controlled by stands of yellow poplar still in their pole timber stage. The track reaches the second iron bridge, this one over the whitewater end of Mill Creek, at mile 2.5.

To the left of the bridge, a blown-out swirlhole and plunge pool at the base of a cascade invite some to swim in warm weather. To the right, Mill Creek's final run slides to a surprisingly large Chattooga pool, carved from two directions and dark green where it's over your head. Just upstream from the confluence, rock banks pinch the river into a long raceway known as the narrows. Here, during summer drought, you can stand on the sloping slab and touch the low bluff on the other side with a long hiking stick.

During low water you can follow the slanting rock upriver beside the narrows, straight ahead and quickly back to the trail. When the river is up, follow the footpath straight ahead from the bridge slightly less than 0.1 mile to its apparent end. Here the track turns 90 degrees to the right, then ducks under rhododendron down the short pitch back to streamside trail. Now the level walking closely parallels the noticeably smaller river, offering numerous good views of the calm, clear, shallow Chattooga as it slowly lapses seaward over yellow sand and cobbly bottom. The treadway ties into road grade, where it rises away from and then falls closer to the now-faster river. At mile 3.2 an easily viewed cascade flies into bright white foam above the glinting green of its pool.

Beyond the cascade, the route ascends sharply for a few rods to standing rock before dropping back down alongside the Chattooga again. The walkway gradually gains elevation above the river, then switchbacks higher onto narrow sidehill path. From here the hiking gently roller-coasters on steep slope through the year-round verdure of rhododendron and small-needled hemlocks; the occasional elderly specimens of the latter were part of the primeval forest before logging. At mile 3.8 the treadway switchbacks up onto former road through largely deciduous forest composed primarily of yellow poplar. Two-tenths mile beyond the switchback, the track angles away from the last views of the river.

The course continues on a mild upward gradient to the place where the trail splits at mile 4.4. Used more frequently by incoming walkers, the left fork leads to a church; the path straight ahead or to the right is the designated trail. This final stretch, predominantly level or slightly downhill, offers the smoothest walking of the hike. After skirting the brow of a steep slope dropping precipitously to the river, the remainder of the footpath follows a woods road through hemlock, white pine, and hardwoods, including an unusually large hickory component.

This route is scenic year-round, but it is especially so when the hardwoods are dormant, when the views of the river, the cliffs, and the nearby ridges are wider and more numerous. Across the river to the east, a nearby string of mountains arches and rolls toward the north. Eons ago, the Chattooga sliced through the lower slopes of the two nearest and southernmost peaks, Polly and Bull Pen, leaving behind a broad band of high bluffs: Chattooga Cliffs. For most of the first mile, looks to the right across the river focus on the steep slopes of Polly Mountain. Further along, from mile 1.0 to mile 2.0, Bull Pen Mountain tilts sharply to its high point only a half mile away.

Brushy Mountain stands to the east a short distance before the second iron bridge. Nearly a mile beyond the second iron bridge, views to the right (120 degrees) frame the uplift of Jacks Knob. Two prominent peaks, Terrapin and Whiteside, are clearly visible from the path's final 1.5 miles. To the east or southeast, depending on your location, big, broad-shouldered Terrapin Mountain (4,460 feet) towers above the other nearby peaks. To the north-northwest and farther away, look for the unmistakable mesalike crown and large expanse of gray cliff face on Whiteside Mountain (4,900 feet).

The last few times I hiked this trail, the long, single spans of the iron bridges sparked lively debates concerning their method of placement. Because roads come close to both bridges, some thought fancy trucks with cranes lowered the bridges into place on their concrete buttresses. Others insisted the job could have been accomplished only by helicopter. The Highlands Ranger District settled the dispute: helicopters placed the bridges pretty as you please across the creeks. The district office has a picture on the wall to prove it.

The Loop

Curling up and to the left away from the main route at 0.7 mile, the loop finishes a 1.8-mile oval back to the Bull Pen Bridge trailhead. The 1.8-mile total includes the first 0.7 mile on Chattooga Cliffs Trail. After it turns away from the trail, the loop gradually gains elevation on a good spring wildflower slope. The track soon switches from cut-in path to road grade, from predominantly deciduous forest to white pine, hemlock, and rhododendron mixed with the hardwoods. The easy walking reaches a picnic table at the turnaround/parking area end of a short spur road at mile 1.4. The remainder of the loop follows the spur 60 yards downhill and to the right, then turns left onto Bull Pen Road.

Nature Notes

If you walk this trail during the warm weather of late spring and summer, you will probably observe the doddering flight of tiger swallowtails as they patrol up and down the Chattooga. The swallowtails you see fluttering up and down river are definitely males, and they are definitely not flitting about aimlessly as you might assume. Males patrol (the word used in butterfly guides) particular routes or territories, usually along streams, in search of mates. The winged stage of this butterfly is characteristically short: males have a maximum life span of approximately 12 days, females a paltry 72 hours—not even enough time to join the males for a quick drink at the sandbar.

This large (3⅛ to 5½ inches across), black-striped yellow butterfly with swallow-tailed hindwings is one of the most familiar and widespread insects in North America. Its range is immense. The northern limit stretches from central Alaska southeastward across Canada to the Atlantic. To the south, it includes all of the eastern half of the

United States and much of the Great Plains east of the Rockies.

One of the few butterflies capable of hanging upside down on a flower, this species favors largely deciduous forests along streams. From north to south across its vast range, this swallowtail produces from one to three flights or generations per year. In the Southern Appalachians, caterpillars resulting from the third flight bundle up in overwintering chrysalises.

As you walk this trail or others along the Chattooga, you may see congregations of several butterfly species sucking at the wet riverside sand. Lepidopterists (butterfly experts) call these groups mud puddle clubs. Newly emerged males from each flight seek moisture and mineral ions from the wet sand. The last time some friends and I hiked this trail, we saw a promising green pool below and dropped down for a swim. At water's edge, a doe lay dead from a large neck wound. Insects milled around the wound, but they were neither flies nor maggots. Instead, a colorful mud puddle club of sixty to seventy butterflies, most of them tiger swallowtails, were drawing moisture and ions from the gash. We passed on that pool.

Slightly larger than the male, the female comes in two color phases—a yellow form, like all the males, and a mimetic black form. The black phase is an assumed Batesian mimic of the distasteful pipevine swallowtail. The males prefer to mate with the blonds, but birds attack the black mimics at a significantly lower rate. Thus the female tiger swallowtail teeters on a genetic fence, and both forms are maintained in the population by different selective advantages.

Short sections of Chattooga Cliffs and its loop offer good spring wildflower displays where the treadway rises well above the river onto largely hardwood slopes. By late April, the Catesby's trillium is both the most common and most colorful of the show. Also known as rose trillium, this member of the Lily family normally attains a height of 4 to 12 inches. Its characteristic three leaves, only 2 to 4 inches long and often wavy edged, are relatively short compared to those of other trilliums likely to share the same habitat.

The strongly recurved flowers, which almost always hang at or below leaf level, range from white tinged with pink to dark pinkish red. The corollas turn deeper pink or darker pink-red as they age. Like the leaves, the petals of the 1- to 1¾-inch-wide blossoms are wavy margined. Bright yellow anthers curling from the center of the nodding bloom complete the easy identification.

During most years, this perennial begins blooming here by April 20. By May 15 only a few ragged and dark pink flowers remain. About the time the Catesby's petals have faded and fallen, the Vasey's trillium (much less common on this trail) begins

blooming, especially along the loop. The Vasey's is readily differentiated from the Catesby's at first glance: the Vasey's is much taller, its broad leaves are significantly larger and lack wavy margins, and its noticeably wider flowers—a rich carmine color—hang well below leaf level.

Directions

Chattooga Cliffs has either-end vehicular access. Its southern trailhead at Bull Pen Bridge can be most

Catesby's trillium

easily reached from Access Points 1, 2, and 3; its northern trailhead off Whiteside Cove Road can be most easily reached from Access Points 2 and 3. (See Access Points on page 130.)

Southern trailhead at Bull Pen Bridge

Access Point 1: From the NC 107–Bull Pen Road intersection, travel dirt-gravel Bull Pen Road approximately 5.4 miles to the small pull-in parking area and bulletin board to the right of the road immediately after the Bull Pen Bridge over the Chattooga River. Pull-in overflow parking is located to the left of the road a short distance beyond the trailhead.

Access Point 2: From the NC 107–Whiteside Cove Road intersection, travel paved Whiteside Cove Road (turns dirt-gravel after approximately 6.0 miles) for approximately 7.5 miles to its ending, three-way intersection with Bull Pen and Horse Cove Roads. Turn left onto dirt-gravel Bull Pen Road (Horse Cove Road is paved and to the right) and continue approximately 3.1 miles to the small pull-in parking area and bulletin board to the left of the road just before the Bull Pen Bridge over the Chattooga River.

Access Point 3: From the Horse Cove–Whiteside Cove–Bull Pen intersection, travel straight ahead on dirt-gravel Bull Pen Road for approximately 3.1 miles to the small pull-in parking area and bulletin board to the left of the road just before the Bull Pen Bridge over the Chattooga River.

Northern trailhead off Whiteside Cove Road

Access Point 2: From the NC 107–Whiteside Cove Road intersection, travel paved Whiteside Cove Road slightly less than 4.0 miles to a small lake on the right side of the road that affords (weather permitting) a wonderful view of Whiteside Mountain. Two-tenths mile beyond the lake, turn left onto the gravel road marked with a "cemetery" sign. The number 1108 appears on the back of its stop sign, and the numbers 103 and 151 on a tree (if it is still standing) to the right of the entrance. A paved private driveway heads up and to the left of the gravel road's entrance.

Access Point 3: From the Horse Cove–Whiteside Cove–Bull Pen intersection, turn left onto dirt-gravel (may be paved in near future) Whiteside Cove Road and proceed (pavement begins after approximately 1.5 miles) approximately 3.4 miles to the right turn onto the gravel road marked with the "cemetery" sign. The number 1108 appears on the back of its stop sign, and the numbers 103 and 151 on a tree (if it is still standing) to the right of its entrance. A paved private driveway leads up and to the left of the gravel road's entrance.

From "Cemetery" Road

Follow the gravel road to the fork at 0.1 mile. Chattooga Cliff's usually unsigned northern end is the old woods road that ties into the outside (right) of the right fork 10 to 15 yards beyond the split.

Something will have gone out of us as a people if we ever let the remaining wilderness be destroyed.... We need wilderness preserved—as much of it as is still left, and as many kinds—because it was the challenge against which our character as a people was formed. The reminder and the reassurance that it is still there is good for our spiritual health even if we never once in ten years set foot in it. It is good for us when we are young, because of the incomparable sanity it can bring briefly, as vacation and rest, into our insane lives. It is important to us when we are old simply because it is there—important, that is, simply as idea.

—Wallace Stegner

The Idea of Wilderness

WILDERNESS ADVOCATES see the Wilderness Act of 1964 as the most foresighted land-ethic legislation since the formation of the National Forest System. The concept of designated wilderness represents a progression of concern, a hard-won belief by the majority that some parcels of the earth should have their own heritage, should be allowed to become what they will, unmanipulated by humans. This act of preservation, a tithing of wildness for ourselves and for the future, is an important but as yet paltry beginning reparation for our abuse and misuse of the land and its life.

Those who oppose the concept of designated wilderness view it as a radical step that locks up resources. Let it be emphatically stated to them, however, that the idea is often a matter of preference—a matter of zoning really. Either we can choose to continue opening large areas of our Southern Appalachian forest to road building and logging in order to satisfy the incessant demands of a world crowded with people chanting more, more, more, like a mantra. Or we can choose to preserve, to lock up diversity and beauty—clear, unsilted streams, magnificent forests, views into wild and natural land—by designating significant tracts as wilderness. Even though the physical resources of these areas would no longer be available for extraction, we can still use them—recreationally, spiritually, scientifically—in their natural state.

Unlike Alaska and the western states, the central and eastern regions of our country have only three categories of federally owned wild land—national wildlife refuges, national parks, and national forests—where federal wilderness designation is possible. Within that immense expanse of our country east of the Rockies, from Texas to South Carolina, from Nebraska to Pennsylvania, federal ownership of those three types of wild land constitutes less than 5 percent of the total land mass. Some states within that region, especially those with flat topography and good soil, have little or no opportunity for wilderness.

Within that less than 5 percent, only certain areas—those that are roadless, predominantly publicly owned, and large (usually at least 5,000 acres)—are qualified to be considered for a roadless inventory, the first step toward designation. Once an area is inventoried as roadless, it still has to be sufficiently scenic and undisturbed—and often economically useless—for there to be enough support to continue the qualification process.

Although percentages vary from state to state, congressionally mandated wilderness within that region east of the Rockies is, at best, somewhere between 5 and 10 percent of the federal wildlands. Thus, designated wilderness over much of our country is a small fraction of a small fraction: two to three-tenths of 1 percent of the total land base. Even in our relatively wild South, with its mountains, swamps, and forests, the figure remains below 1 percent.

Unlike large sections of the Midwest, the South fortunately still has the opportunity for more wilderness. Our best opportunity lies within the national forests of the Southern Appalachians—the South's largest concentration of publicly owned land.

Especially in the highest and most remote mountains, road building and logging in the steep-sloped Southern Appalachians is destructive and costly. Bulldozing and stabilizing roads in this high-rainfall, mountainous terrain is so expensive that the federal government must subsidize it. The road building and logging damages watersheds, leaves the forest less diverse, harms certain wildlife species, and keeps the land in its ecological infancy. Spending money to subsidize destructive logging that yields little of the national lumber output makes neither ecological nor economic sense. This is especially true where we are further fragmenting the small amount of unprotected public land that remains wild and natural.

We are always faced with difficult land-use choices; designating wilderness is just one among many. But today at a time when the pace of life is increasingly frenetic—when ocean levels, global temperatures, and human populations are rising; when acid rain is falling and ozone layers are disappearing; when our collective actions lead to the daily extinction of species—it makes good sense to spare a few more teaspoons of wildness as havens for life and for human hope and renewal, protected both for and from us.

The Wilderness Act

The Wilderness Act of September 3, 1964, established the National Wilderness Preservation System, the first of its kind in the world. The idea of wilderness means different things to different people. Some describe any patch of woods bigger than their backyard as wilderness. Others won't call an area true wilderness unless it meets rare conditions: that it takes at least a week to walk across the longest part of it, that there is no sign of human habitation even from the vistas, and that all of the original predators are still on patrol. Knowing that the term is nebulous, as much spiritual as physical, the framers of the law attempted to define the qualities and purposes of wilderness. The following are salient ideas from the act.

A wilderness:
- is an area of undeveloped federal land retaining its primeval character and influence, without permanent improvements or human habitation;
- has at least 5,000 acres of land or is of sufficient size to make practicable its preservation and use in an unimpaired condition;
- generally appears to have been affected primarily by forces of nature, with the imprint of man's work substantially unnoticeable;
- is hereby recognized as an area where the earth and its community of life are untrammeled by man, where man himself is a visitor who does not remain, and which has outstanding opportunities for solitude or a primitive and unconfined type of recreation;
- is devoted to the public purposes of recreational, scenic, scientific, educational, conservation, and historical use;
- is preservation that will secure for the American people of present and future generations the benefits of an enduring

resource of wilderness—unimpaired for future use
and enjoyment.

What is permitted in wilderness?

▪ Primitive recreation such as dayhiking, backpacking,
  and camping
▪ Hunting and fishing in accordance with state and
  federal laws
▪ Collecting berries, nuts, and cones for personal use
▪ Scientific research compatible with wilderness values
▪ Primitive facilities, if critical to the protection of the land
▪ Nonmotorized wheelchairs

What is prohibited in wilderness?

▪ New road construction
▪ Timber harvesting
▪ Structures of any kind, except those primitive facilities
  deemed necessary to protect the land
▪ Mechanical transport (bicycles, wagons, carts)
▪ Public use of any motorized vehicles or equipment
▪ Removal of plants, stone, or moss for personal or
  commercial use
▪ Removal of historical or archeological artifacts by the public

Wilderness Additions

At 10- to 15-year intervals, each national forest revises its Forest
Plan—a detailed public document charting the course of forest management. After much hard work and input from disparate sources,
the Forest Service publishes the Draft Forest Plan. A public comment
period of no less than 90 days follows the release of the draft. After
this additional period of lobbying by the public, the Forest Service
adjusts the draft, then issues the Forest Plan, usually within a year of
the draft's printing.

The Forest Service makes its recommendations for further preservation—new wilderness, wilderness additions, scenic areas, etc.—

in the Forest Plan. While members of Congress can initiate wilderness designation at any time, they usually wait for the Forest Service recommendations and sufficient public support before sponsoring wilderness legislation. That's where you come in; if you want additional wilderness, you must write letters, make phone calls, or send e-mail to make your wishes known. You cannot gripe at the Forest Service if they propose wilderness and their endorsement dies beneath the dust of disinterest.

In its soon-to-be-completed plan, South Carolina's Sumter National Forest will recommend a 1,969-acre addition to the Ellicott Rock Wilderness. This addition, a long curving strip of forest defined by state line, road, and river, extends the current boundary along the North Carolina line to Highway 107, sends it southward with the highway to Burrells Ford Road, then follows the north side of Burrells Ford Road to the Chattooga. This expansion would flank both sides of Fish Hatchery Road and complete the encirclement of the non-wilderness Walhalla Fish Hatchery and the nearby picnic area. The Forest Service has designated this tract for wilderness before—and nothing happened. Sumter's Draft Forest Plan is scheduled for completion by the fall of 2002.

Georgia's Chattahoochee National Forest will also offer an enlargement to the Ellicott Rock Wilderness, this one a modest 700 acres. Starting at the Burrells Ford Bridge, the proposed addition runs along the northern side of Burrells Ford Road to the southwest past Carey Gap to a ridgeline west of Heddon Creek. The boundary then rollercoasters with the ridgecrest away from the road northward to Drip Nose Mountain, where it turns east and rejoins the existing perimeter. Chattahoochee's Draft Forest Plan is scheduled for publication the same time as Sumter's, by the fall of 2002.

The Forest Plan for North Carolina's Nantahala National Forest is not currently under revision. The arduous process may not begin again until the year 2004 or 2005. Since their plan is not under revision, the Forest Service has made no recommendations for future wilderness in the Nantahala. North Carolina's portion of the Ellicott Rock Wilderness, however, has already been extended to Highway 107, private property, and Bull Pen Road in every direction possible.

North Carolina's piece of the rock will never expand beyond its current boundaries.

The Chattahoochee National Forest also intends to recommend four additions—Tate Branch, Patterson Gap, Shoal Branch, and Ben Gap—to the Southern Nantahala Wilderness. Besides the four extensions, the Draft Forest Plan will propose a new 5,300-acre wilderness, referred to as Joe Gap by the Forest Service, south of and across FS 32 from the recommended Patterson Gap addition. The western side of the 1,087-acre Tate Branch addition abuts the east side of Tallulah River Road. Beginning near the road at the Towns–Rabun County border, the potential expansion proceeds along the current wilderness to the northeast atop Pot Gap Ridge to Steeltrap Knob. From Steeltrap the line ranges southward with the ridgecrest to FS 54A, sticks with the road around the western flank of Chestnut Mountain, then strikes out cross-country southwestward, generally on ridges, back to Tallulah River Road south of Tate Branch Campground.

Totaling 1,200 acres, Patterson Gap lies immediately to the east of Georgia's easternmost edge of the wilderness. Patterson Gap's western boundary is the present wilderness perimeter atop Grassy Ridge; FS 32, its southern limit, winds eastward until it comes to the white of private property. The eastern border bends with the right-angle turns of private property north-northeast across Drive Ridge to the wilderness boundary at the North Carolina line. The final line, the northern one, heads straight west with the state and wilderness borders back to Grassy Ridge.

Both Shoal Branch (412 acres) and Ben Gap (1,293 acres) are located west of the Appalachian Trail. Due south of Hightower Bald, Shoal Branch is the small parcel of Forest Service land sandwiched between wilderness to the north and private property to the south. The Ben Gap tract is situated along the southwesternmost edge of Georgia's share of the wilderness. This extension would move the Southern Nantahala's boundary to the southwest from its current perimeter atop the ridgecrests of Eagle Mountain.

The boundaries of North Carolina's share of the Southern Nantahala Wilderness have plenty of room to roam, and they are itching to move toward the nearest road. Every wilderness advocate who has unfolded the Southern Nantahala map has imagined more wilderness, has wished for fuller and more mature boundaries to the north. Since the Nantahala National Forest is still several years away from finishing its Draft Forest Plan, we can expedite the process by making our wilderness wants emphatically known. I would like to make my recommendation here and now. This time around, I would be pleased with one addition—a logical, modest, yet significant expansion. Starting at Deep Gap, this addition would follow the flow of Kimsey Creek downstream to FS 67 near the Standing Indian Campground, then fill out the wilderness all the way to the west and south sides of FS 67 to Mooney Gap. This addition would preserve Standing Indian's botanically rich slopes, many of them north facing and mesophytic. (See the Nature Notes for Lower Ridge Trail, pages 101–104, for a description of the area's diversity.)

A substantial expansion in North Carolina, plus the four small parcels in Georgia, would push the Southern Nantahala over the 30,000-acre mark—bragging size—a size worthy of the designation wilderness. An expanded Southern Nantahala (currently 23,714 acres) would join Cohutta–Big Frog and Joyce Kilmer–Slickrock and Citico Creek as the largest wildland gems among the National Forest wildernesses strung along the Southern Appalachians, the old Cherokee country. At 30,000-plus acres, the Southern Nantahala would become the second-largest single National Forest wilderness in the South (Georgia's Cohutta is largest), and would join a very short list of wildernesses (Forest Service administered) of that size in the eastern United States. Even if the Southern Nantahala were to reach the 30,000-acre plateau, however, it would still be large only in comparison to the conspicuously puny. In the eastern third of our country, many National Forest wildernesses preserve fewer than 7,000 acres; the majority keep the bulldozers at bay from tracts smaller than 11,000 acres.

Everyone living in the Piedmont of Georgia and the Carolinas has witnessed the asphalt assault, the gray glacier gobble and grow. We have all watched the bulldozers push one woodlot after another into the oblivion of burn-and-bury piles and winced as the red and raw earth sluiced into our streams. Even in the mountains, For Sale signs bristle along the byways and an alarming number of new roads rip up the slopes toward the ridges.

Our numbers continue to proliferate faster than kudzu. The populations of Georgia and North Carolina, the states that share the Southern Nantahala, mushroomed 3.1 million from 1990 to 2000. Daily, the media hammers us with the latest onslaughts: urban sprawl, energy blackouts, global warming and the climate change to come; rainforests falling beneath the weight of our immoderate demands; a witches cauldron of accumulating chemical pollutants we can't pronounce, remember, or even quite comprehend; acceleration of accelerating technological change; mass extinctions soon to be caused by the biological phenomenon of modern man; the planet's human population seething toward the swarming stage; and on and on. Our only home—the wondrous revolving, evolving earth—is under siege; it is crying "uncle" to largely uncaring ears.

The point of all this ranting and raving? We, we humans, need wild space for solace, refuge, beauty, and hope. The rest of the earth's life requires rapid human cultural evolution to survive with any semblance of its current richness. One facet of this evolution, the focus of this guide, concerns the preservation and use of publicly owned wildland. As our planet-trampling numbers fly off the graphs and our stress and enmity increasingly manifest themselves in mindless rage, our demand for green space of all kinds will escalate. We will need more of the green silence and the long trail for our health, hearts, and spirits. What remains of the biota, our nonhuman neighbors from bobcat to black-gum, needs living room to survive in unthreatened numbers.

We need as many types of greenways, parks, preserves, forests, wildlife management areas, wild rivers, and recreation areas in as many places as possible. We also need as many unroaded sprawls of wild wilderness where they are practical and possible, on large tracts of publicly owned land, primarily federal. As Henry David Thoreau so succinctly stated, "What is the use of a house if you haven't got a tolerable planet to put it on?" A tolerable planet is an ark for all of its inhabitants; it has numerous wild places set aside for the sanity of the imagination and for the enrichment of the body and spirit.

A tolerable planet nurtures the spirit of adventure of the many, not just of the few who can afford to fly to faraway places. People who want to live on a tolerable planet must take the time to communicate their concerns, voice their opinions, lobby for their beliefs. If you don't, who will?

Wild Rivers

By the early 1950s, after decades of nonstop, hell-for-progress river transformation—dam and wing dam construction, levee building, channelization, and pollution—a few pioneering environmentalists noted that the myth of superabundance was still alive and well and was threatening our country's remaining wild rivers. At first, the river advocates spoke with no more force than a small gathering tributary, but gradually their headwater branches flowed together into the mainstream wildland preservation movement. In a few short years that movement would help erode the bedrock power of the impounders.

In 1955 the Bureau of Reclamation sought congressional approval for the proposed Echo Park Dam, to be built on the Green and Yampa Rivers within Dinosaur National Monument. This project was triply arrogant, sure to anger environmentalists. The dam would drown sections of two wild rivers, bury thousands of acres of wilderness, and once again test the tensile strength of the National Park System. With all this at stake, a coalition of conservation groups and concerned citizens waged, for the first time, a highly publicized, highly effective, nationwide battle. The Echo Park struggle gave birth to the modern, mass-media environmental movement. The fledgling movement swayed public opinion and won the victory against that one dam, in that one place.

But the conservationists scarcely had time for a celebratory slap on the back before they suffered a major defeat. Saving a river for its own sake was not yet a universally accepted ideal. The Bureau turned around and dammed the Colorado River's Glen Canyon—the sacrificial lamb for sparing Echo Park—with little opposition. Finished in 1963, the Glen Canyon Dam drowned an unimaginably beautiful, 185-mile-long chasm—a fairyland of flatwater paddling that had been open to everyone. The mystical landscape now lies beneath the stagnant waters of Lake Powell, named after the indomitable one-armed Major John Wesley Powell, the first Colorado River runner. Wallace Stegner, who floated the canyon before its entombment, described Glen as "once the most serenely beautiful of all the canyons of the Colorado River."

Emboldened by their victory at Echo Park and saddened by the inconsolable loss of Glen Canyon, increasingly organized conservation groups began the grueling effort to preserve some of our last

remaining wildlands and wild rivers. By the late 1950s, a few outspoken dreamers realized that piecemeal opposition to development and the almost daily threat of new dams was not enough. The country needed a positive alternative—a nationwide system for river protection. In the early 1960s, a time of increased ecological awareness coupled with a new political climate, support for wildland preservation grew rapidly. The efforts of the two collaborative forces came to fruition in 1964—a watershed year for wildland passage and promise. That year President Johnson signed the National Wilderness Preservation Act, establishing the first system of its kind in the world. He also signed the Ozark National Scenic Riverways into law, creating our first national rivers. The same year, the first permutation of a wild rivers bill, the Wild Rivers Act, reached congressional committees. Because it focused solely on saving the magnificent rivers of the West, the Wild Rivers Act failed to win backing from key conservation groups and congressional leaders.

Lick Log Falls in the Chattooga corridor

In the mid-1960s, following still another mind-numbing proposal to inundate another national treasure, this time the Grand Canyon itself, the fight for free-flowing streams escalated, and citizens began to oppose dams at scores of sites across the country. With political momentum and public opinion on their side, increasing numbers of people turned their energies to the fate of our last unspoiled rivers.

In his 1965 State of the Union Address, President Johnson called for a comprehensive rivers bill: "We will continue to conserve the water and power for tomorrow's needs with well-planned reservoirs and power dams, but the time has also come to identify and preserve free-flowing stretches of our great rivers before growth and development have made the beauty of the unspoiled waterway a memory."

With the President's approval, Secretary of the Interior Stuart Udall (who had been among the last to marvel at Glen Canyon's sinuous alcoves) directed the Department of Agriculture to identify still-wild rivers, or sections of rivers. Starting with 650 candidates, the list was quickly culled to 67, then further pared to 22 rivers for detailed field study. Various wild river bills eddied about in Congress before finally surfacing as an inclusive, nationwide system, one embracing the "scenic" and "recreational" rivers of the East as well as those in the West. On October 2, 1968, the Wild and Scenic Rivers Act become Public Law 90-542. The legislation began with the following words:

> It is hereby declared to be the policy of the United States that certain selected rivers of the Nation which, with their immediate environments, possess outstandingly remarkable scenic, recreational, geologic, fish and wildlife, historic, cultural, or other similar values, shall be preserved in free-flowing condition, and that they and their immediate environments shall be protected for the benefit and enjoyment of present and future generations. The Congress declares that the established national policy of dam and other construction at appropriate sections of the rivers of the United States needs to be complemented by a policy that would preserve other selected rivers or sections thereof in their free-flowing condition to protect the water quality of such rivers and to fulfill other vital national conservation purposes.

The act continues with this salient passage:

> Each component of the national wild and scenic rivers
> system shall be administered in such a manner as to
> protect and enhance the values which caused it to be
> included in said system without, insofar as is consistent
> therewith, limiting other uses that do not substantially
> interfere with public use and enjoyment of these values.
> In such administration primary emphasis shall be given
> to protecting its esthetic, scenic, historic, archaeologic,
> and scientific features. Management plans for any such
> component may establish varying degrees of intensity
> for its protection and development based on the special
> attributes of the area.

Once Congress decided to broaden the bill to include the less-
than-pristine Eastern rivers, the legislation required language to rank
the varying degrees of wildness. The framers of the act decided upon
three classifications—wild, scenic, and recreational. A national wild
and scenic river might qualify for all three designations along its
length, as is the case with the Chattooga. The act defined the following three categories:

> 1) **Wild river areas**. Those rivers or sections of
> rivers that are free of impoundments and generally
> inaccessible except by trail, with watersheds or
> shorelines essentially primitive and waters unpolluted.
> These represent vestiges of primitive America.

> 2) **Scenic river areas**. Those rivers or sections of rivers
> that are free of impoundments, with shorelines or
> watersheds still largely primitive and shorelines largely
> undeveloped, but accessible in places by roads.

3) **Recreational river areas.** Those rivers or sections of rivers that are readily accessible by road or railroad, that may have some development along their shorelines, and that may have undergone some impoundment or diversion in the past.

Initially, the bill protected only eight of the twenty-two rivers: the Middle Fork of the Clearwater in Idaho; the Eleven Point in Missouri; the Feather in California; the Rio Grande in New Mexico; the Rogue in Oregon; the Saint Croix in Minnesota and Wisconsin; the Middle Fork of the Salmon in Idaho; and the Wolf in Wisconsin. Unlike many of the Eastern rivers, most of these rivers were already on Federal lands, none of them were deemed of national importance, and perhaps most significantly, none of them were slated for Federal hydroelectric development. Twenty-seven other potentially more controversial rivers were named to be studied for possible inclusion in the wild river system. In the southeastern states, only three other rivers besides the Chattooga were initially designated for study. The Chattooga was the only Southern Appalachian river proposed.

Environmental Guidelines

Before the Hike

■ **Limit group size** to no more than eight for backpacking and no more than ten for dayhiking.

■ **Split large organized groups** into two or three smaller parties, allowing the groups to go to different destinations, travel opposite directions on the same loop, stagger their starts, or do whatever it takes to avoid overwhelming everyone and everything in their path.

■ **Educate large groups**, especially children, about the evils of littering and cutting across switchbacks.

■ **Plan ahead**—remember that rivers with waterfalls and swimming holes, such as those on the Chattooga, and major trail junctions with level ground and nearby water will be heavily used during warm weather holidays and weekends.

▪ **Take a lightweight backpacking stove** so you won't have to build fires for cooking.

▪ **Repackage food supplies** in sealable bags or plastic bottles so there will be fewer boxes and tinfoil pouches to burn or carry.

On the Trail

▪ **Travel quietly.** And, if you can, take breaks away from the trail to preserve solitude and to keep other hikers from having to hop-scotch over and around your gear.

▪ **Don't litter**—not even the smallest of candy wrappers or ciga-rette butts. If you pack it in, pack it out—all of it.

▪ **And don't be a hider**—a person whose consciousness is caught midway between right and wrong. The undersides of rocks should be salamander sanctuaries and tree hollows should be wildlife dens— not beer can repositories. And no one wants to see your misfired banana peel draped over the flame azalea.

▪ **Remember that organic scraps are definitely litter.** Orange peels, peanut hulls, apple cores, and campsite compost piles crowned with eggshells and spaghetti noodles are not welcome sights in the wilderness. Carry these organic scraps out or, if you are planning on having a fire anyway, burn them. If there is no way in hell you are going to carry out an apple core, at least give it a good downslope heave well out of sight of the trail.

▪ **Carry a plastic bag** with you. Help pick up what those uncar-ing louts have left behind. Take only pictures and litter; leave only footprints and good karma.

▪ **Take your dump** *du jour* at least 100 feet from the trail and at least 150 feet from a campsite or water source. Dig a cat hole with boot heel or plastic trowel, then cover everything up completely—please.

▪ **Stay on the main trail** (preceding precept is the notable excep-tion), and do not cut across switchbacks. Cutting across switchbacks tramples vegetation, starts erosion, and encourages more shortcut taking.

▪ **Step to the high side of the trail** so you don't cave in the lower side when stepping aside to let other hikers or backpackers pass.

■ **Don't pick, pluck, dig up, or cut up any flowers**, plants, or trees, not even the tiny ones you think no one will miss. Let offenders know of your disapproval gently and tactfully, at least at first.

No-Trace Camping

■ **Don't use worn out, naked-ground campsites** where the entire area is bare earth with eroding soil, damaged trees, and exposed roots. Let these areas heal. Use existing, well-established campsites in acceptable condition. Better yet, move well away from the trail and make a no-trace camp that will rarely, if ever, be used again.

■ **Do your best to camp 100 feet away from trail or stream.** It is often difficult, if not impossible, to camp on flat ground 100 feet away from both path and stream while walking a trail that closely parallels a watercourse. One side of the trail is too close to the river; the other quickly tilts into a steep-sided slope of rhododendron. Bending one rule, however, is better than breaking two. Where the river is shallow enough, try fording the Chattooga to the bank opposite the trail, then tuck in as far as you can. That way your camp will be well over 100 feet from the trail and maybe even 100 feet away from the river.

■ **Don't cut standing trees** or pull up or beat down vegetation to make room for your tent or tents. Fit in, tuck in—don't hack in.

■ **Don't enlarge an existing campsite.** There is no need for large groups to circle the wagons against the night. Again, fit in and tuck in.

■ **Absolutely no campsite construction**—leave the blueprints and hard hats at home: no boot bulldozing, trenching, digging latrines, hammering nails in trees, etc.

■ **Use biodegradable soap** and dispose of waste water at least 100 feet from camp and 150 feet from any water source.

■ **Don't wash dirty dishes directly in a spring or stream.** Don't use soap on yourself or your clothes directly in a spring or stream.

■ **Don't bury trash or food scraps.** Animals will dig them up.

■ **Don't spit your toothpaste on campsite vegetation.** After a month of drought, heavily used sites look like bird roosts.

■ **Make your campsite look at least as natural** as when you found it. Replace branches, twigs, and leaves cleared for the sleeping area.

■ **Keep length of stay to one or two nights**, if possible.

■ **Wear soft-soled shoes in camp.**

■ **Avoid building campfires.** Take a lightweight, backpacking stove for cooking. If you do start a fire, keep it small and use only dead and down wood. Leave the saws and axes at home.

■ **Erase all evidence of a campfire built with no fire ring.** Scatter the ashes, replace the duff, and camouflage the burned area.

■ **Don't build fire rings**—tear them down.

■ **Never build a fire on a dry, windy day.**

Backcountry Courtesy

■ **Leave radios and CD players at home** or bring headsets.

■ **Don't take a dog** into the wilderness unless it is well trained. Even then, carry a leash so you can control your animal when necessary. Leave behind dogs that may growl or bark at other hikers. Do not take aggressive dogs—canine weapons—into the wilderness for protection. Creating stress for other hikers is unconscionable. If you fear being accosted on the trail, learn one of the martial arts, buy a can of pepper spray, or stay at home. But do not selfishly inflict your yapping, snarling dog on other hikers.

■ **Take consideration**—do nothing that will interfere with someone else's enjoyment. It is insensitive to enter the wilderness with a very large group that will completely overrun and overwhelm other hikers.

■ **Keep as quiet as possible.** Drunken parties, war whoops, and loud radios are frowned upon, and downright rude.

■ **Remember that campsites are first come, first served.** Don't whine, argue, or try to crowd in if someone already has the campsite you really wanted.

■ **Help preserve the illusion of solitude**, for yourself and others. Make yourself as unobtrusive, as invisible, as possible. Use earth-tone tents and tarps and, if possible, camp far enough off the trail so that other hikers can't see you and vice versa. Never camp smack on the trail so that other hikers have to wind through your sprawling encampment just to follow the trail. Also, if possible, take lunch and rest breaks off the trail.

Backpacking the Appalachian Trail—an American tradition

Adopt-a-Trail

THE U.S. FOREST SERVICE "Adopt-a-Trail" program gives individuals, friends, families, and organizations the opportunity to do something worthwhile: to become Forest Service volunteers. The Forest Service provides a pat on the back, perhaps a patch, and all the equipment—saws, shovels, axes, shin-guards, plastic bags—you could possibly use or carry. Volunteers provide the time, energy, and enthusiasm needed to clean up and trim out their adopted trails.

The Forest Service, and indeed all those who use and respect the wilderness, will greatly appreciate your help.

If you are interested in becoming the foster parent of a wilderness or wild river trail, or a section of trail, call or write the appropriate ranger district. (See the following section for addresses and phone numbers.)

Addresses and Maps

THE ELLICOTT ROCK WILDERNESS SURROUNDS the exact spot where the borders of Georgia, South Carolina, and North Carolina come together. Georgia's portion of the wilderness lies within the Chattahoochee National Forest's Tallulah Ranger District. South Carolina's share of the wilderness is preserved within the Sumter National Forest's Andrew Pickens Ranger District, and North Carolina's piece of the rock is located within the Nantahala National Forest's Highlands Ranger District.

The Chattooga National Wild and Scenic River begins in North Carolina, then forms the border between Georgia and South Carolina as it flows to the southwest. The ranger districts responsible for managing the Chattooga are the same as those listed for the Ellicott Rock Wilderness.

The Southern Nantahala Wilderness stretches east-west along the Georgia (Chattahoochee National Forest)–North Carolina (Nantahala National Forest) boundary. In Georgia's part of the wilderness, the Appalachian Trail serves as the dividing line between ranger districts—Tallulah to the east, Brasstown to the west. North Carolina's allowance of wild land is generally split along the Macon County–Clay County line. South and west of that boundary, Clay County's designated wilderness is administered by the Tusquitee Ranger District. North and east of that line, Macon County's share of the Southern Nantahala is managed by the Wayah Ranger District.

For more information, contact the following offices:

Sumter National Forest

USDA Forest Service
Supervisor's Office
4931 Broad River Road
Columbia, SC 29212-3530
(803) 561-4000

USDA Forest Service
Andrew Pickens Ranger District
112 Andrew Pickens Circle
Mountain Rest, SC 29664
(864) 638-9568

Nantahala National Forest

USDA Forest Service
Supervisor's Office
P.O. Box 2750
Asheville, NC 28802
(828) 257-4200

USDA Forest Service
Highlands Ranger District
2010 Flat Mountain Road
Highlands, NC 28741
(828) 526-3765

USDA Forest Service
Wayah Ranger District
90 Sloan Road
Franklin, NC 28734
(828) 524-6441

USDA Forest Service
Tusquitee Ranger District
123 Woodland Drive
Murphy, NC 28906
(828) 837-5152

Chattahoochee National Forest

USDA Forest Service
Supervisor's Office
1755 Cleveland Highway
Gainesville, GA 30501
(770) 297-3000

USDA Forest Service
Tallulah Ranger District
809 Highway 441 South
Clayton, GA 30525
(706) 782-3320

USDA Forest Service
Brasstown Ranger District
P.O. Box 9
Blairsville, GA 30514
(706) 745-6928

Maps of the three national forests, the two wildernesses, and the Chattooga National Wild and Scenic River are available from the Forest Service offices for a small fee. The Southern Nantahala Wilderness map is entitled *Southern Nantahala Wilderness and Standing Indian Basin*. The map detailing the Chattooga and the Ellicott Rock Wilderness is entitled *Chattooga National Wild and Scenic River*. An Ellicott Rock Wilderness map is also available; however, I do not recommend it.

Topographic Quadrangles (1:24,000) are available from the United States Geological Survey: US Geological Survey Information Service, Box 25286, Denver, CO 80225 (1-888-ASK-USGS).

Index of Trails

Chattooga National Wild and Scenic River

Ellicott Rock Wilderness

Southern Nantahala Wilderness

Index of Nature Descriptions

Animals, Birds, and Butterflies

Trees and Shrubs

Wildflowers and Ferns

Italics indicate illustration